Navigating the Divide

Navigating the Divide

Selected Poetry and Prose

Linda Watanabe McFerrin

Foreword by Joanna Biggar

Alan Squire Publishing
Bethesda, Maryland

Navigating the Divide: Selected Poetry and Prose, Linda Watanabe McFerrin is published by Alan Squire Publishing, an imprint of the Santa Fe Writers Project.

Printed in the United States of America.
ISBN (paper): 978-1-942892-14-4
ISBN (epub): 978-1-942892-15-1
ISBN (PDF): 978-1-942892-16-8
ISBN (mobi): 978-1-942892-17-5
Library of Congress Control Number: 2019936749

All translations are by Linda Watanabe McFerrin unless otherwise noted.

Excerpts from "Ithaka" on page 178 are from Constantine P. Cavafy, translated by Thanasis Maskaleris, *An Anthology of Modern Greek Poetry*, Nanos Valaoritis and Thanasis Maskaleris, eds. (Jersey City: Talisman House, 2003).

Excerpt on page 286 is from Zora Neale Hurston, *Tell My Horse: Voodoo and Life in Haiti and Jamaica* (New York, HarperCollins, 1990).

Jacket design and cover art by Randy Stanard, Dewitt Designs, www.dewittdesigns.com.
Cover photo by Alison Wright.
Author photo by Lowry McFerrin.
Copy editing and interior design by Nita Congress.
Printing consultant: Steven Waxman.
Printed by API/Jostens.

First Edition
Ordo Vagorum

More Praise for *Navigating the Divide*:

What can I say about the teacher I credit for teaching me how to write and, more importantly, how to believe in myself as a writer? And not just by guidance as rigorous as it was infinitely patient and tender, but also by the example of her own wonderful work. I'm thrilled to see the artfully curated selections in this volume; there's no genre, it seems, that this writer hasn't mastered and made her own with her signature style. Grace. Understatement. Authenticity. Immense power. Comedy and tragedy. Gorgeously transparent writing. You'll find all this and more in pages that seem almost to turn themselves.

—Rebecca Foust, Marin Poet Laureate emerita and author of *Paradise Drive*, winner of the Press 53 Award for Poetry

This surprising, sui generis author's name—*Linda Watanabe McFerrin*—is itself an invitation to travel. Scents of the East, and of her native California, infuse her words. In prose and poetry, they swerve and mount magic mountains, then dive into dark abysses, into places where cultures mingle, mix, and match, unexpectedly. I have long admired Linda's professionalism as a journalist and teacher, and am now privileged to discover her most personal and creative side.

—David Downie, author of *The Gardener of Eden*

Navigating the Divide is a fascinating expression of inner and outer travels through Linda Watanabe McFerrin's poetry and prose writing. It can be easily read randomly as an anthology, perhaps allowing synchronicity to choose the selection and speak to you.

—Jean Shinoda Bolen, MD, Jungian analyst, activist, author of *Goddesses in Everywoman*, *The Tao of Psychology*, and *Crossing to Avalon*

Linda Watanabe McFerrin is a sorceress, a seer, a seductress who pulls you close until you too are navigating the divide between worlds seen, felt, and conjured. Reading her work is an immersion, an experience that can leave you both unbalanced and nurtured, but certainly moved.

—Larry Habegger, Executive Editor, *Travelers' Tales Books*

For Lowry McFerrin,
my kind co-pilot

Acknowledgments

Many thanks to the wonderful editors and literary professionals who have been so kind, supportive, and appreciative of my work and to the publications in which selections in this volume have previously appeared, including:

- *American Fiction*
- *Atlanta Journal Constitution*
- *The Berkeley Poets Cooperative: A History of the Times*
- *Burning the Midnight Oil: Illuminating Words for the Long Night's Journey into Day*
- *By the Seat of My Pants: Humorous Tales of Travel and Misadventure*
- *Camellia*
- *Canary*
- *In Search of Adventure: A Wild Travel Anthology*
- *I Should Have Stayed Home: The Worst Trips of Great Writers*
- *Japanophile*
- *Nimrod International Journal of Prose and Poetry*
- *Passionfruit*
- *St. Petersburg Times*
- *San Francisco Chronicle Magazine*
- *San Francisco Examiner*
- *San Francisco Examiner Magazine*
- *Santa Clara Review*

- *Sierra Songs and Descants*
- *Southern Poetry Review*
- *Venturing in Southern Greece: The Vatika Odysseys*
- *Wandering in Costa Rica: Landscapes Lost and Found*
- *Wandering in Bali: A Tropical Paradise Discovered*
- *Wandering in Paris: Luminaries and Love in the City of Light*
- *Wild Places: 20 Journeys into the North American Outdoors*
- *WorldHum*

...as well as the following books from which poems and chapters have been excerpted:

- *The Impossibility of Redemption Is Something We Hadn't Figured On*, Berkeley Poets Workshop & Press, 1990
- *Namako: Sea Cucumber*, Coffee House Press, 1998
- *The Hand of Buddha*, Coffee House Press, 2000
- *Dead Love: A novel about Japan...and zombies*, Stone Bridge Press, 2010

Contents

Acknowledgments ix
Foreword: Many Faces, Many Voices xiii
Introduction: One Door Closes xxi

Part 1: Love, a Refuge

Sometimes the slant of sunlight on the hills... 3
Her Smile 4
His Hands 5
A Little Night Music 6
Dante, Mayo, and the Libidinous Finns 10
Stranger 15
Strangers 16
Lawrence, Cortés, and the Attraction of Gold 25
Lost Pines 29
Selections from *Namako: Sea Cucumber* 30
Amma 55
Selections from *The Hand of Buddha* 56
Kato 83
Selections from *Dead Love* 84
Post-Apocalyptic Valentine 92

Part 2: Back to Asia

A Calendar 95
Her Luck 96
The Dojo – Lesson 1 97
Bamboo Basket 98
Shanghaied by the Past 99
China-jin 105
Relics 107
Legacy 108
Selections from *Namako: Sea Cucumber* 110

In Tokyo, Finding the Kami Way 117
Shinkichi's Tale 123
Selection from *Namako: Sea Cucumber* 125
Selections from *Dead Love* 130
One Thousand Cranes 143
Selections from *The Hand of Buddha* 144
Ikebana: Woman with Flowers 164
Onnagata 165
Sakura-no-sono 167
Containment 169

Part 3: Death and Shadow

Night Movement 173
In Vatika 174
Nightfall 180
Selection from *The Hand of Buddha* 181
Dark Parent 198
Selection from *Namako: Sea Cucumber* 199
Selections from *Dead Love* 215
A Ghost Reflects on the Ninja 225
Selections from *Dead Love* 226
The Time of Figs 236
Enchanted Piazza 237
This August 241

Part 4: The Edge and Beyond

The Dragon 245
Lost in the Okefenokee 247
Selection from *Namako: Sea Cucumber* 251
The House 266
The Lure of Hoodoos 267
Let's Phosphoresce by Intellection 273
Snake Karma 274
Running the Lion City Hash 279
Bali Belly on The Bukit and the Zombie Apocalypse 285
Hunger 290
Selections from *Dead Love* 291
On the San Joaquin 318
Inside the White Gorilla 321

Foreword: Many Faces, Many Voices

When asked by Rose Solari to make selections from Linda Watanabe McFerrin's entire œuvre, and to edit this ASP Legacy Volume, I was honored and delighted. Linda and I have been colleagues and friends for years, and I greatly admire her writing.

I met Linda while editing stories after a writing workshop on the Canal du Midi in 2005. It was a propitious beginning to a wonderful collaboration that so far has included many trips, ten anthologies, and a deep friendship. It was also the perfect way to get to know a woman whose name is legendary in San Francisco Bay Area writing circles: as the founder of the immensely popular Left Coast Writers group which meets at Book Passage bookstore; as a beloved teacher whose workshops are regularly oversubscribed; and as a mentor to dozens of successful and grateful authors of bestselling and award-winning books.

Before beginning this project, I already knew that Linda came from a literary family of mixed ancestry—Japanese, Italian, Welsh; that her childhood was spent in England, Japan, and many parts of the United States; that she writes travel stories, personal essays, short stories, novels, and always poetry and that she began putting her adventures on the page and sharing them with others in the first grade. I knew, too, that there had been a turning point when she left behind a life in the corporate world to commit herself full time to writing. That transition is beautifully described in the essay "One Door Closes." But you discover a lot of entirely new things about a writer by plunging into the full scope of her work. In Linda's, I found a kaleidoscope: lyrical beauty; aching precision; humor; a respect for form and tradition, alongside a willingness to cross boundaries and convention; a drive to travel far physically and artistically, to seek the bizarre, the surreal, the unknown.

This volume has been compiled from a wide variety of Linda's publications, but has drawn heavily from four key books.

- The volume of poetry *The Impossibility of Redemption Is Something We Hadn't Figured On* (1990), in which her luminous images and distinct voice are already established
- *Namako: Sea Cucumber* (1998), a fictionalized memoir of the childhood years Linda and her family spent in Japan with one of her most memorable characters, her formidable Grandmother
- *The Hand of Buddha* (2000), a short story collection that gives voice to a wide array of voices, cultures, and characters, some drawn from Linda's life, some the lives of others she has met and embraced
- *Dead Love* (2010), a zombie thriller novel with deep Japanese roots that also reach around the world; its shape-shifting supernatural characters embody many of the author's "on-the-divide" proclivities: the zeal for adventure and danger, the thin edge between the real and unreal, the blurry lines between life and death, the supremacy of love

To help the reader appreciate such a richness of material, the book has been structured around four broad themes, each comprised of several genres.

Part One: Love, a Refuge. A man named Lawrence—tall, lean, lithe and sexy, often seen with long golden hair—appears throughout Linda's work. He is Lowry McFerrin, whom she met while in college and married soon after. Their experiences, travels, passions, and ideas about love reverberate in her work—as in these lines from "Sometimes the slant of sunlight on the hills":

> ...our bodies, calipers,
> curled drowsily
> toward one another
> flame red
> twin tulip petals tipped
> in scarlet
> in that refraction
> our kisses multiple and
> so inflected that
> the sun comes riving into
> our plain souls
> suffusing us.

But beyond romantic love, Linda explores its many other dimensions. In the short story "Strangers," which takes place on a train, she captures the temptations of infidelity, and in many pieces creates perfect-pitch eroticism. There is dangerous sex with vampires; kinky sex in Japanese "love hotels"; forbidden love, perverted attraction, and adolescent desire. These come together in "yuki/snow," when a teacher is banished because of a homosexual affair and confesses an inappropriate love for a student, Ellen. She meanwhile discovers her own feelings for a boy as they huddle in a collapsing igloo:

> Then his mouth was on mine, and I felt his sorrow—the sobs that I wouldn't hear this time entering my mouth and falling into my throat. I closed my eyes, and we were spinning around and around, giddy music box dancers under the revolving constellations.

Even beyond the infinite permutations of love and desire, the reader will also find in these pages the kinds of love—adult for child, child for parent, love for oneself—that make love the ultimate redemptive force.

Part Two: Back to Asia. While acknowledging the primacy of Japan in the author's life and writing, this section also takes the reader much further afield, as is evident from the first essay, "Shanghaied by the Past." Part history and part family history, it illustrates how the historical and the personal always intertwine, and how boundaries are always blurred.

> This is the Shanghai my mother remembered—the Shanghai she called home until 1937. It was a dazzling world to child and adult alike, a world filled with chauffeurs, dressmakers, pastries, parties, movies, movie stars, and electrifying sporting events; but there was also poverty and prejudice to which my mother, a daughter of a Welsh professor of English literature and a Japanese actress, was hardly immune.

Beyond China, the book ventures to Singapore, Hong Kong, Malaysia, and Indonesia but always finds its author's deep Japanese roots. In the travel essay "In Tokyo: Finding the *Kami* Way," the reader visits modern Tokyo, but also tours Shinto shrines where *kami*, or spirits, shelter. Grandmother's Japan, with ancient traditions, values, and rituals, coexists with the realities of modernity. Images of Hiroshima and Fukushima singe these pages. The reader plunges as well into the places and characters of *Dead Love*: upscale Tokyo, where the protagonist Erin Orison seeks her missing father; dangerous Tokyo with its bars, nightclubs, and pleasure palaces introduced to Erin by Ryu, her bodyguard; and all the crevices between in the Tokyo of Clément, the slippery ghoul who loves her. It is easy to find the formation of Linda Watanabe McFerrin, the woman, here.

It is also easy to find in this mix, including poetry, the artistic forms that give rise to her unique, Japanese-infused aesthetic. There are glimpses of Japanese theater in the ever-changing faces of a personage like Clément, in Linda's use of her character, Erin Orison, as the author of some of her poems; traces of a Hiroshige woodcut wave gathering force, awaiting the perfect moment to break in the controlled passion of Grandmother; the precision and understated beauty of haiku in Linda's poetry. Hear "Ikebana: Woman with Flowers":

> ...Gold is the color of sorrow.
> "We have gained much. We have lost so much more."
> The afternoon hours tent around her—
> kimono of patterned emptiness—
> the way green tea brushes porcelain.
> Each leaf-blade, a knife, cuts the silence
> with thought precisely incised into the void.

Finally, there is the powerful art form manga, whose drawings form the basis of wildly popular graphic books worldwide. It seems a perfect fit for the pulsing urban beat of *Dead Love*. So perfect, in fact, that renowned manga artist Botan Yamada did an illustrated version of the chapter entitled "How He Fell for You."

Part Three: Death and Shadow. Embracing the dark is as central to Linda's art as is giving expression to love. Death weaves through her work as it has her life—a childhood marked by the early death of a younger brother, then the death of Grandmother. Most tragically, she and Lowry lost their only child shortly after birth. Later came the death of both of her parents, followed by that of her beloved sister. These losses lace her writing. This section begins with the poem "Night Movement," followed by the essay "In Vatika," both reflections of grief after the death of her infant daughter, Marissa.

There are depictions of cold-blooded death, too: ninja assassins in Nijo Castle; a posse of mob assassins in Kuala Lumpur; ritualized voodoo killing in Haiti.

Death itself seems a creature of darkness, where many other elements reside in shadow—soul sickness, sorrow, evil. Secrets, too. "Our hidden and forbidden selves" find their own reflections in the dark of Carnivale in Venice, in the travel essay "Enchanted Plaza." Fracturing love and despair are both captured in the poem "This August." Evil manifests itself in many forms, as well, including in that monster of selfishness, Iyemon, antihero of a folktale in "yurei yashiki/ghost house." Darkness also encompasses sorrow and shame, as Erin learns from the dance master Hiroshi Nakamura in "Hide and Seek."

> ...The high-pitched twang of a single string cut through the other instruments, full of blame. Now the movements were *butoh*, drawn from the dance that came from the war, from the suffering and shame of Nagasaki and Hiroshima.

And yet, and yet. Even from the bottom of pain, decay, and sorrow, there is a way to beauty through words. From "The Time of Figs":

> ...Wasps comb the remains. Days are short,
> stubby things now, barely utilitarian,
> and the nights have stretched into
> wide dark umbrellas folding us
> into starry linings.

Part Four: The Edge and Beyond. This section begins with the poem "The Dragon," whose last lines are:

> My jaw unhinges
> like a python's
> and the squealing piglets,
> saints,
> the vast array of shadows that I paint
> slide
> in.

It ends with the travel essay "Inside the White Gorilla," a surreal trip through Paris where a dead albino gorilla finally closes its pale blue eyes.

In between is the poem "The House," in which Linda reveals her survival strategy.

> If you must own a house,
> do not live in it.
> If all else fails,
> travel often.

And travel she does, always to the distant, difficult, dangerous. Often, these are places inhabited by reptiles: alligators in the Okefenokee, a hallucinatory iguana in the desert, lizards, lethal snakes everywhere. These beasts are guardians of the dark places, places she must—we all must—dare to go. But beyond the actual landscapes she ventures into—the jungles, swamps, deserts—are the psychological ones. Everywhere she is peering over the edge, then leaping beyond.

In terms of language, this leads to experimentation, dizzying hallucinatory scenes, surreal worlds. In those worlds, creatures of other dimensions, such as ghosts, ghouls, zombies, and *kami* live, and there they can interpret reality. In "Akishima/autumn island," the child Ellen meets a *kami* who offers a glimpse of the afterworld where newly departed Grandmother has gone. In several excerpts from *Dead Love*, zombies and ghouls debate if they are figments of others' imaginations, or if every figment of imagination can exist in this world.

This is a space of "double exposure," Linda says in the travel story "The Lure of Hoodoos," where external and internal landscapes seem to superimpose. This is the dwelling place of the free spirit, where it's easy to get lost, but where creation and new visions arise beyond the edge.

Yet there is more. Going to and beyond the edge is often the hallmark of a solitary explorer whose body of work is the legacy of her explorations. But Linda is also a great teacher, determined not to leave anybody behind, and her legacy is vast.

The woman I first knew as a legend in the San Francisco Bay Area writing community has been a regular presenter at such events as the annual Litquake Festival, San Francisco's Bay Area Book Festival, and the Writing Salon, as well as a perennial instructor at the Book Passage Travel Writers & Photographers

Conference and the Writer's Center of Marin, to name only a few. And her net reaches wider—as panelist, speaker, judge, contributor to many NPR broadcasts, and as workshop leader from Hawaii to Bali, from Japan to Costa Rica, Greece, and beyond.

The common thread of these activities is what inspired Linda to found Left Coast Writers—the need for writers to form communities, to help, inspire, and teach one another. Her own list is long, and the number of successful protégés stunning. Among them: Kunal Mukherjee, author of *My Magical Palace* (HarperCollins, India); Marin County Poet Laureate emerita, Rebecca Foust; memoirist Jason Rezaian, author of *Prisoner: My 544 Days in an Iranian Prison* (HarperCollins); Rosemary Gong, author of the perennially popular *Good Luck Life: The Essential Guide to Chinese American Celebrations and Culture* (HarperCollins); and *New York Times* bestselling memoirist and novelist Jasmin Darznik.

As Darznik, who could be speaking for all Linda's pupils says: "Linda is one of those people whose teaching, like her writing, draws deep from the well of who she is—smart, funny, and, above all, generous. Her mentorship set me on a path I could never have found by myself. I'm grateful to her beyond words."

—Joanna Biggar

Introduction: One Door Closes

Put me last.

Call it the caboose—the final car in a train that you don't want to miss. Maybe you've run just fast enough to catch up with it and hop aboard as the train pulls out of the station. You grab the end ladder, the one behind the back wheels, and then you are on it...but just barely. It was like that when I joined the Berkeley Poets Cooperative. I was on that last car. I'd missed the wild and crazy sixties, the seventies, what I thought must have been the cool, Telegraph Avenue street poetry days. They were history. The year was 1984, and I'm well aware of how fortunate I was to catch the tail end of the Co-op's incredible ride.

Did I mention that I was a zombie at the time? Well, at least that is when I began writing about them. I was wandering through the post-apocalyptic ruin of my still-young life, having lost my newborn daughter. She died in my arms in the hospital. I was living in the East Bay, in Oakland, after dropping out—first from the fashion industry, then from the art world—to start a family. Cruel joke, and the last time I tried that. The only thing standing between the absolute end and me was some volunteer work I was doing for The Hunger Project and a blank book that my husband had wisely given me. I had writers in my family. My grandfather was a Welsh journalist in pre-war Shanghai. My aunt was a screenwriter. One of my uncles was an American war correspondent, and my mother would have liked to have been a poet or maybe a novelist...if she didn't have her hands full with the four children, whom she seemed to like a lot more than her writing. I was encouraged to write, and I loved doing it, but only for school or for pleasure.

In 1984, it had become something more than that. The pages of that blank book would become an empty wasteland I would first puzzle over, then use as the space to create a map back. I'm not sure what provoked me to call up the people who organized the Berkeley Poets Cooperative. I'm certain my hand shook as I dialed the number.

"Hello?"

"Hi, this is Gail."

"Is this the Berkeley Poets Co-op? I was thinking of..."

"Yes, come on over. We'd love it if you joined us." Gail. Does she know that I will always love her for that?

Not everyone was as welcoming as Gail. It didn't matter. Gail is generous and generative enough to mother a huge tribe. She and Charles, the Co-op founder, lived together, and although they weren't married at the time, it was immediately clear that these two were very much in love. That love permeated their poems and filled the space around them. To me, tottering as I was on the verge of disintegration, it was manna. They made it a comforting and colorful space, as did Carla and Jamie and Gerry and Elise and Chitra, too, when she briefly joined the group.

Every week I would bring some horrid little poem to the meeting, and the other poets would chop it to bits. I liked that. It suited my frame of mind. I learned to ignore the less than pleasant people in the room, and I did overcome my fear of the Bruces—Hawkins and Boston—long-time members whom I found both brilliant and intimidating.

Fireflies after thunder
for Lowry

Fireflies after thunder:
lights winking on as if
life scattered kisses—dandelion-light—
into the dark cloud damp,

and they have stuck there
on a flypaper of shadow,
on a moment that, like a shade drawn,
counts itself down.

And the moisture rises up,
a hand's heel pressing into my cranium.
Fireflies follow, their flickering lights—
Hatchlings, a contagion—touch of life and death
that I now carry inside me.

I can see why the Co-op thrived for all those years. In general the sessions were thrilling—full of risk and dread and elation. Charles and Gail were the perfect hosts. Charles is a fantastic editor. Any of us could volunteer to work with him on the BPCW&P anthologies, which I did. I sometimes think of that first experience after all these years of editing books. Charles is a genius. Everyone was opinionated. Not a lesson was wasted. I still don't understand why more people didn't seize the opportunity to work with Charles on those projects.

By the time Charles and Gail moved the Co-op to Dana Street, I'd decided to pursue a graduate degree in creative writing at San Francisco State University, so I started studying language poetry with Barrett Watten, contemporary women's poetry with Kathleen Fraser, and memoir with Michael Rubin. Anne Rice's husband, Stan Rice, was department chair at the time. Stan was a poet and an artist, though I also took a short story class with him. For my oral exams at the end of the program, I chose John Ashbery, whom I interviewed; William Shakespeare, whom I could not possibly interview; and Yukio Mishima, whose work Michael read and studied just so that he could serve as my examiner. I did well. I earned the degree. Not long afterward, Michael died, and I realized how sick he had been when he tackled Mishima—a complex, darkly driven writer—for me.

In 1990 the Berkeley Poets Workshop and Press published two chapbooks: *the reason for nasturtiums* by Chitra Banerjee

Divakaruni and my first book, *The Impossibility of Redemption Is Something We Hadn't Figured On*—the last to come out from the Co-op before Gail and Charles moved north to Nevada City. I switched shortly thereafter to prose, both fiction and nonfiction. I wrote for newspapers and magazines for years. *Namako: Sea Cucumber* (Coffee House Press), *The Hand of Buddha* (Coffee House Press, and *Dead Love* (Stonebridge Press)—my ultimate zombie exorcism—are among my book-length titles. I'm still in touch with my favorite Co-op members. Bruce Boston turned out to be something of a mentor. I have him to thank for the direction that led me to place as a finalist for a Bram Stoker Award. Every so often—not often enough, though—I see Charles and Gail, and I've been delighted to have them as speakers and members of my own writers' organization, Left Coast Writers, now in its seventh year.

It turns out that the last car of the train is as good as any on a trip like this one. I tell that to all my students these days. Last car or first, take a chance. Run for it. Jump aboard. The journey regretted is always the one not taken.

Freight Train

The freight train moans toward the docks
just as I cry, working my way into my metal future.

There is no door in the bright sky
from which God descends on a cloud of steam.

But there is an ocean close by.
It creaks with ships.

On my black track, I clatter toward oblivion,
find solace in the vast wings of the albatross.

—Linda Watanabe McFerrin

Part 1:

Love, a Refuge

Sometimes the slant of sunlight on the hills...

as here
the new light fingering its way
into a darkened chamber
into sleep
crisp morning licking
at the pillowcases and
the sheets to drive
us out

our bodies, calipers,
curled drowsily
toward one another
flame red
twin tulip petals tipped
in scarlet
In that refraction
our kisses multiple and
so inflected that
the sun comes riving into
our plain souls
suffusing us.

Her Smile

It is long
like a knife,
(her smile)
but curved:
an eastern slyness;
(more a scimitar)
one thinks of
bursting cardamom pods,
a sudden fragrance,
aromatic,
or of cloves ground in a palm.

Most often
it is veiled
because it is suspicious
to be small,
to have lips like persimmon,
(inside, like a pomegranate)
caving in,
like a fruit under mouths.

It is shy
in the way of
dates,
how the sweetness retreats,
a dry nest of sustenance
remaining.

His Hands

The way cold porcelain is—
their movement
clean as knives
splitting pears.
Girls would give blood
for those hands.

His handshake,
the spread of his palms...

"You will live a long life.
Some woman will fall in love with your hands."

A Little Night Music

(travel essay)

It's impossible to escape the sun on the Côte d'Azur. Heat plays strange tricks, leeches the will, and drives everything crazy. Like the lavender—the tips of the shaggy lavender wands tickled my waist. Lawrence's hair, a van Gogh–orange, winked in and out amid the purple-gray blossoms, made him seem like a miniature of the dazzling sky-borne brute.

"It smells just like soap," he laughed, fiery beard brushing my knees, kisses let loose to wreak havoc. "The lavender smells like soap."

Later, in Grasse, a medieval town embedded in the rocky heel of the Alpes-Maritimes, we visited the great perfume manufacturers, found other scents. We learned how many tons of flowers it takes to produce an ounce of fragrance.

"Imagine all those flowers dying for one silly dram of perfume," I raged, remembering Saint-Raphaël—the lavender scent teased up by the breeze, Lawrence's petal-soft lips, the prick of his mustache and beard on the inside of my thigh.

"Insanity," he agreed. "I prefer my bouquet on the stem."

He toyed with my hair, making dark loops and coils. Passion filled my horizon again. But the jealous sun chafed, muscled in, dealt out headache and exhaustion. Too tired to enjoy one another, we moved on, a pair of sweaty palms exploring the coast.

At a café in Sainte-Maxime, a teenage waitress made a pass at Lawrence. Stringy-haired coquette, head cocked like a ragdoll, she slid her hands into her jeans, grinding this way and that. A crooked smile crept across Lawrence's face. His hands strayed from the table. But a demon wheeze seized him. He sneezed into a white pocket handkerchief and headed for the restroom. He returned green-faced. Too much coffee, not enough sleep.

"I think I've caught something," he reported. "It feels like a flu."

"In this heat?" I wondered. I noticed he was shivering.

Lawrence was ill, and I get cranky when he is unwell. He's helpless, a child. I dragged him through stations, pushed him onto trains. I couldn't fault his reluctance. We struggled with suitcases and baggage pushed in and out of train station lockers and an endless gnawing in French.

"Un franc, monsieur. Il faut payer."

Two women, the pay toilet attendants at Sainte-Maxime, barred his way to the restrooms, demanding their fee. Lawrence paid them, stood at a rail station urinal, his back to the gate. The old girls repositioned themselves on their extra-high stools. They spied over his shoulder, elbowed one another. One raised an eyebrow. One winked.

Saint-Tropez. Cannes. Antibes. Always, we found ourselves back on the trains, in compartments gasping under a tyranny of armpits and sweat. On our way to Monaco, we sat across from a couple of nuns. They rolled their rosaries around in their clean, old hands. I thought of the young waitress in Sainte-Maxime, hands in her pants, and of the two pay toilet monitors, of myself. Jarring contrasts and strange correlations. Six women reach toward one another across a chasm of philosophy and time.

Then, we were in Nice. The sun, a big copper gong, smoldered high overhead in a wrapper of haze. The sea was a vitreous blue. We sat on deckchairs, our backs to the city—behind us, the Promenade des Anglais. A river of old people with hair like batting, complexions like broken geraniums, drifted by. On the other side of the promenade, a seawall of multifloored buildings rose, curved around the coast, chalky fronts peering out over the Mediterranean Sea. Further down the beach, the tangle of trash cans, brown bodies, paper sacks, and food crowded in a ghetto of flesh and debris. Nice, like a thick grenadine, trickled over us.

We squandered an afternoon at the water's edge. Yellow buoys bobbed on the water's surface. A young fisherman sat on the end of the pier, his pole dipped halfheartedly into the shallows. The sun fell behind the dome of the magnificent Hotel Negresco. A flag mounted upon the rotunda seemed to clutch at it as it went. It was muggy, still warm. Soon enough, we would be on another train, in another couchette, on our way to Geneva. The humidity sheathed us like a second skin. The night air brought with it a separate chill.

"Lawrence, are you cold?" I asked, noticing the goose flesh on my own bare arms.

He didn't respond. He was writing busily in his journal. No doubt he was stringing together metaphors, similes to describe the sun. He pointed to his subject of study, that red-shelled beetle creeping out of the sky. On the beach, sunbathers clumped together, trying to share one another's warmth. They refused to relinquish their hold on day even as it slipped out from under them. The first artificial lights twinkled on.

Umbrellas closed. The last sun worshippers wound themselves around and around in sweaters and towels. At our backs, the city awakened, gaily decked in tiaras of light. We walked along the darkening lip of sand. My hands fumbled under Lawrence's clothes, hunting for remnants of fever, the shreds of warmth hidden within him.

Lawrence slid his hands into my jeans.

"Ew," he said with a shudder, "cold ass."

"Cold ass, hot snatch," I said smartly, moving his hands.

Point of ignition, I could feel the flame leap.

"You devil," he hissed.

"C'mon, Lawrence," I dared, "Let's make a fire."

His mouth was already on mine. I squeezed my eyes shut and held on, clinging like a drowning woman, wanting to bring him down, too. I tried to push through the rack of his ribs, press toward his heart, toward the tented wings of his lungs. It was his breathing that filled the cavity of my chest. Soothed by his warmth, the rhythm of his hips. His life was a river that snaked into me, ran the length of my limbs, spilled heat.

Later, his arms still around me, we sat for a while, like nesting boxes, looking out toward the shadowed horizon, braced against nightfall. A few feet away, the cold sea sucked at the land. Music whined, petulant, from one of the clubs. It hung plaintively over us for a moment, wafted out over the black waves, dissolved.

We fled inland, toward the trains.

Dante, Mayo, and the Libidinous Finns

(travel essay; excerpts)

"Il y a des mains pareilles à des feuilles capturées. Et d'autres qui parlent sans arrêt dans leurs collerettes de rires."

—Jehan Mayoux, *Au crible de la nuit, 1948*

There are hands that resemble captive leaves. And others that, trapped in their quicksand of laughter, speak without cease.

Finland is Western Europe's northernmost country. Further north than much of Siberia, it hangs, with Sweden, from the horn of the cold Arctic Circle, one of a pair of saddlebags straddling the Gulf of Bosnia. All winter the days are locked in darkness. In summer, the nights are white, the watery light leaking into dreams and slumbers. It was June. I was traveling in Scandinavia with Lawrence. Night after night I wrestled with the flickering glare. Sleep-starved, I stumbled from smoldering midnights to shimmering noons, a somnambulist trapped in the endless river that flowed between those twin cauldrons. Lawrence moved through the marathon days with an animal zeal, feasting on big bowls of herring and sour cream, guzzling down strong aqua vitae as if it were water, as if the bleak memory of winter—of hibernation and silence—were locked within him, an unspoken warning and inescapable goad. Paris was our next destination. I longed for it.

Traveling by train, the trip to Paris from Orebro, Sweden, would take thirty-four hours. I sleep well on trains. The dark rattle of a rail car has always been soothing to me. But we had a problem with bookings, and at the Orebro station, instead of the comfortable bunks of a first-class compartment, we were faced with a cramped glass-doored cabinet. Four seats upholstered in dirty brocade crowded two of the facing walls. The green floor was marbled in grime. When we slid open the door, an explosion of sulfurous, sweet-heavy heat engulfed us.

"Lawrence," I hissed, "this is not a couchette."

"I see that," Lawrence replied, his blue eyes darting beneath the gold flutter of lashes taking in the whole picture...

The first man to enter was handsome, young, and quite tall, with long, dark hair and eyes like a Siberian husky. He sat next to me. The second, also tall and angular, had curly, blond hair and skin as pitted as a lunar sea. He took the seat next to Lawrence. They appeared to be companions, or at least countrymen, for they spoke to one another in Finnish, a kind of staccato clucking. One of them had a deck of cards. It was quickly opened, and they began to play a strange game reminiscent of liar's dice. The corridor outside the compartment was beginning to fill up. Faces peered in, assessed the occupants, and moved on. A river of students eddied and swelled, parting finally to reveal two girls. One was a plump redhead, her cherub shape squeezed into a pair of black jeans and a black T-shirt. The other was a frail blonde with a face like a Botticelli Venus, except that there was a carnal glint in her eyes when she spotted the dark-haired Finn and pushed open the door...

The girls got up often, leaving the room in slipstreams of their scents and returning to catch the attention and, occasionally, a remark from one or another of the two Finnish men. They were invited to join the card game and participated in a halfhearted way. In this limbo, the train sweated its way into Copenhagen, disgorged some of its passengers, clattered through a few more dreary suburban miles, and was loaded, in Gothenburg, onto a cross-channel carrier. It was a cumbersome process, complicated by the presence on this ferry of a duty-free shop. The Finns evaporated like phantoms at dawn.

"They're gone," I barely breathed.

"They're at the duty-free shop." Lawrence replied sagely.

"Lawrence," I warned, "I have to sleep."

"It will get easier," he replied. "It will get darker. We're moving toward the sunset."

I smiled tiredly, thinking of the drawn look of my sleep-deprived face, the lines etched into the corners of my mouth. Behind Lawrence the sun was setting in a bright scarlet gash.

"You look like a nefarious poppy," Lawrence continued, his hands resting on my knees. His eyes fixed me in a blue-gray gaze as riveting as two metal spikes. I could smell the beer and whisky on his breath. "I can see the sunset reflected on your face. I like seeing it this way—indirectly." His hands moved over my thighs.

Behind him the sun bled red onto the black eyebrow of earth. The dark Finn leaned over the arm of my chair.

"It is really a remarkable sunset," he said in a clipped British English. His lapse into English scared me. It had an eerie effect—like a ventriloquist's puppet, echoing Lawrence.

"She's tired," Lawrence said, addressing the Finn. "She needs to sleep."

"Yes," came the Finn's voice, so close to my ear that I felt it was in my own head. "Yes, I can see that."

I thought I was dreaming. I felt a great vault open beneath me, felt myself falling, again, into an abyss under the spell of language. Darkness closed over me.

When I awoke it was to a world of shadows. Lawrence was awake, his face alight with jack-o'-lantern laughter as he surveyed a diabolical scene. A full moon, or nearly, washed the compartment in ghostly light. Next to Lawrence the blond man was beginning his descent, a long slow slide toward the faux malachite of the floor. He was aided in this by the powerful legs of the redhead. The soles of her feet, now angled against his hip, exerted a purposeful pressure as she unconsciously claimed the entire banquette for her own. Obliterated by whisky and beer, he colluded with her intentions, in unknowing self-sabotage. We watched as he slid from his seat, folding over himself like a jackknife, falling to the floor unconscious. Once crumpled onto the larger space, he began to unfurl like one of those small paper flowers that, placed in a bath of water, blossom and open. He uncurled slowly, his recumbent form carpeting the floor like an exotic animal skin, his head resting lightly on the toe of Lawrence's shoe. If Lawrence were to move his foot slightly, the curly blond head would hit forcefully against the sharp metal rim of an adjacent wastebasket. I noticed that Lawrence was laughing soundlessly, tears rolling down his cheeks.

"Look," he managed to rasp, indicating the compartment's far corner.

I turned reluctantly from the Finn, so delicately balanced upon Lawrence's foot, to observe that the tender blonde Aphrodite had grasped the hand of the other sleeping man and was moving it slowly and rather thoughtfully over her small breasts. He twitched slightly, like a large dog dreaming. Then murmuring something, he slowly rolled toward her, covering her body with his. His hands, in the darkness, looked like white foraging rodents. She slithered beneath him, finding the fork in his body, and lodged herself there, arching into him in the timeless maneuver that undoubtedly fostered Rome's greatest engineering accomplishment.

His response was predictable. They had formed an inseparable sandwich, fused into a coupling of delicate pressure and delectable glissades. Then we watched as a pair of hands so fair they appeared to be gloved pulled the man's jeans down over his hips and loins, and the marble-white mirror image of the near-full moon glistened in the compartment's dim corner, rising and falling in an ancient and irresistible rhythm. It was shocking. It was exhilarating. It was as if the night had become effervescent, the compartment filled with fairies. Outside, moonlight, like a dreamy lichen, furred the furrowed fields in silver. Lawrence's sleepless visage was Mithras-like. Mirth mantled him in glittering light. A profound hilarity seemed to well up inside me, the way as children, laughter gathers and threatens in the dark bole of a church.

In a rush of soft groans, purring and pleasant animal sounds, the movement in the chamber's corner stopped, the participants parted, rearranged themselves and exited, trysting again in the corridor for a slow cigarette. Lawrence, cradling the head of the man at our feet, eased it past the metal rim of the wastebasket and onto the floor. A breeze rolled in through the windows, thinning the civet-thick scent of sex that now blanketed the compartment. I fell asleep again in the darkness.

Morning, sour and bright, awakened me. Lawrence was sleeping, finally surrendered to the dark wave that had gathered on the other side of the leaves of his energies. At our feet, the blond Finn slept, curled into a fetal position, his sallow cheeks still pressed into the dirty floor. Next to me the other man slept also, dark brow furrow-less, forehead smooth as an infant's. The redhead, like a selkie, was combing her long siren hair. The blonde nymph's seat was empty...

One by one the others awakened. Activity swelled again in the corridor. Sleepy heads lifted. Students rose from bed rolls hastily thrown here and there in the halls. The blonde girl returned. A babel of languages surged in through the door behind her. Her return awakened the man asleep on the floor. He rose and looked about sheepishly, his face coloring with crimson as he climbed into his seat. The dark-haired Finn watched him in amusement and offered a few encouraging words in their language. Lawrence, at last yawning and stretching his legs, said a cheerful good morning to all in English.

The dark-haired Finn looked over at me. "You are feeling better?" he asked.

"Yes," I said warmly, raising an eyebrow. "And you?"

"Oh, yes," he said smiling. "Much better."

Lawrence cleared his throat and looked at his watch. "Nine forty-five," he said. "Nearly thirty-four hours. We have witnessed the sunset. We have lived through the night."

We lurched forward and stopped in a fitful progress. The trains were backed up and delayed. In this manner, we rolled slowly toward the Gare de l'Est. Around us graffiti rose in monstrous swirls on the concrete lips of the platforms. We slid toward the rude din of the station, sucked into the terminal darkness, arriving at last in Paris.

Stranger

Strangers
intoxicate me
when, too close,
the current of their lives
streams into mine.
Friend or foe,
I want to let them in.

You, I have met before,
staggering under
the impulse of acquaintance.
Lines of composition,
my eye traces
the path of your egress.
The sparsity of our
communion beckons.

Trying to push
flesh into flesh,
thrusting toward
a moment that crumbles,
disintegrates,
before it can complete,
suggesting only
that other entering
when all the outlines
are erased.

Strangers

(travel essay)

The allure of strangers is, for me, the allure of travel. The mysterious beckons—what we do not know. Maybe it is an intrigue, a shade drawn, a brocade curtain dropped. Curiosity is kindled. Small flames lick up. Appetites ignite. Potent and passionate, this fire destroys homes. I have scars from old firestorms. But my pyromania is a thing of the past. Still, there is no thrill like the first wicked little tongue of flame. It can appear anywhere. It smolders in a stranger's dark eyes, in lips full and soft, in a shadow that appears on a certain man's face at a particular time of day.

I was leaving Antwerp behind. The rail car rocked and rolled on its carriage, shaking me up. Outside the train windows the landscape rushed by, rain-soaked and dark. Antwerp had been gloomy, the weather bad. Peter Paul Rubens's rosy nudes seemed to sulk, petulant under a murky pall. Lawrence and I had ventured out under big black umbrellas until the damp and cold crawled under our clothes, spreading icy hands over our flesh. But the weather drove us indoors. We retreated to the warm cocoon of the hotel room, to the ministrations of kitchen and staff. We spent two days between sheets, until they were thick white ropes, twisted and knotted; days punctuated by the gloved knock of the bellman, platters of smoked eel, delicate wines, pastry crumbs.

"This rain won't let up," Lawrence said, leaning into his arms, his weight against the window casement.

I was watching the hard line of his back, ass, and thigh, the way muscle bunched and stretched with each movement, the white sheen of bare skin.

"I'm leaving for England tomorrow." He turned toward me.

"Why?" I asked, "Can't take anymore?" Fingertip to my breasts, I traced each nipple, watching them rise and harden under my touch.

"Hardly," he said, leaning over me, replacing my hands with his.

"Maybe I'm not finished with you yet," I said.

"Maybe not, but I've got to work."

"Fine," I murmured into his neck. "I'll take the train."

I took the train. Antwerp to dreary Ostend—I leaned back into the train cushions' dingy velour plush. Most of my body ached. The chill had finally weaseled its way into my core. My limbs thrummed in exhaustion. Part of me craved still more attention. That morning I had noticed how my nipples had darkened, become deeply russet. Other changes—breasts and lips swollen. A delicious languor filled me. I was leaking sex.

Thunder? Or was it the train roaring along its track? The low rumble rose, not in the distance, but beneath me like a flapping sheet of metal, noisy and grim. On the shape-shifting horizon, an arrowhead of tiny black birds shot heavenward. A cuckoo nest looked cockeyed, balanced precariously, high in a tree. The cows never looked up from the high grass that they'd settled in. Ramshackle houses. Rail tracks crisscrossing. Rust rail on rust. Fat bundles of sheep buried deep in grass. And the gray curtain of rain draped over all.

A long-haired young man walked down the aisle past me, backtracked, hoisted his bag up onto the rack over my head. His jeans brushed my cheek when he did this. He smelled of vanilla and bay rum.

"You don't mind?" he asked in English.

"Oh, no, not at all," I replied.

He sat across from me, right ankle resting on left knee, pushing his long brown hair behind his ears. I looked back out the window. His gaze followed mine.

I'd left Lawrence in Brussels. Apprehensive, I was having one of my panic attacks—my heart racing like a featherweight stockcar, slapped with its decals—old memories, old wounds.

Even now, anxiety stabbed with the thought of Lawrence standing, strangely alone, two suitcases and his briefcase stacked neatly beside him. I reminded myself that I'd see him again, in England. Sudden and vivid, the recollection of our dinner at a restaurant in Antwerp—champagne cocktails, a golden Sancerre, much wine. I saw Lawrence's white business card, illuminated in his hand, like some auspicious and mysterious sign in a Cocteau film. The card looked luminous in the shadowy dining room, a ghost object, something drawn from another world or from a magician's hat, like an egg or a live, kicking rabbit.

"So, where are you headed?" the young man asked.

"Huh? Oh, Ostend. I'm taking the ferry to Dover."

"The ferry? That's a long ride."

"I mean the hydrofoil," I corrected myself. "I'm meeting someone in England."

"Someone?" he asked playfully.

"Yes," I mumbled. "Someone."

Outside, the cows huddled in one corner of a rainy field. They were red-spotted. Their large pink noses quivered as the train clattered past them. I saw my own brown eye flash past, reflected in the window on a background of clay and white houses, the protective coloration of the collective. My eye looked dark and mysterious, an inquisitive brown orb sliding thoughtfully over the landscape, over farm and hamlet alike. The young man's visage was reflected in the window, somewhere behind mine—his face, curious and attentive, his hair, softly umber—a cloud in the back of my mind. I had seen Lawrence this way, in the train window, reflected on rivers and castles along the Rhine. I had drawn him twice, once as an Egyptian with kohl-rimmed eyes, because I saw the suggestion of this in my own eye and in the deep creases that crawl from the corners of his. I told him that I would begin to draw him then and that I would draw him eight thousand times. He told me that would take thirty years, at one image a day. I have thirty years; but I drew him twice, thinking to make it fifteen.

"I'm getting off at Bruges," my compartment companion announced. "Have you ever been there?"

"No," I answered, looking at him closely. He had a handsome face, tawny lips, beautiful white teeth, a compassionate smile.

"It's like Venice, very romantic," he said.

"Really?"

"Yes, you could even have lunch there," he added. "My treat."

His invitation, the sincerity of his voice, kindled a response in me. I felt its pull—the stranger's desire to connect.

"I don't think so," I said. "I'd be late. I have to meet someone."

He nodded and smiled. "I see," he said.

The train pulled into Ghent. A line of shabby buildings sagged mournfully on either side of the track. The black-trunked chestnut trees with their tattered, rust-tipped leaves provided only a partial curtain. The train pulled out. The brick became modern. We passed through secluded coverts. Trailers nestled in them like little white eggs—more clay and white houses, clay and white cows, and the ominous gray of the sky.

The young man, whose name was Michael, told me about his career as an ecological engineer. He was exuberant. He was full of fire. He asked me, again, about lunch. I was hungry. I'd had nothing to eat but a cookie and coffee at around six in the morning. Again I declined. But I liked the way he would smile out the window and watch me from the corner of his eye. I regretted my rush.

One cannot, of course, see much of Bruges from the rail station—wet streets, shiny asphalt, more cloud covered sky. It didn't look much like Venice, but it was charming, a city of very old houses. Michael got off there. Reaching up for his bag, he looked down at me.

"Last chance," he said.

I smiled and shook my head no.

I missed him at once. The rail car seemed empty and forlorn. I sneezed twice. "Damn this cold weather," I thought. "I'm catching a cold."

Outside, the landscape was flattening—Ostend, dirty Ostend, opening onto the channel, the crossing to England.

The ferry terminal was not attractive at all. Was this what one was to expect crossing over? Everyone looked equally bad in the urine-yellow light. I had yet to purchase a ticket to Victoria Station and another from Eustace Station. There'd be a cab ride, too, in between. I had no idea of time. I changed money. A certain criminal air hung over everything. After the efficiency of the trains, the ferry operations seemed tardy and mediocre. Not so bad, I supposed, if one had only to do this once, this second-class sort of steerage, as if large herds of cattle were daily shuttling back and forth.

"It's a long way to England," I thought. "Red Rover, Red Rover, send my lover over to Dover."

It was clear, when they announced the first movie, that I had boarded the wrong vessel. I was not on the high-speed hydrofoil. I was on the ferry—the slow boat to Dover. Too late to turn back, the seamless gray of channel and sky stretched before me. I sulked in the cabin, pressed around by large families, by children running about. I read for a while. I slept fitfully. Roused by my hunger, I got up from my seat and foraged, found nothing to my liking in the cafeteria. I bought Belgian chocolates, for gifts, at the duty-free shop thinking I'd eat some of them. I got wedged into a line. Someone was shoving behind me—a young man in a black leather jacket.

"They're pushing behind me," he explained. "Cut it out," he yelled over his shoulder, hazel eyes full of laughter. I considered the broad backside of the person in front of me and decided to hold my line. Still jostled, I paid for the chocolate with large bills and made my way back to my seat. He followed and took the seat next to mine. He had a guitar. He had a small knapsack on his back. Six gold hoops of diminishing size glittered on the lobe of his right ear. I would have guessed him to be nineteen, but the fifth of vodka that he'd bought at the duty-free shop suggested he might be older than that.

"Name's David," he said. "Wanna play cards?"

I looked at him, at my book, at the featureless horizon outside the window, at the vodka, and said "Okay."

We played a childish game. We played "War." He snapped up my cards with a wide grin and gusto. Occasionally, he'd take a pull from the vodka.

"Do you play the guitar?" I asked.

"Yeah," he said, taking a break from our card game to plunk out a few notes. It sounded nothing like music. "I'd play a song for you," he said. "I'd play a song for you, because you're so pretty."

He placed his hand on my thigh and leaned toward me. The thick brown curls of his hair smelled of sweat and dust. A silver chain swung from his shirt. It had a funny charm on it that looked like a boot. His breath smelled faintly of liquor, liquor and the Belgian chocolates that I'd bought. I reached out to touch each of the tiny gold hoops that gleamed on his ear. He rubbed his jaw voluptuously against the back of my hand. I was surprised at how soft it was.

When we disembarked at Dover, David hovered protectively at my elbow, using his body as a barrier between me and the crowd of other passengers. The guitar on his back made him dangerous. The night was rainy and black. The famous white cliffs of Dover were ash-colored ghosts hunched in darkness. We stood in long lines under fluorescent lamps, waiting for passport stamps and instructions. We all boarded a bus to the train station. David sat next to me.

"I've missed my train," I said.

"We're both going to London," he said happily. "We'll keep one another company."

"Yes," I agreed. He scooted closer to me on the seat. "Yes, that'll be fine."

Once at Dover Station, we found that the last train would leave in ten minutes. It would let us off at Victoria Station. We'd both need to catch cabs or the Underground to Eustace Station to get on with our journeys, but there would be no trains out of Eustace until the next morning. We could not stay all night at the station.

"We can share a cab," David insisted, showing me the paltry cash he had on hand.

"And a room?" I asked.

"Well?" he smiled shyly, his fingertips stroking the back of my hand.

I must have smiled sympathetically, because he grabbed my hand quickly and said, "Come on. Come on, now, the train will be leaving."

"Wait," I said. "I have to place a call."

"Not now," he insisted.

"There is someone waiting for me," I said.

I found a telephone booth and stepped into it, trying to figure out how to use it. I hadn't enough change. David loaned me twenty pence, his face worried as I made my connection.

Lawrence's voice: "What happened? You weren't at the station. No, don't risk the hotels in London. Stay where you are. Find a place for the night."

We talked on and on and David faded, a ghost, a waif drifting reluctantly off to the last train. I didn't even see him leave. I heard the train pull out and knew I must find a place for the night in Dover.

The station was deserted. It had a sorrowful, funereal feel. David's puppy-like zeal had been comforting. I felt lonely. The station master grew kinder as the crowd thinned. At last, he pointed toward an embankment on the hill above the station.

"There'll be a bed and breakfast up there," he said. "Or you can check out the Priory, right across the street."

Yearning for charm and intimacy, I climbed the steps to the street above and crossed it, dodging puddles and a sudden couple of cars, to the line of tall, narrow buildings, each with its sign, "Bed and Breakfast."

Selecting one, I walked hopefully up the front stairs. A florid, bleary-eyed woman met me at the door. She had on a thin cotton robe that came to her knees, white socks, and slippers. Knots of varicose veins, purple and green, marbled the stone-colored flesh of her calves. A bonnet of curlers and pin-curls capped her head.

"Oh, yes," she said in answer to my questions, "I'll show you the room, then."

She climbed the cramped stairway with great difficulty, her slippered feet catching often on the frayed, floral carpet. The room was dreadful—dirty and drab.

"I was also thinking about the Priory," I said, turning to where she stood in the doorway behind me, hands on wide hips. "Do you know it?"

"Oh, yes," she remarked critically. "I don't think you'd like it. New owners and all. You can still smell the paint."

"Well, I need to check it out," I replied. "I'll probably be back."

I was back on the cold street, the promise of new paint my sole comfort.

The Priory was a crowded matchbox of warmth. Rosy faces, glowing in firelight, turned toward my entrance. I found the manager, a thin, dark-haired man, and explained my situation to him.

"Been to the hill, have you?" he laughed. "Well, we'll set you up. Jeffrey, show this lady one of the rooms."

Jeffrey, who was serving beers at the bar, was fair and muscular. He had spiky blond hair that stood up from his head and seemed to ignite in the firelight. A faint golden stubble covered his jaw. I followed him up a meandering staircase, past other landings, to a small white door. The room was small also, but crammed with a large pine armoire, antique table, and chest drawers. The four-poster bed was nearly buried under a down comforter covered with a delicate rosebud pattern. The room had a clean porcelain bath and the smell of fresh paint—white trim, soft aqua walls.

"It's perfect," I sighed. "How much?"

"Twenty pounds," was the prompt response.

"I'll take it." I was elated.

Jeffrey walked into the bathroom. "Lovely bath," he said proudly, "right in the room. You'll probably want that."

I wondered, for a moment, if I now smelled like David—sweaty and faintly alcoholic. A vague nostalgia stirred.

"Can I pay you now?" I asked. "I have to catch a four a.m. train."

"'Course," Jeffrey answered. "Hardly worth sleeping. Come on out back, and I'll show you how to leave in the morning. There'll be no one up at that hour."

He led me downstairs and took me out back to a little fenced garden where a prim white gate opened onto the street. It was windy and wet. Leaves and blossoms, whipped to a frenzy, released a sinuous fragrance—the foliage dripping, the night bitter cold.

"This'll be it. Would you like me to wake you?" he asked. His blue eyes held something behind them: chaos, the first sign of a blaze.

"I don't think so," I said. "But thanks, anyway."

We were turning to leave when I stopped him. "Listen," I ventured, "I'm starving. Any chance of some food?"

"Sorry, no," he said. "The kitchen's been closed for hours. Maybe a package of chips." Disappointment edged his voice.

"I'll pass," I said glumly. "How about some white wine?"

"That I think can do," he responded shortly. We both went inside.

As Jeffrey did not come up with the wine, I hopped into the bath. "Probably pissed off at me," I thought. The bath was a luxury, after the arduous day. Blowing my nose into toilet paper, I knew that I really was catching a cold. I coddled myself, admiring my body in the herb-scented water. I took my sweet time. I was just getting out when I heard someone knocking. In mild irritation, I put on a robe and opened the door. Jeffrey stood in the hall with a large service tray. He had untied his tie and unbuttoned his collar. His eyes twinkled with merriment. On the tray was a platter of toast, chicken liver pâté in a big, clumsy bowl, and *two* glasses of white wine. He smiled gallantly.

"I've put something together for you," he said. "Hope you like it."

I looked ruefully at the two glasses of wine.

"I've changed my mind," I said. "You can wake me at four."

"Great," he exclaimed. "Let's drink to it."

"Oh, all right," I surrendered. "Come on in. But remember to wake me at four. I have someone waiting for me."

Lawrence, Cortés, and the Attraction of Gold

(travel essay; excerpts)

Traveling south from Mexico City, we crawled past fields of sugar cane and rice, through maguey-haunted landscapes. The car belonged to Arturo, our shaman-like guide...

Arturo was dealing a series of tales like cards from a soothsayer's deck. He conjured the Olmecs, the plumed god Quetzalcoatl, Spanish *hidalgos*, and the ancient city of Tula. But I listened with only the slightest attention. My focus was fastened on Lawrence. Lawrence leaned on the frame of the open window, letting the wind cool his sunburnt eyelids. Under the narrow brim of his Panama hat, his eyelashes looked golden. His beard and mustache, ignited by the bright sunlight, made him look as though he were fashioned of gold, and I thought of Cortés as I studied Lawrence with fascination.

Cortés went to Taxco looking for gold. He'd heard that the Tlahuica, the Native Americans who inhabited the area, paid their debts in blocks of solid gold. In the eighteenth century Taxco became a boom town. Silvery, argonaut fortunes were built there. Remote, it stayed beautiful...

The nine of us stayed at the Hotel Los Arcos, in rooms that were once monks' cells, and listened at night to the rattling chains and incantations of the candlelit Easter processions. The night was full of prayers to saints and virgins. It was full of chaste desires. Not surprisingly, of course, some of us were still virgins at the time.

No longer a virgin, I sat between two men in the back of a station wagon on this ascent to Taxco.

Will's moody power filled one side of the car; Lawrence's golden brilliance the other. As we climbed, I felt that we wobbled back and forth between the opposing axes like a misloaded carriage that was, at any moment, in danger of toppling over the road edge and into the canyon below. A light rain began to come down, compliments of Tlaloc, god of rainfall.

Taxco was as I remembered it—steep, cobblestone streets, the twin-towered coronet of the Santa Prisca Church, the pious accommodations of converted monasteries. When we arrived at our home for the evening, Cecelia peeled herself from her seat, headed straight for the lobby, and then to her room trailing a calamine slipstream. She promised to join us before dinner, at eight o'clock, in the lounge.

"You'll be eating at David's," Arturo advised us. "I know you will like it, señores."

"Come on, Arturo," Lawrence pleaded. "You must join us for a pre-dinner drink."

"Señores," Arturo demurred. "I am tired."

"I can't kick off the evening without you," Lawrence insisted. "I need more of those spellbinding stories."

"Well, señores, since you insist," Arturo shrugged. He cast a smug look at Will, who was too busy with suitcase, camera, and bags to notice. "I will join you."

"Great," Lawrence said. "Then we'll see everyone in an hour. We'll just put our bags up in the room."

Our room was white and monkishly simple. The floor was a rich red terra cotta. There were a few sticks of furniture made of charcoal-black wood and dry straw and a puritanical bed without bounce.

"Hardly the iniquitous den I had hoped for," I said sadly.

"It'll do," Lawrence replied, winding his arms around me. "These friars were a frolicsome lot."

We showered quickly, skin to skin, while outside the rain came down. We could hear it splattering off the veranda.

Lawrence lathered up—lean as a racehorse, high strung, and well hung.

"Look," he said toweling me dry. "Let's play parlor games. Let's play pin-the-tail-on-the-donkey."

"All right," I said warily. "Where's the donkey?"

"You are," Lawrence laughed. "Come over here."

The monk's bed had only slightly more give than the terra cotta floor. There were no lights overhead. It had gotten dark. Just a table lamp and a couple of candles. We opted for candles and fell asleep side by side. I woke up to pitch black. Lawrence was awake, eyes wide, staring into the darkness.

"Did you see him?" he asked in a whisper.

"Who?" I asked.

"The Mexican Moses," he answered.

"Uh, oh," I thought, searching his face and sniffing the air for intoxicants.

I remember the peyote on Xochicalco. Had Lawrence popped a few buttons?

"I saw a thin, bearded man, in a huge sombrero," Lawrence said. "He was standing right there in the corner. The sombrero was electric. It had cacti with luminous spines all over it. Rattlesnakes wound their way over the brim. There were lariats on it, cattle skulls, and bottles of tequila that glowed in the dark. He wore a serape. He looked straight at me. His eyes looked like water. I thought I'd fall into them."

This was very strange. Lawrence was conjuring visions like a starving mystic, and all I could think about was his downy ass!

"Lawrence, I didn't see any Moses," I said.

"Well," Lawrence replied, "I'd swear it was real."

"Just hallucinating," I concluded.

"Hallucination," Lawrence accepted.

"Lawrence," I reminded him, holding up my travel clock so he could see the numbers and hands in the darkness. "What about Arturo? We can't stand him up."

"Damn," Lawrence exclaimed, springing up. "Arturo. We'll hurry. Come on."

We dressed quickly and opened the door. The hot, floozy breeze gushed in. The night sky was curtained in lead and silver. Beneath it, the tile roofs of Taxco glistened, masked in watery shadow. We stood a few moments watching the sky prepare for the late-night pyrotechnics, then descended the steps and found our way to the cocktail lounge and Arturo. He had also changed clothes. He wore one of those Mexican shirts with embroidery down the front on either side of the buttoning placket. Cecelia was with him. She wore a Mexican blouse trimmed in lace. A colorful cotton skirt covered her bug-bitten legs.

"Anyone seen Will?" I asked casually.

"He is gone," said Arturo simply.

I thought I detected some pleasure in his voice. This was one more mystery to ponder.

Lawrence and I ordered drinks. Lawrence ordered a drink for Arturo. Once we had them, Arturo said, "Señores, you know I will not join you for dinner. I have my place and you have yours. But I'm glad you insisted upon a drink. It has been an interesting day."

"Yes," Lawrence agreed. "I just saw a Mexican Moses."

The fire leaped in the fireplace. Outside, raindrops exploded like small bombs on the swimming pool surface. Arturo did not even bat an eye at Lawrence's claim.

"You know, señores," he continued calmly, settling back into his chair, "there are many witches in Mexico."

Lost Pines

This year the Japanese beetle
has attacked my pines.
I will sell no trees this Christmas.
My wife works diligently,
makes baskets from the dead needles—
and me, with nothing to put in them.

Selections from Namako: Sea Cucumber

koji/orphans

Sara liked giving to others. When she was a small girl in Shanghai, she gave all her toys away to the children who begged in the city streets. "Street urchins," she called them, adding proudly, "they were my friends." Sara told us that she would come home from her boarding school for the holidays to a Christmas tree surrounded by presents. By January, when she returned to school, not a gift was left in the house. Grandmother let Sara know that she felt it was thoughtless and frivolous to give away all her gifts, but she continued to buy them for Sara every year, and Sara continued to hand them out to the first poor children she could find.

Sometimes Sara even gave our things away without asking. Once she gave away all of Mimi's old stuffed toys to a dirty, blonde neighborhood child. We discovered this when we found Mimi's battered, black-and-white bunny in a mud puddle far from the house. I brought it home and told Mimi that she had to take better care of her toys, but Mimi knew nothing about it. That's how we discovered what Sara had done. It wasn't so bad that Sara had given the old toys away; Mimi didn't play with them anymore. But the child that she'd given them to was dirty and careless. Mimi would have nothing to do with this girl even before she had mistreated one of Mimi's favorite stuffed animals. Mimi was furious with Sara for days.

I thought it was probably a good thing that Grandmother was leaving Akishima to her brothers instead of to Sara. Sara most likely would have given that away, too.

So Sara was moping about those old clothes and mourning their return when Ineko-san mentioned the orphanage in Hokkaido. She was trying to be helpful, of course, but she made things much worse.

Hokkaido is the wild, almost-forgotten island just north of Honshu. Floating between the Sea of Okhosk and the Sea of Japan, it is linked to Honshu by ferry across the gray Tsugaru Straits.

The Hokkaido orphanage was a small one, run by a handful of Japanese nuns who took care of around twenty parentless children. They had no source of support except their own labor and the meager contributions provided by the region's scant population. Ineko-san had a brother who lived and farmed in Hokkaido. Through him she discovered the orphans. Every year, she gave them rabbits, vegetables, fish, and whatever extra clothing she could spare. She told Sara that the orphans could really use our old clothing. The Hokkaido winters were cold, and the next one was fast on its way.

Ineko-san's suggestion had an amazing effect on Sara.

"Oh," Sara exclaimed, "yes, Hokkaido. I've been to Hokkaido. We went there one summer when I was a child. That is the land of the Ainu."

The Ainu, Sara told us, were the original inhabitants of Japan. They had blue eyes, wore little clothing, and were covered with hair. The Ainu lived in Hokkaido's deep, primal forests, in communities high in the mountains and in villages along the cold coast.

"They are far more Russian than Japanese," Sara continued. "They keep history alive through their oral tradition. They are the tellers of marvelous stories."

Naturally, based on Sara's account, we wanted to go to Hokkaido. We expected a wonderland full of magical Ainu, but it wasn't like that at all.

Hokkaido was a desolate place. Volcanic peaks, coarse and craggy like brutal stalagmites, climbed into the cold gray sky. Along the lonely coastline, thin cranes flapped, long necks like matchsticks, and heads capped in a fiery, sulfurous red.

We all went together on that first orphanage visit. Our crossing over the Tsugaru Straits was rough. We had to wear heavy coats to keep out the damp, clammy hands of the fog. The roads went from gravel to dirt to mud and sometimes to almost no road at all. Most of the landscape was unfarmed and untamed; where farms did exist, they were of the most primitive kind—mud huts or shacks with rickety tools scattered or hung about them.

The orphanage, at the end of a mire-clogged road, must have once been a farmhouse. It was made of straw-filled mud and the roof was thatch. Looking like wings, a couple of barracks-like buildings with tin roofs butted up against it on either side, giving the orphanage a cruciform shape. One wing served as the dormitory, the other as the refectory.

We got there at noon, later than we had planned. The nuns gave Gene and Sara a hurried but courteous welcome, then ushered us into the dining hall to have lunch with the orphans. When we entered the lunchroom, one extremely thin little boy rushed up to Sara and grabbed her hand.

"Okasan?" he asked, desperately pulling at her.

"No, not your mother," the shortest Japanese nun said kindly, bending down to the small child and gently prying his hand loose.

"Come now, let us have lunch," she said.

He trotted obediently beside her, looking plaintively back over his shoulder at Sara, the question of "Mother?" still in his eyes. Sara's mouth hung open, still formed around the "Yes," she wanted to say but did not.

"He does that with every woman who comes in the door," the other nun said apologetically. "He's been here for months. His mother is dead, but he thinks she is coming to get him." Sara looked very sad.

We sat down to a lunch of white rice and chicken and various kinds of fish. I noticed the orphans ate rice and vegetables—mainly turnips and carrots. They were the thick, tough kind of carrots—the kind we usually gave to Mimi's rabbit.

"Why don't you tell that boy that his mother is dead?" I asked the nun who'd stayed with us.

"We've tried to tell him his mother wasn't coming," she said.

"But you didn't actually tell him?" I demanded.

Sara's eyes looked as if she were suffering. "Ellen," she said, "that's enough."

"Well, I'd tell him," I said. "I'd tell him she's dead, and she'll never come. I wouldn't let him go on hoping for something that won't happen. It's ridiculous," I added frostily. "It's worse. It's pathetic."

It seemed cruel to let the boy continue to believe that each woman to walk in the door might be his mother. It seemed to me that the most horribly hopeless thing was his hope. "I'd tell him," I repeated. "I'd tell him the truth."

I visited the orphanage three times after that with Sara, and that little boy always ran up and ambushed her with the same pitiful question. Then finally, one visit, he was not there to greet us with his wretched little wishes. Sara said nothing, but I watched her eyes move like silent sentinels over the haggard young faces that surrounded us, searching the rows of children for him. Sara was afraid to ask where he was, but I wasn't.

"Oh, it's so very sad," the nun murmured in response. "He got sick, and he never got better. He grew weaker and weaker. I'm so sorry. He's dead."

"That's what happens when you feed someone lies," I said hotly. I thought of the orphan waking every morning with the hope that his mother would come for him. What must he have felt as each day unraveled into the next? What does it feel like to lose hope piece by piece, without explanation, until there is nothing left?

I knew it was wrong not to say anything. But I never did tell him the truth. I never screamed, "Stop it. Stop it," when he attached himself to us. "This is Sara. She isn't your mother. Don't you know your mother is dead? She's not going to come." And Sara never said anything either. No, we never slammed him brutally in the face with the truth to save him from the heartbreaking disappointment that his hope brought him to, over and over again. Instead, we let him believe, so that we could pretend that his mother was still alive. That made me think we were cowards.

namako/sea cucumber

Splack.
...splack.
...splack.

Anne was a silhouette in front of the sun-smeared windowpane of the biology lab of the American school. Outside, the snow was piled high. She stood on a box, holding negatives up to the light, loudly snapping her gum. "Ummm, these are pretty weird." Splack.

"The inside of a frog testicle." Splack...splack.

"Wow, urine crystals."

She was looking at our biology slides, and wasn't concentrating on how she put them back into their tray. She was getting them all messed up. We were alone in the spotless, clinical brilliance of the science lab at the American school—Anne and me and my squid...

I WALKED OVER TO THE windows. The late sun had cast them in bright topaz. I picked up the box that Anne had been standing on earlier.

"I'm going to draw one of these," I said, scrupulously positioning the box at the foot of one of the lockers. I had to stand on tiptoe to reach the particular jar. I climbed down cautiously, mindful not to slip or drop it. I had selected it long ago when it had made a brief appearance during a lecture on coelenterates. It was my favorite creature. The jar seemed to have a life of its own. It threatened to slide from my hands. I walked over to one of the lab tables and set the glass container on top of it, surprised that the hand that had gripped it was not wet. Had

I imagined a wetness? Only the dull smell of formaldehyde lingered on my fingers and on the flat of my palm.

The brown thing in the jar looked like a long pouch fringed at the mouth with whisker-like tentacles.

"This is a sea cucumber," I said. "It is an animal. Doesn't it look a lot like a vegetable, though? It's even named for a vegetable. It must be horrible to be so strange that nobody knows what you really are."

Anne leaned close to the jar in which the cucumber dangled quiescently, so close that her long lashes appeared to brush the glass. Next to the embalmed form, her face looked pale, like a small moon. "It's so awful looking," she murmured, with the hushed appreciation generally reserved for only the holiest things in church. "What are you going to do with it?"

"I'm taking it home with me," I reported with great satisfaction. "Mr. Graham told me I could."

Anne looked up quizzically, and then back at the jar, as though she were trying to draw some connection. I offered no explanations. I wrapped the jar in my woolen, navy blue sweater and slid it into my bag. We didn't say much on the way home. Anne surprised me by getting off the bus at my stop.

"I'm walking to your house with you," she declared.

The dry snow crunched under our boots. It looked like dirty lace trimming the sides of the road.

"Are you going to show that to anyone else?" Anne asked suddenly. She had on a pair of green earmuffs that, along with her big dark eyes, made her look especially childish.

"Yes. I'm going to show it to Sara. I think she will like it. Don't you think I should?"...

I KNEW AS I ENTERED the *genkan* and took off my shoes that something was wrong. Gene was home. He stood in the kitchen, leaning against one of the counters. I thought he would get the neat white sleeve of his shirt dirty on the usually sticky surface. Ineko-san was standing in one corner of the kitchen, sniffing into a handkerchief that she held up to her nose and mouth. Sara sat in one of the kitchen chairs, her back straight as a rod, her face colorless.

"I'm home," I announced hopefully, as though I expected this would somehow break the spell under which they seemed frozen. Sara turned her head and stared at me as if she couldn't quite place me.

Gene said, "Ellen, your grandmother has had a stroke. The doctor's just been here."

Ineko-san sniffed loudly in her corner of the room. I noticed the faint smell of disinfectant and medication that was Dr. Kimura's signature.

"Is she all right?" I asked, feeling my plan to surprise Sara crumble. Selfishly, I wanted Grandmother to be fine so that Gene could go back to work and Sara would get out of that chair and Ineko-san would stop her sniveling and I could show Sara the sea cucumber.

Gene said, "The doctor says she's doing all right. Ineko-san will be staying; I'll need you to help her out."

"Okay," I said simply. I went and stood next to Sara, my arms wrapped protectively around my book bag.

I wanted to pull out the sea cucumber and show it to her. I imagined her face filling with wonder. She'd like it. She would be profoundly amazed. It was my little creature. I'd found something as strange as anything Sara had known. Instead, I did nothing. Sara reached up and pushed back the hair that had settled across my forehead. The movement had a mechanical quality, as though she had brushed at a moth.

"There's a good child," she said tonelessly. "Your grandmother's very ill, Ellen. Why don't you go look in on her?"

"All right, Sara, I will," I responded and fled from the room. I fled from the people frozen there, from the meticulous knot of Gene's tie, from Ineko-san's crumpled white handkerchief, from the loose-fitting platinum rings on Sara's left hand.

The metal doorknob was icy. Grandmother's room was icy as well. It was like walking into a refrigerator. The heavy curtains were drawn. Puffs of mist seemed to form with my breath. The smell of medication assailed me. Grandmother lay on the bed under a thick shell of patterned silk coverlets. Her face, helmeted with steely-gray hair, was barely visible at the head of the bed, and her thin, bed-jacketed arms stretched on either side of her on top of the heavy futons, so that she looked like a pharaoh or the top of a marble sarcophagus. Her breathing was shallow, her face motionless—a mask—the flesh of her body draped so sparely over her bones that I thought I could almost see through it to the bed beneath her. The frigid air of the room scratched at my throat and lungs when I breathed. I felt it was cold enough to make my nose bleed. Unable to stand it, I wanted to leave. Then Grandmother's eyes opened, depthless, like two broken bits of black glass. Her mouth pulled at the corners, stretching her thin lips across her teeth as if she were trying to speak, and her gaze moved down toward her hand. It was opening and closing stiffly and the effort was making her arm shake. She seemed to want something, but I wasn't sure what. Fearfully, I put my own hand in hers, and when her fingers closed around mine, the strength of her grip frightened me. Her hand was cold, like the room, like the silk covers beneath it. Suddenly, I realized that my hand was locked in a vise. Grandmother's hand was not going to open. I was trapped. Then her eyes closed, and I stood beside her for a long time, staring into the lineless map of her face.

"What do you want from me?" I asked the face of the demanding old woman who was so acutely critical, who thought that I had no soul. Then I asked it in Japanese.

All around me, playing hide and seek in the silence, were whispering voices. "What do you want? What do you want?" they echoed like gossips mocking me over a fence. "She doesn't know. No one will tell her," they tittered. The voices grew louder and louder. I wanted to put my hands over my ears, but Grandmother's fingers were still gripping mine. I felt dizzy. It was as if I'd ascended to an enormous height and the air was so thin that I could not get enough. I felt hollow and light-headed. I could no longer feel my body.

This must be what a ghost feels like, I thought, as the world started spinning and consciousness seemed to start to slip out from under me. Then I heard my grandmother's breathing cutting through the low buzz of the voices. In and out, in and out, in long, muffled rasps, like a door creaking open and shut, pulling me back to the bedroom. I let it bring me back to the bedside, let myself be soothed by the laboring saw of her breath. Then the voices subsided, and Grandmother's hold on me loosened a bit so I could pry my hand free.

I walked shakily to the window and peered through the curtains that she kept perpetually drawn. The last droopy daylight was eking away. Then I tiptoed from the room, closing the door behind me, my footsteps soundless in the *tatami* hallway.

The rest of the house was silent too. In my empty room, I opened my book bag and eased out the jar containing the sea cucumber, unwinding the sweater I'd wrapped around it. Sitting cross-legged on my bed, I studied the specimen. I turned it around and around. The sea cucumber bobbed sadly in its mordant bath. I imagined it must have floated somewhere at the bottom of the sea like that, passive and silent, like something asleep. Or maybe when it was alive, it had moved, finding its way across the slimy ocean floor, eating and thinking and dreaming the way all animals do. It didn't seem right for living things to pass silently from existence with their secrets still locked up inside them. Grandmother was like that. So was Sara. And in a way, I was just like that too. Suddenly I wanted to smash the glass against the wall of my bedroom, releasing the thing from its prison of pickling liquor. Instead, I sat helplessly on my bed, clutching the jar's flawless surface.

deshi/apprentice

"How is your grandmother?" Mr. Graham asked.

"Oh, she's better," I said. "It was just a mild stroke." Grandmother was recovering under Dr. Kimura's care, regaining shaky ground.

"And do you still think the doctor is trying to kill her?"

"I know what I know," I said.

"Hmmm," said Mr. Graham. "Well, you know your own mind. I like this one, Ellen," he continued, changing the subject completely, taking a long drag on his cigarette.

We were seated in the parlor of Mr. Graham's house. Deshi slipped silently into the room. He placed a platter of fruit on the table with a deferential nod in my direction. Deshi was Mr. Graham's houseboy. He must have been only a few years older than me, and he treated me like a queen. Deshi had high cheekbones and delicate features. His sloe eyes widened and narrowed with feline intensity. He slid in and out of rooms like a moonbeam.

"I'm going to draw Deshi," I said.

"With or without clothes," Mr. Graham quipped. Then he caught himself. "Yes, of course you are," he laughed. "You are going to draw the world. Such a talent." I felt my ears burn.

"But, regard your present assignment."

My assignment was the long-legged, narrow-hipped form of a naked woman poised on the verge of a high dive. Her nipples, rising from a pair of perfect, globed breasts, followed the point of her chin. I'd used white highlights and ocher oil pastels to suggest sunlight on burnished flesh. I had loved drawing her. She was radiant.

"I don't know if I approve of the poetry, here," Mr. Graham observed, his green eyes gathering in a squint. "It's a little off-putting. And the crayons, the oil pastels, are terribly messy."

He rubbed his thumb and forefinger together as if trying to clean them. Then he rose from the desk. Mr. Graham wore a short cotton kimono over his dark-colored slacks. He had on socks and corduroy slippers.

"Have some fruit, Ellen," he said indicating the platter that Deshi had placed on the table. "I'm so glad you could come to lunch."

"Deshi," he said, addressing his white-coated houseboy. "Please bring sake and something for Ellen to drink."

Deshi vanished. As Mr. Graham had suggested, I addressed the platter of fruit. Deshi had arranged wood shavings around the fruit in a fine balsa nest. I grabbed a big peach nestled in the excelsior. The peach was juicy and sweet, an unexpected treat in the middle of winter.

"They're hothouse peaches," Mr. Graham explained. "They're from Kyoto. They're lovely when they get here, but Deshi brings them to perfection. He wraps each one in a tea towel. He broods over them like a hen over its eggs until they have ripened completely. Deshi never loses a peach."

Deshi had made a small cross at the top of each peach so the skin would peel off in four leaf-shaped swaths. Eating them must have been an art as well, one that I hadn't mastered. I wrestled with the slippery softball-sized fruit. The peach juice drizzled down my forearm.

"What's the right way to eat these?" I asked, my hands growing stickier with every bite.

"Simplicity's best," Mr. Graham responded cryptically. He dabbed my chin with a napkin. "In a few moments, we'll have the surprise," he added warmly, "but first I must have my sake."

Deshi entered on cue with a plain wooden tray. He poured hot rice wine from a rough pint-sized carafe into an equally rustic cup, then raised a second extravagantly painted porcelain bottle aloft.

"And some plum wine for you?" Mr. Graham inquired. I nodded. I was never allowed to drink wine at home. Deshi filled a cordial glass almost up to the brim with a thick amber liquid.

The plum wine was sweet and syrupy. It fell in a burning waterfall down through my body. I was suddenly warm and deliriously happy sitting in Mr. Graham's house with Deshi as my attentive handmaiden. At school, Mr. Graham was pretty discreet and controlled, but his preferential treatment embarrassed me.

"I prefer you when you aren't self-conscious," Mr. Graham observed, watching me over his cup.

Deshi brought more sake and Mr. Graham finished a second bottle.

"So, Ellen," he asked, draining the thimble-sized cup in a single gulp, "do you like my house?"

I was very impressed with Mr. Graham's house. It was lovely: *tatami*-carpeted, simple—like the best Japanese homes. And it was full of wonderful things: books, cameras, microscopes, magazines, rocks. Deshi had arranged them all into small works of art. The resinous smell of pine and cedar perfumed the rooms.

"This house," Mr. Graham continued, "is a haven—a haven from girls and white gloves and the pressures of mothers to marry. It's a haven from business and expectations, from social engagements and parties and proving a great disappointment. Which I have. I always have."

Mr. Graham shook his head sorrowfully, poured and consumed one more small cup of sake.

"I inherited this house from a college friend," he continued. "He was living here in Japan. I inherited Deshi too. His name isn't even Deshi, really. That's what my friend named him. My friend was here on a fellowship. He was studying Japanese drama. I think "deshi" means dresser or something—an assistant in the Kabuki theater. So, it was a joke calling him Deshi. But a good joke, hmmmm?"

Mr. Graham was getting plastered. He leaned against a bookcase trying to smoke his cigarette, almost knocking over a silvery nautilus shell balanced on a delicate lucite stand, when Deshi entered with more sake.

"Thank you, Deshi," he said with a slight slur of the "s."

"Where was I? Oh, yes," he remembered, continuing his soliloquy.

"My friend went back to the States before long. He hated being alone. And I was his beneficiary. I got his house. Great friend...great friend.

"I'm thirty-three years old," Mr. Graham confessed suddenly with a sour laugh. "I'm thirty-three and I hide here. I am stranded in life. I hide here because I don't know what else to do." His voice rose and broke on a high note. He immediately tossed back another cup of warm sake.

Mr. Graham was drunk as a piper. I was a little high, too.

"Well," he said, "let's look at the surprise, now, shall we? Deshi, a little more wine."

I noticed the slightest hesitation on Deshi's part. He made one more trip to the cupboard. The surprise was a box wrapped in brown tissue paper. It was tied with a green raffia cord.

"I wrapped it," Mr. Graham proudly announced. "Deshi helped." He winked. "Open it," he commanded.

I tore through the wrapper.

Inside the box was a stack of old illustrations of the strangest birds I had ever seen. One was a pink flamingo with a big orange beak that looked like Jimmy Durante's nose. Its long neck was looped like a bow. Another was a small-eyed white ibis. It had a beak like needle-nosed pliers. A wood stork, its featherless head a grisly, iron-clad helmet, an elegant crested night heron, and a stout pelican, its pendulous pouch full of fish, were also among the pictures.

"It's a gift from me," Mr. Graham said leaning toward me. "Strange birds for a very strange girl." His hand came to rest on my knee and moved up to my thigh.

"Don't do that," I said lackadaisically. The plum wine was working on me. I felt good, and his hand felt good, gently massaging its way up my thigh.

"All right, Ellen," he said. But his hand continued to move up my leg.

I've always wondered who invented the dress. Dresses remind me of lampshades. It's easy to get up inside them. Mr. Graham's hand reminded me of a moth fluttering in between a lampshade and a bulb.

"Don't do that," I repeated without much conviction.

Deshi stepped into the room with more sake. Noting that Mr. Graham had his hand up under my skirt, he reddened. He made a very deep bow. Mr. Graham drew back his hand.

"Of course you are right, Ellen," he said quickly. "You are only the artist. You are the artist, aren't you?" His speech was ginny and muddled.

"Yes," I said, trying to look righteous. "I am the artist."

"Of course you are," he repeated. "No need to take umbrage. No need." He leaned closer to me and he began stroking my hair. "Forgiven, I hope," he said.

I didn't reply. I was watching Deshi watch us.

"Of course I'm forgiven," he muttered, his hands still caressing my head. "Yes, you are the artist, my dear. You are the artist. We have time for a little more wine," he added, falling back onto the soft-pillowed couch. "One more glass of wine. Then, Deshi, call a cab. It's time for Ellen to leave." He half-swooned onto the cushions. Deshi moved swiftly to his side and propped him up on the sofa. Deshi reminded me of a puppet master in the bunraku puppet theater. Grandmother had taken me once to see the bunraku puppets in Tokyo. They were life-sized puppets that looked disturbingly human. The bunraku puppeteers manipulated them onstage in full view of the audience. The puppeteers were dressed all in black and the audience had to pretend not to see them moving the puppets around. As with anything where one pretends long enough, soon the puppeteers really did become almost invisible. They disappeared into the background. I saw only the puppets moving, as if by their own volition. Deshi rearranged Mr. Graham into a polite position on the couch. Mr. Graham now looked rather composed.

"Ellen," he said, "I'm so sorry to say good-bye to you this way, but Deshi will take care of you. Deshi, call Ellen a cab."

Deshi dipped slightly and fled from the room. He was mortified by Mr. Graham's sudden collapse. I heard his voice on the telephone requesting a cab.

"Good-bye, Deshi," I said later, at the door. Deshi nodded very politely, stepped out, paid the driver, and darted back into the house quick as moonlight disappearing behind a drawn curtain.

Two weeks later, a dreadful thing happened.

"Ellen, I want to talk to you."

Gene stood in front of me holding my biology notebook. I already felt sick to my stomach. That morning I hadn't been able to find it. Later, in school, I'd asked Mr. Graham if he had given it back.

"Of course," he said carelessly, taking a drag from his cigarette. "You had two drawings for me this time, remember?"

"Yes, I remember," I said crossly, "but I thought you might have it. You see, it's missing. I can't find it."

"Well, hadn't you better?" he asked with an eyebrow raised. "It could prove very embarrassing."

"Yes. Yes, I have to find it. I must have just misplaced it."

And now here was Gene, my father, holding the very notebook, the one full of drawings of naked and near-naked women. They had replaced the crustaceans and mollusks that had once been my subjects of study. Those easily explained why phyla and their members had been replaced by my anatomical explorations of *homo sapiens* of the female gender.

"Ellen, I think this is yours," Gene said, indicating the red spiral-bound notebook.

"Where did you get that?" I stammered. I could feel the blood rush to my face.

"It was on the sidewalk in front of the house."

It must have slipped out of my book bag.

"Is it yours?" he asked.

What could I do? Tell the truth? Certainly not.

"No, it's not mine," I lied, trying to remember if I'd been stupid enough to put my name in it. Gene saw right through me, of course. It wasn't enough to deny ownership. I had to produce a believable suspect. "That notebook is Anne's," I blurted out. "Anne must have dropped it out on the sidewalk. Gee, I doubt if she knows it's missing."

"Really?" Gene asked rather coolly. "Whose drawings are in it?" I was sure he didn't believe me.

"Anne's drawings," I said. "It's her notebook. It must be full of her drawings."

"Well, if it's Anne's, I think she'll be sorry to discover it lost."

Gene must have been terribly disappointed in me. I wasn't even doing the honorable thing.

"I suggest you return it to her as soon as you can."

Gene handed the notebook back to me. I grabbed for it, but he didn't release it at once.

"I don't know what to think," he said softly, still hanging onto the notebook. "I didn't show this to Sara. I trust, Ellen, that you know what you're doing." I took back the notebook.

"I'll tell Anne that you found it," I mumbled.

"Tell Anne that you found it," he said. "That way she won't be embarrassed."

"Yeah, thanks," I muttered and ran to my room, threw myself on the bed, and covered my head with a pillow. I couldn't believe that Gene had looked through my notebook, a notebook full of the pictures I'd drawn for Mr. Graham. I thumbed quickly through it, just to torture myself. Yes, it was my notebook all right, raw and uncensored, with my signature style in every one of the drawings. I was sure that Gene knew that it wasn't Anne's, but he hadn't argued with me. He hadn't accused me. He just handed the notebook back. He was probably just as embarrassed as I was. Maybe I could pretend that I'd actually broken my hand several months before and hadn't been able to draw. Maybe I should break my hand to add an element of truth to the story. I concluded that this was a pretty ridiculous idea; one that indicated just how desperate I was. I couldn't look Gene in the eye after that, and tried to avoid him, though I noticed that he seemed to handle me with a great deal of care. He began to treat me with special attention. It was as if I had all of a sudden become some kind of person, someone that he could no longer ignore.

In the end, I gave the notebook to Mr. Graham and told him that he could keep it. I told him about Gene's finding it. I didn't tell him that I lied and said it was Anne's.

"Did you tell him about me?" Mr. Graham asked. "Does he know why you drew those pictures?"

"Of course not," I answered. "Do you think I wanted to get in more trouble?"

"Well, good. Very good," Mr. Graham said sagely. "Ellen, I think you're a very wise girl."

yuki/snow

(excerpt)

It had been snowing for weeks. We'd known it was coming. There was always something different, a certain smell, a precise quality to the look and feel of the air that would tell us a storm was on its way. Grandmother was bundled up in aqua- and clay-colored sweaters. The large wood stove near the kitchen was stoked every morning against the chill until it glowed like a red coal. We were warned not to touch it. The mountains of harvested sunflower stalks were blanketed in snow. We hadn't seen the plowhorse in weeks. Ineko-san had pulled the heavy silk futons down out of the closets to be used as quilts, and we lay at night crushed beneath them, like little bugs, flattened and pinned. Jars of canned foods from the store began filling the cupboards. Sara took us to the big *machi* and bought us two ski sweaters apiece. We saw less and less of the other children outside of school. They now stayed closer to home...

I could see Sara in the kitchen, over the counter, at the kitchen table, calendar, train schedules, and magazines in front of her. She was planning a trip to Akishima in March, at Grandmother's request. Grandmother's condition was worsening. She was very ill, but was still insisting on going to Akishima.

Standing at the counter with one of Ineko-san's blue aprons wrapped around him, Gene was making a big mess with a huge pile of shellfish, moving back and forth between counter and stove, cutting the heads off shrimp and slipping them out of their wafer-thin jackets of exoskeleton, pulling off runny blue veins, then rinsing them in a colander. They were shiny and gray, with big heads festooned with antennae and a pair of beady, accusing black eyes. It was actually the first time I realized that shrimp had heads.

For years, our dinners on Saturday nights were steak, salad, and shrimp cocktail, but the shrimp I knew were thumb-sized, pink commas, in no way related to living creatures anymore than a steak conjured up the vision of cattle. Heads, legs—these things were out of the question to me. Now, seeing Gene chop off those whiskery heads with a single whack of his knife shocked me. It also intrigued me. A strange tickle rose up in my stomach every time the knife fell. It was dizzying to think about it. Gene scooped up a handful of the shrimp heads and jackets and dumped them into the trash. Sara shuffled papers.

"Well, I think it's horrible," she said flatly. "It's like a witch hunt. It's so cruel. They're riding him out of town on a rail. The man is convicted and sentenced without even a trial."

"It does seem that way, Sara," I heard Gene reply. "But think about this: maybe he doesn't want the exposure. Think of all the old bones that digging of that kind tends to bring up. Maybe he doesn't want them to investigate further. Maybe there are other unpleasant things that might be exhumed."

Curled up in the armchair, I was only pretending to read my book. Sara and Gene's conversation was much more interesting.

"What do you think, Ellen?" Gene asked suddenly, as if he knew that I'd followed the entire conversation. "You know Mr. Graham pretty well, don't you?"

Gene, I thought, was starting to figure things out. He had a suspicious mind. I figured that this was because he was a sneak.

"Not that well," I mumbled. For children, recalcitrance usually works as the perfect diversion.

"Gene," Sara interrupted impatiently, "You know Ellen has always loved Mr. Graham's class. I'm sure she holds him in the highest regard, and I know she's going to miss him."

Sara's brow furrowed. She did not even look up when she said this. She had been reabsorbed by the schedules and calendars. Gene raised an eyebrow, whacked off one more shrimp head, and looked over at me, the slightest of smiles on his lips. He couldn't hide it. Gene admired danger and narrow escapes.

I slipped out of the armchair and sauntered into my room, willing myself to show no reaction. Once in my room I threw myself down on the bed. I would really miss Mr. Graham. He was more than a teacher. He was a friend. I'd found some kind of balance with him. My perspective and his seemed to meet and connect in our peculiar fascination with things odd and troubled. Yes, Sara was right. I would really miss him. I wondered how he was feeling. I could see him sitting at his desk, head in his hands, Deshi no more than a shadow upon the wall behind him. I took out the curious Audubon prints, his gift, which I treasured. I settled upon the featherless, red-eyed face of a turkey vulture and studied it.

"Mr. Graham, Mr. Graham," I whispered sadly.

Later, when the house was quiet, Sara in Grandmother's room, and Gene gone for a visit to Mr. Nielson's, I picked up the phone and dialed Mr. Graham's number.

"Yes," Mr. Graham's voice crackled into the phone.

I choked on my response. I had expected to hear Deshi's softly melodic Japanese greeting. The disorder was upsetting. Where was Deshi? "Mr. Graham, it's me. Ellen," I managed to rasp out at him.

"Ah, Ellen," he said, his voice slow as the vapor of one of his cigarettes. "You've heard."

"Mr. Graham," I blurted out, not knowing where the sentence was going to go, finding a block in my throat. "Mr. Graham, I'm so sorry."

"Oh, Ellen, don't be silly," he said softly. "It was my mistake. It was Miss Ibsen, the PE teacher, you see. What a fool I was. I asked her to dinner. Quite a mistake. A beautiful specimen, Ellen, just like your drawings. Absurd, however, to think that a dream and reality would have anything in common. I just didn't perform as she so dearly wished. Not a pass, you see. And so she blamed Deshi and my rather "perverse," as she called them, preferences. Oh, hell hath no fury like a woman scorned. Turned me in. Just like that. Blew the whistle. Made all sorts of accusations about my history. Implicated Deshi. It was all very ugly. Of course, I couldn't contest it. I'm guilty in so many other ways. It's justice."

"No, it's not," I said sharply, "I hate PE, and I hate stupid Miss Ibsen. Why did you even ask her over?" I whined. "I'm your friend. You have Deshi."

I heard the sigh on the other end of the line.

"A mistake," he whispered. "An error. You know, I thought for a moment, just one, that I could pretend to be normal. You know what I'm saying, don't you?"

Yes, I knew what he meant. I thought of the sea cucumber in its fragile glass prison. I thought of my own sense of hopelessness.

Then, quite a different question occurred to me. "Are you in love with Deshi?" I asked.

There was a silence on the other end of the line.

"Don't be ridiculous, Ellen," Mr. Graham whispered huskily, "you know it's you that I love." He punctuated this with a self-conscious snicker that broadened the distance between us.

"What will you do?" I asked.

"Oh, I will leave. Travel, I think. There is so much of Asia I haven't seen. So many places one can go, places where a man can disappear entirely. I've always been a ghost anyway, haven't I, Ellen? You sensed it. I could tell by the way you watched Deshi and me. Deshi knows it too. I am the one who didn't. Now I do. I finally know that I'm dead, the mere after-image of something that has already passed from existence."

Mr. Graham was drifting, even over the phone, becoming morbid. I was worried about him. "I'm coming over," I said. "I can't now, because I'm grounded. But I will as soon as I can."

"Don't bother, Ellen. You won't find me at home. Just the boxes. Deshi's packing everything. I will leave swiftly. No long sad departures."

"But will I see you again?" I asked, the cloud of unhappiness blooming, pulling wet and thick at the front of my throat.

"I don't think so, no," came the dreamy voice on the other end of the phone. "No, that's very unlikely."

"I won't forget you," I swore, wanting to somehow fix him forever in a place where he could not be destroyed.

"As I am?" he laughed, "or as you have made me in your mind?"

"Both," I said hotly.

"Yes, of course, both. The artist. The strange, often imprudent artist. Good-bye, Ellen," he said.

"Oh, oh, good-bye Mr. Graham," I managed to choke out, long ribbons of misery delicately making their way down my face.

"Good-bye, good-bye, Mr. Graham," I sang sadly to myself as I hung up the phone, putting him away forever with the black receiver falling gently back into its cradle.

I heard soft footsteps on the *tatami* of the hall. "Ellen, *daijobu desuka*? Are you okay?" came Ineko-san's question, coupled with a look of concern.

"Yes, yes, Ineko-san, *daijobu*, I'm okay," I sniffed, wiping my nose on the back of my hand.

"Yuki," Ineko-san said softly, pointing toward the thick mist of white that was swirling outside the window, surely mistaking my tears for tears of regret over taking Mimi and Gray out for their ascent of the mountain of compost and being grounded.

I saw the soft flurry of snow. It fell in feathers, laced itself over trees, bearding the pines—a fuzzy, swirling, soft cloud of white, covering everything, destroying it all as the white, like a great wall, climbed.

BAD THINGS COME IN THREES. That is what Sara always said, and that is exactly what happened. I was grounded, Mr. Graham was dismissed, but I didn't think about Sara's old saying. That's why I didn't even anticipate the third thing, didn't know it was forming while I brooded that day. I didn't suspect it when the small stones chipped at my bedroom window at night in the last hours of the last day of my punishment. It must have been close to midnight. Mimi was fast asleep in her bed, snoring fuzzily into her pillow.

The first little stone hit the window with a click. It could have been the wind. It could have been icicles breaking or snow melting and falling from the eaves. Then the next few little stones hit the window, one after the other—tic, tic, tic—a simple code methodically tapping out a message to come to the window. It continued until I couldn't ignore it. I tiptoed through the dark room and pulled back the curtain. What I saw made me catch my breath. The moonlight from the fingernail sliver of moon had cast all the snow in a pale blue moonscape against the black of the sky. It was so entrancing that I was completely taken off guard when David Vintner's face appeared at the window. I watched his mouth shape words theatrically on the other side of the glass.

"Open the window," he mimed.

I opened it quickly. The cold air rushed in. Our summer screens had been removed months ago.

David put his face close to mine and whispered into my ear. "Ellen, Ellen, get dressed and come out. I have something important to tell you."

"You're crazy," I said, thinking, *what a lunatic*, not trusting, fear catching in my voice. "I'm grounded. It's nearly midnight. It's freezing out there."

"No, it's not," he laughed, moving away from the window and spinning around, face turned toward the heavens. "It's wonderful. Come on, Ellen." He rushed back up to the window. "Please, I have something very important to tell you."

I think it was the tone of his voice, the brightness of his eyes, the way his narrow white face seemed to be blue, hard, and glittery like the moonlit snow. Maybe it was the week of being confined, or the cold pulling up around the sash and the clean smell of night stealing into the room.

"Okay, okay," I heard myself saying. "Just wait right there and I'll be out." I dressed carefully, not wanting the cold to lay an icy grip on me, finding ways to lock in the stored warmth of bed and blanket. I tiptoed through the house while everyone slept, wrapped like dreamy chrysalises in their cocoons of warmth. But as soon as I opened the front door the chill reached in and slapped me, a hand to each cheek where the blood rushed in with warmth, staining them, I imagined, very bright red. Then it entered my mouth, filling my lungs with icy splinters of cold, and the heat escaped in a fine steam from my nostrils and lips. "David," I said as the steamy breath gushed out. "Are you nuts?"

David's eyes were bright. They caught the moonlight. He was very excited.

"Ellen," he whispered, grabbing my hands, "I came to say good-bye. I'm leaving."

The words sat outside my mind and waited patiently for me to give them the command to enter. But I couldn't let them. Something about them was too much. I chose to focus on something else to distract me.

"David, you have gloves?" I said noticing that my own gloved hands were surrounded by his leather-clad ones.

"Yeah," he said proudly. "Nice. From Tad. That's what I wanted to tell you about."

David was pulling on me. We waded through the snow-covered yard toward the back of the house through the rickety white picket gate propped open for the season by a drift of snow. The baseball field had become a winter amusement park where the trampled snow formed paths that circled and ended in snowmen. Melting stockpiles of snowballs that the boys had amassed had turned to ice. The ruined shell of Mimi's igloo hunched in the center of the field.

I was complaining bitterly. "Look, David, this is crazy. It's freezing out here." The hem of my nightgown, which stuck out from under my coat and below the line of my boots, was soaked through. I had on a hood, but the wind wormed its way through the outer layer of my clothing and now had its icy hands on my body.

"Yeah, but it'll be warm here," David said, pulling me down with him against the unbroken half shell of the igloo. "See."

David put his arms around me. Then he said with a drunken grin on his face, "Isn't that better?"

I nodded, shocked out of my mind, surprised to be sitting there in the shell of an igloo with this dangerous, beautiful boy with his arms around me. *What if you were marooned on the moon at midnight in the arms of David Vintner,* I asked myself, supplying the opening line to that favorite game that had somehow wormed its way into the real world. I was brilliantly happy, but at the same time horrified, sensing that something was terribly wrong.

"Tad," David continued his story. "Tad, this guy. He's my

friend. He's been helping me out, spending time with me. Ellen, he knows my dad, too. Says he knew him fifteen years ago, met him in school."

"David, do you mean he knows where your dad is?" I asked, suddenly thinking I'd made sense out of the bits of information David was sharing.

"Well, no, not exactly," David stammered. "But I'll find that out later. What's important is this: Tad's in Tokyo now, and that's where I'm going. I'm leaving, Ellen. I'm going to find Tad. He'll let me stay with him. And then, who knows? Maybe we'll hang out together for a while. Maybe I'll find my dad."

What about your mother? What about Claire? I thought. I was glad those words did not come out of my mouth. There was no place for them in the igloo. They would have melted away the moonscape around us, destroying the thin bridge of ice that now, for the moment, joined David and me. Instead I said, "I'm going to miss you, David."

David's grip tightened around me. Bloated by our layers of clothing, we clung to one another like a couple of ticks.

"I'll miss you too, Ellen," he said gently, his eyes bright, exploring my face, resting on my mouth.

Then his mouth was on mine, and I felt his sorrow—the sobs that I wouldn't hear this time entering my mouth and falling into my throat. I closed my eyes, and we were spinning around and around, giddy music box dancers under the revolving constellations. I caught my breath. He took off his gloves, put his warm hands on my cheeks, and squeezed my face. He squeezed so hard that tears came to my eyes. I felt a couple of errant drops start from the inner corners.

"All this shit about growing up," David said to those teardrops. "It's hard, isn't it? No, it's worse. It's perpetually fucked. I hate being a kid. It's the worst part of life. You, you'll be fine, Ellen. You're pretty tough. You've got Sara, and you've got Gene. They're pretty good parents. Well, at least they care."

"But what about you, David?" I asked, talking from the pinched shape of my mouth, not at all discomforted by it. Wondering when he'd let go of my face.

I must have looked funny talking out of a pinched mouth like that.

"Oh, sorry," he said, releasing his grip. "Me? I'll be fine, too. Better than here. They're killing me here, Ellen. I just have to go. My mom," he laughed, "she's used to guys running off on her. And Claire, well you know she's much better off without me around.

"I'll tell you who I'm going to really miss, though. I'm going to miss you and your family. I wish I were one of you. That would be nice."

Okay, so marry me, I wanted to say. *We'll grow up together and marry, and neither of us will ever be lonely again.*

But David, teeth chattering, was already struggling to his feet, replacing his gloves, brushing the snow from his jeans.

He stretched out a hand and pulled me up next to him.

"I wish we were older," he said.

"Me, too," I replied.

Then David hauled back and with one banshee whoop kicked down the last side of the igloo.

Amma

With my eyes closed
it felt as though
he had one thousand hands.

Shizuka-na kaze
chō-chō no hana-odori.

White egrets over
green mist.

Selections from The Hand of Buddha

A Little Variety

"What this country is losing, what is going the way of the dinosaur, is the good old-fashioned variety store—the five and dime," thought Mona as she pushed her gardening hat down over her fluffy gray hair and charged down the hill into the hustle and bustle of her busy Sunset District neighborhood. Living in San Francisco, with the world virtually at her doorstep, Mona rarely found an occasion to go more than a few blocks to find anything. Walmart and Kmart might be part of the nineties, but they couldn't replace the variety store of her youth. Her neighborhood had one of the last of them.

All her life Mona had found everything she had ever wanted or needed at the variety store, Harvey's Variety Five and Dime, to be exact, including her husband Ed. She smiled when she thought of Ed. Now he was a real find. She remembered that day, two years ago, when she'd met him. What had she gone in for? Several packets of seeds—marigolds, dahlias, bachelor buttons—the kind of flowers that are colorful. Loud, friendly flowers. Not the airy-fairy, fancy-dancy kind. Mona liked flowers that could cheer people up. Snapdragons, daisies—she had plenty of those, too.

On that particular day, April 3, 1992, she stopped first to have lunch—a burger at Jake's—Jake's Diner. Jake's Diner, Millie's Thrift, Clausen's Market—almost every business on Irving Street had someone's name connected with it, and the owners—Jake, Harvey, Millie, Ella and Harold Clausen—were always in their shops, working away. Mona knew them all, too, at least on a speaking-to basis. She chatted with most of them daily. In fact, she chatted with just about everyone she encountered on Irving Street—students, housewives, strangers—the kind of people who were out and about during the day. Sometimes, she'd sit across from the five and dime and watch them come and go—on foot, on bikes, in their run-down, can-no-longer-open-the-window cars. Once she had been entertained for a full thirty minutes watching a kid break into his own car because the door was broken and jammed.

Harvey's Variety Five and Dime, on the opposite side of the street from Jake's Diner, was wedged between Millie's Thrift Shop and Gallagher's Stationary. Mona did a lot of business at both. "Yep," Mona smiled, thinking about the pretty blue paper at Gallagher's. She had time to write letters. People like her had that kind of time, spent the latter part of their lives giving away the things they'd gathered around them in the first half. In fact, it was on people like Mona that people like Millie, of Millie's Thrift, thrived; and by the look of Millie's, crammed to the jambs with merchandise, there were plenty of people like Mona—people with cheap, quirky taste.

"But you know," Mona thought, "even *that* gets better with age." In fact, Mona's tastes represented just what everyone seemed to be looking for. Like the college students who shopped at the thrift store; they were Millie's best customers. They were in love with tacky old things. They seemed to be drawn to them, as if there were something secretly magical about carnival glass and homemade ceramics.

Mona always made it a point to eavesdrop on their conversations. It was like listening to someone talking about you behind your back. They said things like:

"Oh, June, look at this. Can you believe it? My mother had one of these."

"Oh, my, isn't it just too trashy; and look at that silly fringe. Look, if you don't get it, I will. How much is it?"

"Three fifty."

"Three fifty? God, I can't believe it. This place is so fabulous. They don't even know what they have. Scoop it up."

"A bargain."

"Oh, yeah, a bargain." Mona snorted. "One man's garbage... Yeah, life is a bargain." Those cute, sassy kids in their crazy put-together clothes, talking about the fifties as if they were prehistoric—she loved them. They were making her life worthwhile.

The streetcar rattled by—the N Judah car. Mona wondered how long it would be before they replaced the remaining electric cars with greasy fume-spewing buses.

"Just a matter of time," she thought. "Hang on," she muttered, addressing the streetcar. "Hang on."

A few buildings up, across the street, was the old lounge, Bill's Gaslight. Fire escapes dangled from the apartment windows above it, a clutter of ugly balconies.

"Fire escapes," Mona reflected, "are like radiators—unattractive, but ultimately useful." And you had to wait until they wore out to replace them. And that seemed to take a very long time. Like her. She was not wearing out, not at all.

Eating her hamburger on that momentous day, two years ago, Mona was pleased. From her window seat at Jake's Grill she had a good view of Harvey's Variety store. If anything exciting happened, she could pounce. Mona hated to miss things. And she didn't. She never missed a sale, never missed a bargain.

Harvey's Variety was having a sale, a special on seeds, and Mona planned to stock up. But she wanted to savor the feeling, wanted to take it slow, wanted to kind of sneak up on it. She wanted to get the most bang for a buck, and she loved the anticipation. So, she decided to wait. She decided to have lunch at Jake's and wait till the spirit moved her.

In front of the store, out on the sidewalk, Harvey had arranged several trash cans. They bristled with the long handles of various mops and brooms.

"Spring cleaning," mused Mona, imagining herself with a kerchief tied around her head. It was funny. Young girls wore their hair that way all the time. She'd seen them at Millie's, spongy pink dish towels tied around their cropped hair, again validating her life. She straightened her shoulders. Things like that made her feel important. Spring cleaning was Mona's favorite spring ritual, more significant than a month of Easters and Ash Wednesdays.

She was thinking just that. She was also thinking about the seeds, yes, but at the top of her mind was the phrase "spring cleaning." *SPRING CLEANING*—she could almost see it in front of her now, like a big neon sign. The thought had been triggered by all of the mops and brooms. She was musing like that when a handsome young man in a white T-shirt and shorts walked almost past Harvey's and stopped. How odd. He was hauling a huge Hefty trash bag full of clothes. He was dragging it along the sidewalk behind him. The bag was ripping on the concrete walk, and clothes were dribbling from it. He kept stopping to pick up the clothes that fell out, stuffing them under his arm. As the bag became emptier and emptier, the knot of clothing under his arm got bigger and bigger and harder to manage. But the part that Mona loved remembering the most was that, in the midst of all this, he stopped. He stopped as he passed the variety store. He stopped right in front of the trash cans with all the mops and the brooms in them, and Mona could see it, in his head, too, like a neon-tube sign, those words, *SPRING CLEANING*. It really was such an uplifting phrase. Mona thought she saw him relax for a moment. He straightened, then, from dragging his bag and stretched, and she saw that he must be around six foot two, and he had broad shoulders. Well, Mona was out of her seat and across the street in a snap, because she knew an opportunity when she saw one.

She rushed over to Harvey's door and, whoops, she "accidentally" bumped right into the young man, wham, as she tried to rush past him. He looked down at her, somewhat surprised, having no idea where she'd come from. Mona knew that he was sizing her up. And she knew that she was quite a sight in her yellow capri pants, her gardening hat, her plastic fruit-covered sandals with the cotton front of her bowling-style shirt waterfalling over her D-cup breasts. "One thing never goes out of style," she thought with a world-wise chuckle. It looked like all six foot two of him was going to reel backwards, caught up as he was in the middle of private thoughts.

"Young man," Mona said with just the right touch of kindness and humor, indicating the clothes under his arm and the near-empty bag at his feet, "what you need is a shopping cart."

Suddenly he was aware of himself, gently weaned from the image of Mona's goofy hat, the plastic fruit-covered sandals, and the D-cup breasts. He realized that he must also look somewhat ridiculous with the trash bag pooling around his feet and his underarms chock-full of clothes.

"Laundry?" Mona asked charitably.

"Oh, no, not exactly," he answered, still off guard and feeling a little silly. "I was just thinking," he said confessionally, nodding toward the cans full of mops and brooms, "I was just thinking about spring cleaning."

There they were again. Those magic words—like some special code for a decoder ring, a code that meant marvelous things to Mona like sales, bargains, longer days, summer, fresh starts, and six-foot-two guys with their arms full of laundry.

"Oh," she laughed. "And I was running into Harvey's for seeds. You know," she said, patting the top of her hat theatrically, "it's planting time." Mona delivered this with just the right touch of hayseed—a cross between Ethel Merman and Minnie Pearl. She knew how to work her era, knew how to capitalize on that undiminishable source of charm.

"Need any help?" she asked in her most neighborly way.

The young man looked down at her again, running a big hand through his longish sun-streaked hair. Mona liked that he was wearing a kind of bracelet and that his T-shirt had the words "NOT BAD/NOT RAD" on it. She also liked the sweaty smell that floated around him. She wasn't around that kind of smell much anymore.

The young man looked at her as if she had made a truly bizarre proposition. He had dropped a few T-shirts unnoticed, when he ran his hand through his hair. He gazed down at them suddenly conscious of this. "Well, yeah, I guess I could use a little help," he said warily. "I'm just going a few doors up—to Millie's."

Mona smiled a broad, watermelon-red smile. "To Millie's," she said, delightedly stooping to pick up a few sweat-scented T-shirts. "Well, come on then. By the way," she added sweetly, "my name's Mona. And you?"

"Me? Oh, yes, sorry. My name's Ed."

Millie Salinger pursed her lips and squinted when Ed and Mona walked in the door. She fished around in the drawer and pulled out a pair of cat's-eye bifocals. They certainly were an unlikely couple, but Millie was having one of her "feelings." It was as if she had seen them together before.

"Hey, Millie," Ed greeted the thrift store proprietor.

"Just put your things here in this box, honey," Millie said sweetly. "Well Mona," she added, addressing her long-time friend. They'd gone to high school and business college together. "Whatever are you up to?"

Ed dumped the dirty garments into the box, then made his way through the clothing-crammed interior of the shop, finding and focusing on one rack full of T-shirts and another of pants.

"He comes here every week," Millie whispered to Mona, with a nod in the young man's direction. He brings in his soiled clothing and buys things to replace it. "Perfectly sweet guy," she added as if he were in some way handicapped. "Just can't do laundry. Look at this," she said, pulling a pair of gaudy green paisley boxer shorts out of the box on the counter. "I have to wash everything. It's like taking in laundry."

"You trade his dirty clothes for new ones?" Mona asked with concern. It wasn't like Millie to get stuck with the short end of a deal.

"Of course not, silly," Millie said with a wink. "I just use the old stuff to discount his purchase. It's a kind of recycling, a deposit system, like used Coke bottles or something." Mona was glad to hear that Millie and Ed had only business between them.

"He's cute, don't you think?" Millie asked, knowing Mona well enough to have sensed the attraction.

Mona laughed. "He's a doll."

"And young," Millie added, pressing a point. "Twenty-seven years old. Saw it on his driver's license."

Mona looked at her friend and sighed audibly. "Millie," she said "we mustn't hold that against him."

Ed came back to the counter with an armload of T-shirts, three pairs of shorts, and some slacks. "These, Millie," he announced with a wide, winning grin.

Millie counted the shirts and folded the pants. "That's fifteen ninety-five for the lot, Ed," she said. "I give him a bit of a discount," she confided loudly to Mona.

Ed paid the fifteen ninety-five. "Thank you, Millie," he said. "You're a gem."

"See you next week," Millie sang, as she rang up the sale.

"So, Ed," Mona asked when they walked out the door. "So, you never do laundry?"

"No, I don't," Ed replied sheepishly. "I have fabric care problems. Things shrink and change color. It's much easier this way. Millie takes care of everything. And, thanks, by the way, for your help," he added with feeling. "I'd like to reciprocate. If you're here to get seeds, I can help you with that. I'm an awesome gardener, you know."

So they went back to Harvey's Variety Five and Dime and in addition to dahlias and bachelor buttons, Mona bought sweet peas that day. She bought zinnias, pansies, and carnations. She bought corn, tomatoes, zucchini, and eggplant. She bought lettuce and carrots and baby potatoes.

Ed helped carry everything up the hill to her house. He offered to help plant the garden.

All summer long, he watered and hoed in the big plot in Mona's backyard. Mona made zucchini fritatas and tomato salsas. She taught Ed how to do laundry. She made eggplant ragouts and potato pancakes.

And when summer had passed and the garden died back, Ed moved in with Mona.

"Next year," Ed said, one evening in January, folding fluffy, clean towels, "we'll plant bush beans and jasmine. Wouldn't you love to cover that fence with climbers and flowers?"

"Yes," said Mona. "That's a good idea, Ed." She'd lived with bare chain-link for years. A change would be welcome. "We could take the fence down," she offered.

"No, Mona," Ed said thoughtfully. He paused in his folding. "The fence is still strong. We don't need to replace it."

So they covered the fence with bush beans and jasmine, and when fall came again, they were married between it and the garden.

Millie came to the wedding, Bill, too, and Jake and Mr. and Mrs. Clausen. Harvey came too.

Harvey said, "Mona, I don't know what to give you. You can take your pick from anything there in the store. Just take it."

Mona laughed out loud. She'd found the best gift of all right on his threshold.

"Oh, I don't know, Harvey," she said, "you have so many things. Why don't you just surprise me."

Coyote Comes Calling

Sam, aka Samantha Iphigenia Darwin, dba Sam's Wampun Wigwam, Main Street, Sedona, Arizona, was having a coyote week. She hadn't realized this yet. What she did know was this: certain things were going wrong.

It started when she dumped a bottle of the wrong color hair dye on her head. Her amber locks turned brassy blonde. Then she had a flat tire on the way back from Scottsdale where she'd gone to her doctor. Her visit, precipitated by the sudden hyperextension of her abdomen, ended in her gynecologist's assessment that Sam either had a large fibrous tumor or she was pregnant. They'd know for sure in a couple of days. At the time of this pronouncement, Sam's legs were spread, her feet up in the pink potholder-protected stirrups.

"I don't know, Sam," her doctor, Sally, observed, "I fear it's a fibroid tumor."

"What's that? Is it cancer?"

"Well, no. But if it is a fibrous tumor, we'll have to remove it."

"Shit," Sam said, letting out a low whistle.

"On the other hand, you could be pregnant."

"What?" Sam asked, incredulous, fearing a pregnancy almost as much as a tumor. "What will I do with a baby? I'm not even married."

"You can still have a baby, Sam."

"That's not what I mean, Sally. It's just not in my reality. Besides, that would mean the baby was Daryl's."

"What's wrong with that?"

"Doc, Sally, we're talking *Daryl*. You know, Mr. Noncommitment. Fly Boy. Permanent *Puer*. It's like saying Peter Pan is the dad. It's that serious."

"It's not that bad, Sam. Anyway, we'll know in two days."

We'll know in two days. That's what Sam was thinking when a piece of shrapnel jumped up off the road and speared her sidewall. She heard the hissing first, like a snake. She rolled down the window and listened. The snake was following her. Naturally, she didn't have a jack, at least not one that worked. It was that kind of week. She had a spare tire, but she'd broken the jack months ago, lost a part of it when she'd helped Cynthia, her best friend in the world, fix a flat tire in the Coffee Pot parking lot. She kept telling herself to replace it. She hadn't, and now she was "paying the price of procrastination," as her mother would have said.

Fortunately, she was close to Sedona and home when the tire started to go flat. It shouldn't have been hard to flag down some help. However, as luck would have it, her realization of the equipment shortfall corresponded with a certain unpleasant coincidence. At the exact moment that she realized that the jack was not going to work, a certain primer-brown pickup truck appeared on the shaky horizon. It quivered toward her like a mirage. It was the worst thing that could have possibly happened. It was Daryl's truck.

"Your savior again," Daryl said with a wide grin, as he swung his long legs out of the truck. Beau, his obedient hound, jumped out too.

Just what she did not want to hear. But, being in something of a bind, Sam let him change her tire. Sam hated herself for letting him do it. She was sullen when she arrived at her store, Sam's Wampum Wigwam, Main Street, Sedona, and listened to the messages on her machine.

Erly, her helper, had already been in that morning. She had stacked the packages neatly on the counter. Sam was grateful for Erly. Erly was her only support. She was a tough little woman, originally from New York. But she was generous, dependable, and a darn hard worker.

You've got to see beyond the surface, Sam reminded herself, standing in the midst of the room full of trading beads, prayer feathers, and amulets.

"Erly is a perfect example of squirrel energy," Sam thought, stringing totems.

Sam needed a little time with her thoughts. It had been a terrible morning. This baby. What in heaven's name was she going to do? An abortion, probably. Sam couldn't have a baby. She couldn't let an infant into her life. It was hard enough washing her own hair, feeding herself every day. Getting from one place to another was a perpetual challenge. She had trouble staying balanced and managing her own life. How could she do it for two?

The shop door opened. This was a great surprise. It was March, and Sam's Wampum Wigwam survived mainly on mail order at this time of the year. Sam immediately broke into a glossy cover model smile because it was David, her pal, and the man she'd recently decided she'd most like to go to bed with. The thought of her swollen belly ragged at her.

"Hey David," she said cheerfully. "I thought you were in Phoenix this week. What's going on?"

"Oh, I came back early," David said in his soft purr of a voice. David had the kind of voice that could coax eggs out of a rooster.

"Sam," David said, "I have a favor to ask."

"Sure," said Sam. "Anything. What'll it be?"

"Well," he said, suddenly shy (Sam found this endearing), "I wonder if I could get Cynthia's number from you. I'm thinking of asking her out."

Sam felt as though she'd been kicked by a mule in the solar plexus, right over that little tumor.

"Yeah, sure," she heard herself say quickly, to hide her surprise. "I'll give you her number."

She wrote down the number and handed it to him.

She was amazed that her hands weren't shaking. She felt reasonable, even calm. She suspected she was in some kind of shock. Sam saw herself standing on top of Apache Leap. Below her, Cynthia and David were putting around on the green of the world's most obnoxiously situated golf course. It was built over a Native American burial ground. Sam hated that golf course. She, Sam, alias Wiley Coyote, was rolling a boulder to the edge of the precipice. She was going to drop it on the spoony-eyed couple below. She imagined it squashing them both. Then a breeze came out of nowhere, ruffling her hair. It was the "Wind of Karma."

"That boulder," it said, "is going to bounce like a superball. It is going to hit the golf course lighter than angel food cake and bounce back on you with the force of a Peterbilt truck. Don't do it, Sam."

"Thanks, Sam," David was saying. He'd completed his morning mission. He had Cynthia's phone number. He already had one leg out the door. "By the way, I don't know what you've done with your hair, but it looks great."

"Tasteless goon," Sam thought, as he left. But she knew that if he asked her to go out, she'd say yes. Sam felt like she'd taken a ride in the spin cycle.

"What a rotten day," she thought miserably. "What else could go wrong?"

That's when she noticed the squashed package and opened it. She hadn't even seen it before. It was from Bella, the Italian bead manufacturer. Her Venetian trading beads—she'd been waiting for them for months. She needed them to fill one of her store's largest orders. She had a very bad feeling about this. She opened the package. It was filled with glittering powder—sea blue, gold, bottle green—beads ground to dust. On the package wrapper was a note: "This package was damaged in transit. Please file a claim."

There are times when it all gets to be too much for you and you just have to close up shop. This was one of those times. Sam could feel a couple of big fat cow tears running down the sides of her nose.

"That does it," she said.

She turned out the lights and flipped over the sign on the door to read "Closed."

Sam didn't want to see anyone. Not Cynthia, Daryl, Erly, or David. She wanted to be alone. She jumped into her car and headed for home. That's when she saw him, standing at the side of the road. The mangy, yellow-eyed dog; the trickster; the hound of the desert; her new pal—Wiley Coyote. The coyote was standing there, mouth pulled back in a panting grin. Its big yellow eyes connected with hers—full of promise, full of mischief, full of sorrow—and suddenly it let out a quick little yelp. Actually, it was more like a greeting. That is when Sam realized that she was having a coyote week.

"Okay, little brother," she said to the animal. "I get it. I'm out of control. Nothing I can do."

Sam understood totems. She knew that an armadillo at the side of the road meant that she wasn't watching her boundaries, that when mountain lions appeared it was time to take a leadership role. She knew that a lynx meant secrets, a fox camouflage, and she knew that the best posture during a coyote week was what she called "baby in a car crash." You had to go limp and unresisting. You had to relax or you'd really get hurt.

So, Sam took the cosmic advice. She drove to the bakery and picked up a bag of warm chocolate chip cookies. Then, she stopped by her house and picked up some tai stick to roll more than a couple of joints and headed for Cathedral Rock, a powerful feminine vortex, a place on the high red rocks of Sedona where the energy collects and swirls. She climbed until she felt as though she were sitting on top of the world. She could see the Coffee Pot restaurant, HO-scaled in the canyon, like part of a train set. The long line of hoodoos, spires, and minarets of sandstone that crawled along the horizon made her think of the skyline of an Eastern empire.

"Dr. Seuss," she thought. "It looks like a Dr. Seuss landscape."

Sam sat cross-legged on the ground. She could feel the earth humming up under her skirt. She meditated, smoked a joint, meditated some more, and ate all of the chocolate chip cookies. She was thinking of Daryl, of babies, of abortion.

"Everything is a risk," she thought. "None of us is ever really in control. It's all an illusion."

She imagined a cute little cherub that looked just like her—the same amber hair, Daryl's blue eyes. "How could I possibly prefer a tumor to that?" she wondered. "I must be out of my mind." It was true that a baby might send her over the edge, but she was a capable woman. She ran her own business. Daryl or not, she could make it work.

The day slipped out from under her. Evening bore down. It got dark and cold. Sam made an anthill of cornmeal in front of her. She threw a pinch of it over her shoulder: cornmeal offering. With a pocketknife, she ripped open one corner of her down vest: prayer feather offering. She lit the end of a smudge stick, a bundle of herbs tied together with string, and waved it around, letting the sage perfume the air. With the same match, she lit another one of the joints and took a long slow drag. The night snuggled in around her. The stars moved in a little bit closer.

"Daryl," she thought, "is not such a bad guy." Too bad he was constantly taking her out where the water was high or the road too narrow. Careless Daryl generally found some way to expose the people around him to danger. But he did always seem to come through. "Her savior," he'd said. That was a laugh. He was more like her nemesis.

Sam took another drag from her joint, counting coup—the gains and the losses. The problems came tumbling in. The feather-light vest down was lifting and drifting around her in some kind of whirlpool of wind. It looked like snow flurries. She leaned back on her elbows and watched it. She watched the stars come sliding closer, between the down, like little souls settling on earth, filling angel fluff—like babies.

The hard red Sedona rock was digging into the small of her back. The night air was kissing her cheeks. She was happy and sad at the same time. How weird the world was. How beautiful. How full of problems. At some point, you just had to relax. You had to trust someone, even if it was only yourself. That's exactly what she was thinking when the tumor kicked her. She swore that it did. It shocked her. It was a swift kick in her gut, that was certain. She even let out a moan. Somewhere in the cool desert night, the coyotes heard her moan and they answered. One first, then another, in a great chain of song until the night was filled with coyote music. Sam was almost moved to tears by the magic of it. Then the tumor kicked her again, and she let out a war whoop, a laugh, and a big coyote howl.

"Praise the Lord. Hell's bells," Sam shouted in a spontaneous evangelistic frenzy, embracing the possibilities. This coyote week could turn into a coyote life.

Meantime, all around her, the dogs were singing.

God and All the Angels

When Terrell's mama Maiva died, Selita went to the funeral. She sat tall in the twelfth row of the 96th Avenue Baptist Church, as composed as a television anchor woman while everyone else carried on.

She had liked Terrell's mama and Terrell's mama had liked her, so she was glad to be paying her respects. Of course, no one knew that for Maiva, who had crossed over into another world, Selita was the most important person in the room. To the throng that sweated, fidgeted, swayed, and soared to spiritual heights on the wake of Maiva's heavenly transportation, Selita was no more than another of Terrell's many girlfriends.

The most recent one, perhaps, but beyond that, nothing special. She wasn't the most ingratiating, or the prettiest, or the most enamored with Terrell. And she certainly wasn't the only girlfriend in attendance. The knife- and scissors-scored pews of that shabby little church were generously salted with the lovers of Maiva's cherished only son.

With the exception of Selita, none of Terrell's other girlfriends was very much interested in either the personality or metaphysical destiny of his mama, Maiva Quinn. Most of them didn't even like her. And she hadn't liked them. Like a closetful of cheap nylon nightgowns, they seemed only marginally alluring and infinitely replaceable. They had come to the funeral, not for Maiva, but for Terrell, and for the chance to catwalk solicitously back into his consciousness. But for the time being, focused as he was on his mother's casket, Terrell took no notice of them.

The most important woman in Terrell's life was dead, and he felt really bad. The fact that every available seat was taken and the room swollen with family members, neighbors, Maiva's choir and church and card and gardening friends, and so many of the other women in his life made very little difference to him. He didn't notice either how the light trumpeted in that Sunday morning in July through the six frosted panes that towered over the front door of the church to settle like a shine on ebony over the gentle rise of Maiva's brow and cheekbones or how it pummeled the interesting star- and trapezoid-shaped holes in the walls where loose plaster had fallen to reveal the rotting rib-work of lathe. The raggedy interior of the church was gay with the flowers of Maiva's gardening buddies, many of whom had risen to testify to her great character and strength, but Terrell, self-absorbed and utterly miserable, barely noted that.

Maiva, on the other hand, had she been in the body, would have loved the flowers. She would have deeply inhaled the scent of lilies, lilacs, gardenias, and floribunda roses. Her heart would have sprouted sudden tendrils of tenderness at the flatteries of her friends. And she would have clapped, nodded, and "amen'ed" to the Reverend John Wort's sermon about the fact that she, Maiva Quinn, was *expected* in the Kingdom of the Lord. That there was a place set for her at the table of *Jesus*. That her recipe for life would be *welcome* at God's banquet. Maiva would have also loved the way her nasty sister Cora Mae threw herself on the coffin to make her big-skirted, stiff-hatted, sorrowful amends because she and Maiva had been fighting for so many years, and like any big winner, Cora Mae could afford to put on a show. And she would have especially loved that her precious boy Terrell was sitting just a few feet away from her, already missing her terribly, and that his current girlfriend, Selita, was seated, considerately, somewhere toward the middle of the church paying her respects. Selita was a capable and dependable young woman. That made her quite unlike the flighty creatures with whom Terrell ordinarily consorted. That made Selita special.

Beyond the quick sensual survey, and a certain satisfaction with Selita's attendance and other ceremonial details, Maiva's attention—had she been physically present—would have been focused entirely on another feminine entity, this one six years old and wriggling on the seat next to her daddy. This pint-sized being was Terrell's daughter Tina, and Maiva's only grandchild. Something that would have certainly irritated Maiva—the same thing that disturbed both Terrell and Selita—was that Aisha, Tina's mother, was also seated in the front row, clinging possessively to Tina, flaunting her hold on Terrell and making everyone's life a horror. Maiva would have sympathized deeply with Tina, who squirmed away from Aisha and tried to snuggle closer to a father who paid her no attention. Even at six, Tina was aware that she was no more than a pawn. Her mama always made a big fuss over her in front of people and, when they were alone, ignored her. This was very different from the care she had received from her grandmother, who spoiled her both in public and in private; from Terrell, who was not even remotely interested in her; and from the care she was about to receive from Selita, who was to prove as perpetual and immutable as the road between her house and her school.

In her struggle to move closer to her father, Tina accidentally pinched the inside of his thigh with a knobby little elbow, waking him from his sullen reverie. Terrell looked at the thin-limbed, pixie copy of manipulative Aisha and turned to find Selita's face in the sea that swam behind him. She, he thought, could save him from the baby mama who dangled Tina like a baited hook in front of him at every opportunity.

Perhaps it was the counterinfluence of Terrell's indifference and Aisha's shammed devotion that prompted Tina to slide from the pew, high-step up to the casket, and wrestle a place for herself right next to Cora Mae's queen-sized posterior. The casket, which had been purchased from Alex Buniole's Funeral Heaven, was as black as pitch. It had big, gold-plated handles and a lining of fuchsia satin that Tina could just see peeking out at her from the coffin's top. Tina, who could not see over the side of the well-polished sarcophagus even though she got up on her tiptoes, because it was sitting on some kind of stand, was not convinced that her grandmother, Maiva, was really in the dark rectangular box at all. If she were, Tina decided, she'd be submerged—half-drowned in the crocodile tears that Cora Mae was raining liberally into it. Imagining a swimming pool with her grandmother floating upon it on an inflatable raft, a glass of pink lemonade bobbing next to her like a camellia decorating a punch bowl, Tina offered up a prayer.

The prayer is untranslatable, because Tina could not cast the vague shape of her longing into language. But for Maiva, and anyone dwelling in the astral world for that matter, the wish came in clear as a bell. Formless beings prefer formless thoughts. Dead people have trouble with language.

If Maiva had not already stepped across the boundary to the other side, she would have sat up in her coffin, pushed the theatrical Cora Mae out of the way, and wrapped her arms around Tina. As it was, all she could do was send out a comforting vibe so that when Tina finished her prayer and opened her downcast eyes, the white ruffle of her anklet socks looked as frothy as angel wings and the shine in her black

Mary Janes beamed up at her like a kiss. It was this luster that walked with her back to the pew where a much-comforted Tina resumed her place in the fractious embrace of her family.

After the tributes and the sermon, the choir raised its voice in praise of the Lord, and it was this song that carried Maiva finally up the celestial staircase. More plaster must have fallen during that outburst of affection and celebration. Star metamorphosed into trapezoid, trapezoid into rhombus, on the dusty old walls of the church.

When the funeral was over, the congregation stepped outside into the 96th Avenue sunshine. Under a canopy of a baby blue sky dotted with clouds shaped like wispy rosettes, the family and friends of Maiva Quinn touched, knitted, and knotted, embroidering the morning with rich combinations of jubilation and warmth. Aisha stood as close to Terrell as she possibly could, her arms wound tightly around Tina, Terrell disregarding their proximity as the procession of young women with whom he had dallied came up to express their regrets.

In a dizzying parade of scent, short skirts, high-heeled shoes, sculpted nails, and elaborate hairdos, Terrell's ladies sauntered up to offer their silky condolences to Maiva's bereaved boy. Aisha, struggling against this upwelling of her ex-boyfriend's old loves, kept her violet-colored talons firmly planted in the only piece of Terrell's flesh to which she could still lay claim—a much bigger piece, she surmised, than anything those other women did possess. Selita, looking elegant and aloof in her orchid-colored suit, leaned up against her car, a silver Lexus that she'd parked wisely and portentously right in front of the church like a coachman with the perfect exit strategy. The car keys dangling from her manicured fingertips flashed like an approach light on a runway, and Terrell, gratefully honing in on them, made his excuses, untangled himself from the garrote of past encounters and, with a relief that was clear and visible, said, "Save me, Selita. Let's get out of here."

Selita nodded, opened the door for him, and let herself in on the driver's side.

"Where to?" she asked.

"Let's go to the club," Terrell replied, in the misty-eyed middle of that morning, thinking that a Remy was exactly what he needed.

Selita glanced over at Terrell, considering for a moment his handsome face and build, how fine he looked all suited up, the tight curl of his hair. "Lots of girlfriends," she observed coolly, her full lips anticipatory, just a little open, as if poised for a pronouncement.

Terrell, conflicted as always between the good his mama saw in Selita and her physical attractiveness, looked at her and sighed. "Uh, huh," he agreed, straightening a sleeve.

It didn't take Aisha long to project her desires into the vacuum left in Maiva's absence. With Terrell's main gatekeeper gone, she stormed at once the citadel of his attentions. She called him up the very evening of Maiva's funeral to demand that he take care of Tina while she went to get her club on with her friends. Tina was, as usual, the genetic hostage through whom she could exact a ransom.

Of course Terrell said no. She always called him without notice. He had made other plans. His mama had just died. What was Aisha trying to do? His voice rose on the phone. Aisha's voice rose with it.

"You, Terrell, have never been a father to this child. How come you don't care about Tina, huh? She's your baby, too. You're never there for her. It's all about you, isn't it, Terrell? You, and those trifling ho's you hang out with. Maiva may be dead, but you are still nothing but a mama's boy. You just don't have that big skirt to hide behind anymore now that she's gone."

Tina, her hand caught fast in Aisha's angry grip, could not squirm free to cover her ears the way she wanted to—she hated it when her mama talked this way—so she let out a squeal.

"Is Tina there?" Terrell asked angrily.

"'Course she is," Aisha taunted. "You think I hide the truth from her? Cover up for your behavior?"

"All right, all right," Terrell's voice placated. "I'll come and get her." Then he slammed down the phone.

He quickly dialed Selita's number.

Terrell despised the way Aisha used Tina to make him do things for her. The truth was he would have, could have, loved his daughter, but with every step he made toward her, Aisha tightened the noose around his neck. Tina was the trap that Aisha had set for Terrell seven years ago when they were dating. Her plan had failed. She had not managed to catch Terrell, but she had found a way to keep him on an emotional tether. Maiva's love for Tina, Terrell's potential love for Tina—all this kept him bound to her financially and otherwise. Terrell supported Tina, Aisha by association, and physically he tried to keep his distance, tried to run as far away from them as possible. But Aisha knew just how strong the tie was between the father and his child, and when he got too free, too spirited, she'd pull him in.

"Hello?" Selita's voice sounded sleepy on the phone.

"Baby, did I wake you?"

"Um, hmm. What time is it? Oh, I must have fallen asleep. Terrell, I simply cannot drink a whisky in the middle of the day. How are you doing, honey?"

"Me? Oh, I'm straight. It's just that Aisha called me to watch Tina tonight, and I can't. So, Selita, I was wondering if..."

It was so easy for Terrell to slip the yoke, to transfer the responsibility that Maiva had assumed for him to Selita. She was so much like Maiva anyway—caring, thoughtful, and dependable. She was the only woman Terrell had dealings with who had a career. Perhaps that was why the two women had been so drawn to one another. For Terrell, these very qualities presented problems. The only thing that made it possible for him to love Selita at all was her beauty. In this way, she was not a bit like Maiva, at least not to Terrell. In his mind Selita was far lovelier than any of his other girlfriends. Of course, it did not occur to him that this loveliness had to do with something more than physical appearance. That would have disturbed Terrell. He liked to think his preference for Selita had to do with her prettiness.

"You want me to take care of Tina for you?" Selita said warily. She was a little cat-shy after witnessing the pussy promenade at the funeral and not enthusiastic about getting any closer to Aisha.

"Just this once, sweetie," Terrell pleaded. "It's been a hard day. I just can't do it tonight."

"All right, Terrell," Selita heard herself say, regretting almost immediately her acquiescence. "You'll drop her off, right?"

"Yes. Oh, thank you, baby. I'll make it up to you. You know how much this means to me."

"Ummm," said Selita, shaking her whiskey head. She hung up with Terrell and took a shower.

Tina sat quietly in the car next to Terrell. She knew he was taking her to one of his girlfriends for the evening. In the past, his surrogate had always been Maiva. But as Terrell had so crisply clarified, Grandma was gone now. Tina would spend the evening with Selita.

"Mama's gonna be mad if she finds out you took me to your girlfriend's house," Tina muttered.

"You are too young to be in my adult business. Maybe we just won't tell her," said Terrell.

"Maybe. What will you give me if I keep the secret?"

"Girl, where did you learn that blackmail shit? Don't tell me. From your mama. Six years old and you're already trying that blackmail shit on me."

Terrell took the next corner tightly. The car screeched angrily beneath them. Tina knew she'd made him really mad. It scared her, so she wasn't going to say another word.

"You just better be a good girl with Selita," warned Terrell. "I don't want to hear about any misbehavior. And I don't want you talking with your mama's mouth. Look where it gets her—a whole lot of nowhere. Nobody's gonna want to be around you if you act like her."

The problem was that Tina didn't really know how else to act.

One thing Tina didn't have to do was feign surprise when they arrived at Selita's place. It was across town, near a lake that twinkled in a necklace of lights slung all around it from light pole to light pole. The building looked like a beautiful box wrapped in gray paper and trimmed in fancy white ribbon. It had a wide, marble-floored lobby and an elevator that took Tina and her daddy up to the seventh floor. Selita came to the door, kissed Terrell quickly on the cheek, and then smiled down at Tina. She was wearing a freshly laundered white shirt and a pair of black sweatpants. Her feet were bare, and she had gold nail polish on her toenails.

"Well, hi there, Tina," said Selita.

Tina said nothing, stuck her little nose up in the air, and swaggered in.

Selita followed, closing the door on Terrell who had kissed her, gushed bouquets of thank yous, and hurried back toward the elevator.

"I've been on that lake," Tina lied before she had removed her coat. "In a big boat. With my mama."

"Really?" said Selita, already certain that it was going to be a long and trying evening.

"Yes. And we have a big house, too. With lots of things in it. It's not empty like this." What Tina didn't want to say was that she lived in a tiny apartment that was always messy. She saw immediately that Selita's home was neat and so sparsely furnished that everything in it seemed very, very special. The walls were lavender, the ceiling was light green, and most of the furniture was white except for one purple velvet chair that Tina was dying to sit in. The dining room table had been set with napkins, plates, and silverware, and there were candles on it.

"You haven't had dinner yet, have you?" asked Selita, noting the direction of Tina's gaze.

"No. I like McDonald's," Tina said meaningfully. "That's what we always have."

"Well, I don't have that, but I can give you chicken soup and a great big bowl of cut-up fruit—bananas, strawberries, kiwi, pineapple—how does that sound? Oh, I almost forgot—and chocolate cake for dessert."

Tina shrugged. She didn't know what kiwi was, but she liked the sound of the fruit, and of course she wanted chocolate cake. "I'd rather have McDonald's," she complained.

Selita ignored this. In minutes, she had the food set on the table.

"If you used plastic forks and plates, you wouldn't have to clean this up," said Tina critically, as she swung her legs beneath her during diner. She liked the shiny gold and purple design on Selita's dishes, imagined how they'd look piled up on top of one another on the kitchen counter. "And paper napkins are better too, because you throw them away. My mama's beautiful, and she's got lots of boyfriends," she added suddenly.

Selita looked a little startled. "Your mama's very pretty," she agreed.

Tina thought that Selita was also very beautiful, but she didn't like her. She didn't like Selita, and she didn't like her too-clean, fancy house. "I want to watch a movie now," she said.

Selita seated Tina in the purple velvet chair to watch the movie. Tina fell asleep there, curled up in its soft plush lap. That's where Terrell found her when he came to pick her up.

What Terrell didn't tell Selita was that he couldn't watch Tina that evening because he had a date. Lavonne was such a nasty girl. Terrell had forgotten how good bad girls could be, but she had reminded him very quickly at the funeral. A touch here, a tongue there when she hugged him. Her phone number in his pocket. What with the terrible stress of his mother dying, he thought the booty call would be just the thing to perk him up. And he was right. What he hadn't counted on was just how addicting a woman like Lavonne could be. He'd gone out with her briefly a few years before, and he'd dropped her—he'd forgotten why. It seems she'd been around a lot since then; her talents had developed. She was a big girl, too, and quite demanding, the kind that kept a man's hands full in every possible way. Selita's beauty and her charm and attributes paled next to Lavonne's big-breasted, thick-thighed urgings.

Of course, Terrell said nothing of this to Selita. There was Maiva's role to fill for Tina, and Selita seemed the perfect candidate for the job. Perhaps, had Maiva been alive, she would have been appalled by what Terrell was doing, but after all, she knew her son. She'd never interfered with his love life, however sticky things managed to get between him and the objects of his fickle affections. More likely, Maiva would have been greatly pleased and far more interested in what was going on between her granddaughter and her son's soon-to-be ex-girl. Selita was really much too good for Terrell.

Selita could not remember when she'd had a better time with someone than she'd had with Tina. It pained her, naturally, that Tina lied and copped an attitude that could easily make one want to avoid her. But there was something about her that touched Selita's heart. Tina did remind her in the tiniest way of Maiva. Some of her grandma's frank and forceful nature had rubbed off on the child. But what Selita didn't know was that she had actually been captured by Tina's wordless prayer. Tina had sent out a call for help, one that Selita had been chosen to answer. All that Selita knew was that something about the sweet-faced imp of a girl snoring away in the purple chair spoke to her, and this is what prompted her to pay Tina's great-aunt, Cora Mae, a visit.

It was apparent to just about everyone who had known Maiva and who knew Cora Mae that the sisters were absolute opposites. Maiva loved flowers and music and people and Terrell and her granddaughter Tina. Cora Mae loved money and what it could buy. She liked food, big hats, and loads of expensive shoes. She did not trust anyone, least of all her family, thought Terrell was a philanderer, and that her grand-niece Tina was a brat. She did have one thing in common with her dead sister, however. She liked Selita a lot. So when the young woman called her with things on her mind, she was pleased to invite her to tea.

Cora Mae lived in great style in a house in the hills with two surly Dobermans and a big swimming pool. It was this pool that had inspired Tina's coffin-side vision, and it was next to this pool that Cora Mae served her tea.

"Actually, I came to you to talk about Tina," Selita revealed once they'd settled into their teacups.

"Just like her mama and papa," spat Cora Mae. "Ugh, that child is a demon."

"I know it seems that way, but I think it's an act. She has no place to turn. Cora Mae, I went to pick her up at school the other day—Aisha couldn't do it and Terrell was tied up, so he asked me if I'd fetch her and take her home. Well when I drove up, Tina was standing in the middle of the playground and a long line of girls was hurling insults at her. Liar. Stinky. Baby bitch. Their taunts were really quite awful. Tina stood her ground even when one of her tormentors, a very big girl, ran up and pushed her. A teacher came out and broke it all up before I could park and get out of the car. Tina seemed glad to see me. She didn't ask about Aisha or about Terrell, and she didn't know that I'd seen the abuse that she'd taken. On the way home, she told me all about how popular she was at school and how all her friends wished that their mamas were as pretty as hers.

"When we got to the apartment, there was no one at home, so we waited in the car—two hours, Cora Mae, until Aisha arrived. All Aisha could do was swear on Terrell. She was furious with him, furious with me, furious even with Tina. I was just wondering... you've known them for such a long time, is there anything I can do to help Tina?"

Cora Mae was taken completely off guard by Selita's account and by her request for advice. Normally, she would have snorted a perfunctory "Don't think so" and called it a visit. But she had been standing next to Tina at the funeral when the child offered up her unphraseable prayer. The petition had grazed her as it launched heavenward, and like Selita, she had been caught in its potency.

"I don't know," she admitted with a sigh that suited her girth. "Some things are unsalvageable, like the rift between Maiva and me. Nothing this side of heaven could make us see eye to eye. But I know what you mean. That little girl is a mess. She's just like her mama. Unwanted. Unloved. And she's acting it out every hour, every minute. Can anyone get through to that Tina? I don't think so. It will take God and all the angels to save that child."

Cora Mae felt suddenly heavy in her heart and her soul. Such an unpleasant feeling. She just wanted to cry. "I'm sorry,

Selita, I don't think I can help you. I wish I could, but I can't." She pushed back her chair and gathered the dirty teacups. Tina's prayer shot into the galaxy on giant booster rockets and started to unfurl like a banner.

Aisha could see the bond that was forming between Tina and Selita. It troubled her in a strange and upsetting way. Some stammering part of her mind seemed to deem it a very good thing. For Tina, but not for her. She could no longer blackmail Terrell with Tina's emotional needs. She called Terrell. Terrell called Selita. And Selita no longer seemed to be just filling in for Terrell. Selita clearly enjoyed spending time with Tina, even though Tina responded with no particular show of affection. Even so, this attention to Tina made Aisha terribly jealous. She began to compete with Selita, finding, of course, that she herself had a hold on her daughter's heart much greater than she had ever imagined. This lovely discovery should have been enough for Aisha, but she was so consumed by her need to control Terrell and curtail any freedom that he might be able to contrive that she began looking about for some poison.

She found it in Terrell's ongoing fling with Lavonne—Aisha had lots of connections in the same scene as Terrell—and she made it a point to pen the note that would so inform Selita. Late one night, with a profound and satisfied chuckle, she dropped her letter into the mail slot at Selita's apartment. There was no way she'd trust the mail with the mission.

Selita was a little surprised by the crude language of Aisha's missive, but she wasn't exactly staggered by its content. She suspected Terrell of affairs; she knew his past, but she'd been so absorbed with her growing affection for Tina that she'd all but shut his methods of operation from her mind. For a moment she actually considered pretending she hadn't received the letter, worried about what it would do to the support that she was trying to give to Tina. She realized, however, that since it had been written by Aisha, to ignore it would be impossible. Selita called Terrell, told him what she'd discovered, and let him know that it was over for them. All Terrell had to say was, "What about Tina?"

Selita knew she had to tell Tina about breaking up with Terrell. She'd have to explain why she wouldn't be baby-sitting anymore or picking her up from school. This was not something she wanted to do at Aisha's apartment, so she went to Tina's school, waiting outside the chain-link-fenced schoolyard. Children exploded out of the doors at recess, Tina among them. She seemed to have made a friend. The two little girls looked over at Selita where she waved from the other side of the barrier. Tina said something to her new playmate who sat down on the steps while Tina walked up to Selita.

"Why are you here?" said Tina accusingly, as if embarrassed by Selita's presence.

"Well, I just want to tell you that I'm no longer your daddy's girlfriend. I've just been advised that he's seeing someone else."

"So?" mumbled Tina testily.

"So, I'm breaking up with him."

"Just because of another woman. That's how he is."

"Yes, it is, and that's why I can't stay with him."

"But what will you do?" Tina sharply inquired.

"Oh, don't worry about me," Selita laughed. "I'll get along fine without him."

"You'd leave him just like that?"

"You have to, honey, when it just isn't right." Selita had crouched down to talk to Tina. She stood and smiled sadly. "I just wanted you to know," she concluded.

"You're going to leave me, too?" Tina accused. She thrust her thin hands and skinny arms out through the chain-link of the fence. Selita looked down at the little fist of a face clenched with Tina's disappointment.

"Of course not, Tina," she said slowly and gravely. "I'm just leaving Terrell. I'll always be there for you." She took Tina's hands and cupped them between hers—one prayer locked tightly within another. Maiva put her arms around both of them even though she was no longer in the body, and overhead, Tina's big purple banner unfurled. "I love you, Tina," it said.

Kato

Kato, you are my mystery boy.
I think
you are a green poison
seeping into his bones,
giving him everything he needs

—Erin Orison

Selections from Dead Love

The Pachinko Palace

(excerpts)

Ryu's Tokyo was exciting. It was Shibuya with its game rooms, *pachinko* parlors, love hotels, and its boys and girls with torn clothes and bleached hair. His Tokyo was Shinjuku with its high-end Western restaurants, Roppongi's smoking jazz clubs, and Ikebukuro with its sleazy hostess bars. On weekends it was the racetrack at Tokyo Keibajo and Oi Keibajo. Sometimes it was the little boutiques, the fancy clothiers, and the jewelry stores where he liked to shop. At night it was especially thrilling: clubs full of young people not much older than I, where I could dance to techno or trance or trip-hop or ambient riffs, while he chatted with his unsavory pals.

For the next week or so I spent plenty of time with Ryu. Christian's fat check kept the carnival rolling, and I was determined to have a good time, to forget my father and the miserable childhood I'd spent marooned in prison-like schools. Ryu and Tokyo complied. So did opportunity. Three days after I arrived, I had my audition with Hiroshi Nakamura, in his famous dance studio, and I was accepted as one of his students. I'd gone to meet my idol with all the enthusiasm of someone headed for execution. I left on a cloud of euphoria.

My new teacher, my *sensei*, watched me dance—ballet, *butoh*, modern jazz—and said, "You have a talent I have not seen for a very long time." Then he bowed. "I have a part in my new ballet. You will dance for me?" he asked gently.

"I would be so honored," I managed to reply in faltering Japanese, my heart beating a wild conga rhythm.

"We should celebrate," said Ryu with a sly smile when I told him the news.

That was the first night I slept with him. After too many sakes and whiskeys *onzarokku* (on the rocks), I succumbed to his fatal charms, though I thought that I was the seductress.

"Are you tattooed all over?" I teased, loosening his tie, sliding my hand down his torso.

"Wanna see?"

He grinned through his teeth, like a wolf, and unbuttoned his shirt. Tattoos rippled over muscle. He had the most beautiful body I'd ever seen. I was soon to learn that Ryu's sexual tastes were...how shall I put it?...unusual. I was no virgin, but all of my previous experiences were hasty encounters grabbed when my friends and I could break from the manic surveillance of our teachers and guardians long enough to create an "adventure." These were quick, clumsy trysts designed merely to thwart the authorities. Sex with Ryu was nothing like this.

It was a dance, a tango over ice in a midnight-blue sea. In this, as in many things, Ryu was an artist, his satisfaction apparent in the performance of the act. Ryu used various methods to take his partners to the very brink of annihilation and drown them in sweltering salvation.

"Ryu, that was amazing," I murmured, collapsed upon the *tatami* mats, my dress a violet puddle beside me.

We were in the private room of a teahouse; our forms, wicked by candlelight, almost phosphorescent in the darkness; the rice paper screens broken from the force of his body and mine.

Ryu pursed his lips, raised his eyebrows, and silently buttoned his shirt.

After that we were inseparable, my bodyguard and I. He was very good at his job. And I was happy at last. I thought nothing could disrupt the mad paradise I had stumbled into. But one night, an odd incident disturbed my reckless tumble into the watery world of pleasure.

Be Mine

The Japanese gangster, Ryu, appeared to be dead. He lay naked, face up on the heart-shaped bed of the Shakayama Love Hotel. I could see Mura, or what was left of him, standing next to the bed, leaning ominously over my lover and bodyguard's inert form. Both men were reflected in the mirror above the bed. Ryu, spread-eagle, his well-muscled body dressed only in the tattoos that the *yakuza* fancy, was partially hidden by Mura's white-shirted back, upon which a red stain bloomed, bright and fat, like a large cabbage rose. Mura seemed impervious to whatever had caused his injury, and he was obviously up to no good. That is how I'd found them when I opened the bathroom door.

Love hotels are a quirky Japanese institution. Like capsule hotels, which are the size of small coffins and a great place to sleep it off after a night out with the boys, love hotels serve a particular purpose—that purpose is "quickies," a hot snatch of love midday or midmarriage. Some of these hotels are outrageous, with façades capped by turrets and spires reminiscent of tacky fairy-tale castles, ersatz Middle Eastern seraglios, or one of those corny miniature golf courses. The hotels Ryu favored were far more discreet, their tree-shadowed entrances tucked behind stone walls, the parking underground so that patrons can duck in and out without fear of observation. They are no-tell hotels where guests select rooms from a series of illuminated photos on the wall: the harem, perhaps, or maybe the S&M suite. There is no one to judge you as you slide your thousands of yen through a slot in the wall for your one- to two-hour "rest" or *kyukei*, or your *tomari*, the overnight stay.

This was the second or third time I'd been to a love hotel with Ryu. He liked the drama of the surroundings. He liked the privacy. This particular room had a black leather wet bar, stocked with expensive whiskeys and a heart-shaped bed with red satin sheets. It also had a very large, well-appointed black-and-white-tiled bathroom, and this is where I must have been when Mura snuck into the room.

The Wolf Man and the Mule

It must have been close to noon. Outside, on the canal banks, city noise—voices, autos, and bicycles clattering over cobblestone streets—had escalated. Inside Alain's houseboat home the ambient din was reduced to warmish snuffles and murmurs. Sunlight flooded the rooms, bounced off white walls, bleaching black to ghost-gray. Alain had me pinned to the wall, his hands, like his eyes, roaming over every fold and curve of my body.

"Beautiful," he whispered, "compliant. I like that in a woman."

I was far more than compliant. His large hands moved over my body, and it was like striking a flint. He took off his shirt, stepped out of his jeans. He had a lean body, sinewy, but not thin. Somewhere deep within me a trigger was tripped. Maybe it was the way the houseboat rocked on the water, maybe it was the smells of absinthe and licorice drops on his breath or red-light district pheromones raging across canal after canal along with potato chip and mayonnaise smells and the pungent whiff of cat piss. More likely it was the cheese, the chocolate, and the gin, the nakedness of the wolf man and the sweep of his hands. A switch had been flipped. Everything went autopilot.

You might imagine, as I would have if it had not happened to me, that a near-zombie girl would just stand there like a big blow-up doll. Not at all. I am a seemingly will-less creature, and let me tell you, it takes a great deal of will to resist sex. All living things are designed for it. It is their singular purpose. There was no doubt about this in my body. Horny as any bitch in heat, I was down to the basics. I was consumed with a slimy, single-celled reproductive certainty, swamped with a kind of glandular ecstasy. I couldn't fight it. I wanted to crawl up the wall. The world turned hot and juicy.

Imagine that you are eating a peach and it begins eating you back. That's how surprised Alain was when the laconic object of his attentions mounted a counter attack. I wanted to devour him, and I don't mean metaphorically. This is the point at which murder takes place—murder or self-immolation. This is the lust that kills. Remember the praying mantis, the black widow spider, crimes of passion and desire. But something inside me—some ancient parasitic wisdom—prevented me from devouring him. It did not stop me from trying to swallow his tongue. The drooling thought "deliciousness" popped into my head, and my salivary glands sprang a leak.

Meanwhile, I had become a balloon. All my hormones adjusted their levels and discharged. I was inflamed and unstoppable. My breasts, which, I have already explained, were plenty large, seemed to swell. My womb seemed to have opened up like an umbrella, the blood in it beating like a big Vodoun drum. I imagined my lips splitting, oozing blood; breasts spilling milk; innards raining spicy mucilage. I was caught in my own monsoon. I wanted more.

More, it seemed, wanted me, too. I could feel it making a case for itself between my legs at the ark of the Grand Central Orifice. Taking a deep breath that collapsed our cheeks, I sprang, wrapping my legs around Alain's waist. Like a prizefighter caught by a hard right hook, he staggered and very nearly fell. To his athletic credit, he managed to retain his balance. Then we became a kind of carnival balancing act, a two-torsoed creature waddling into the bedroom where we turned and collapsed onto the bed, which, in turn, collapsed under our weight. Kabooooom.

Now Alain was beneath me, his face under mine, his lips red and tasty. I slipped into the saddle, slid onto that brilliantly designed, perfectly sculpted horn. What a ride we had then, my pony and I. Alain was watching me with a mixture of terror and desire. He could no more stop than a male mantis can shake its amorous mate. I was a pole dancer sliding up and down, a jillaroo bouncing along in the Outback, a frigate ship tossed on the Cape of Good Horn. Straddling him, both hands on his chest, I rode him into the sea. I was in some kind of organic nirvana. Mandalas and kaleidoscopes were opening up like flowers deep inside me. Waves of purple and pale chartreuse, plumes of iris and swamp grass, scrolled past my upturned eyes. Lust flashed giddy tattoos all over my flesh in a rose-red flush.

I couldn't actually hear it, but I was wailing like a cat in heat, my caterwauling sailing up and out the window, turning heads all along the canal. The big dopamine hit mushroomed up and into my brain. "Oh, oh, oooooh," I crooned as the dike burst and the waters of the IJsselmeer came in, flooding Amsterdam.

I think it was good for him, too. He lay still for a moment, his face in a grimace. "God," he said gazing up at me in a kind of adulation. "God, that was good. What exactly are you on?" he wondered aloud and put his hand over his eyes.

I sat looking down on him, my body suffused by a delirious glow. A silky endorphin parachute was carrying me back to the bed. I was paralyzed and couldn't move. Not unusual for me, but I had also found peace and a strange form of union. In Alain, I'd touched some lost part of myself. I was transformed forever. That's how I became Alain's slave.

I never really recovered.

Glow, Little Glow Worm

"Let's wait here for a moment," he said.

The sounds of pursuit had dwindled off in the distance and then fallen away. We were in a small clearing walled in by the long smooth trunks of trees wreathed in curling creepers from the jungle floor and drooping lianas spilling down from the leafy canopy overhead. Clément leaned his skinny dead body against a tree, the leafy trailers parting slightly before coming to rest on his narrow shoulders.

"I love the jungle at night," he sighed. "It's so alive."

He was not winded at all, though he had run quickly, carrying me for what must have been miles, and his voice had an otherworldly sound to it. It had become so clear and resonant, not the sharp scratching of sibilants that generally issued from the mouths of his various moldering incarnations.

"They will kill it though," he added. "Humanity. Like a great plague or a virulent infestation, man will devour the world. He will hack it to bits and set it on fire and cover it with his excrement. Even now, these trees, these very vines, are ghosts. I should know. I live on the refuse. I and the flies and the rats and the other vermin that man so despises, hypocrite that he is. Who, if he had this garden to walk in, would give it up, would kill it? What kind of fiend?"

Clément shook his head, gazed up at the blinking fireflies and down at the stiff and claw-like fingers of the dead Malaysian's hands. "If I had it, I would treasure it and worship it. I would never let it go."

He moved one hand toward me, pawed at my forearm with it.

"You are so beautiful, Erin, like this forest—so alive. I want to keep you, so I have made a net to imprison you. A faulty net, it seems, and full of holes."

He continued to poke at me with the stiff hand and fingers. He was all bones and skin. The old man's already meager flesh was loose and beginning to form gray blisters. This was a monster wooing me. I moved my arm—not much, just a bit—to put it out of reach. Clément spat out his fury.

"Still spurned like something horribly corrupt. All right, I'm a nose-to-the-ground, corpse-eating ghoul. But why can't I aspire for more than that? Why can't I break the rules? You do. You're a zombie. You're supposed to do my bidding, but you still behave like a vain human bitch. You're as grotesque as I am. More. You're an even bigger freak."

It was strange to see the little brown man rage, almost humorous, and I know that I was grinning because Clément narrowed his nearly hollow eyes and stepped back from me. He caught my gaze and held it, as if he saw his wrinkled, gnomish figure reflected there. Then, he paused.

My face was hot. My cheeks and eyelids beaded with a thin web of perspiration. Above us the fireflies continued to dance, flashing luminous messages at one another in their elaborate courting rituals.

Clément threw back his head and stretched the old Malaysian's neck until it looked like it would snap. "I am not this body!" he raged to the bright beetles overhead. "What am I, then? you might ask," he added turning a keen and evil glare toward me. "I am a sentient being just like you. Just like a cat, a dog, or a rat. Just like a flower, a tree. Just like anything that lives. I'm different, yes, but not inferior. And only with this body can I tell you how I feel. Trees, animals, all living things can communicate in myriad ways. You don't listen. I, a ghoul, can only do this when I have a corpse to project from. I am a prisoner, just like you are—sentience occupying an inadequate form.

"But that," he added, suddenly calm, "is my problem, isn't it? And yours, Erin, is that you are stuck with me. Stuck because I want you, and I am willful, and I will not let you go."

The leer had long since dropped from my face. I didn't find him funny anymore. If I had any feelings, they were lost, hidden in the series of unimaginable options that surrounded me like distorting funhouse mirrors. He had me trapped. There was no way out. And so I did the only thing that I could possibly do at that moment, something dictated not by me, but by my body. I let out a long, slow, steady stream of urine. It rained down between my legs and made a little steaming pool on the damp rainforest floor.

Clément watched this first with a look of shock, then one of surprise. Then, he laughed.

"Pathetic zombie," he said, and shook his scrawny head. "Come on, let's go." And we continued on through the forest.

Post-Apocalyptic Valentine

My heart, my love,
FRAGILE
was on the line
HANDLE WITH CARE
when everything went haywire.
CONTENTS MAY SHIFT UNDER PRESSURE
You, a zombie now,
CONTENTS MAY SPILL UNDER PRESSURE
without a clue about me
or you—
promises all broken and
an apocalypse looming...
URGENT
URGENT
URGENT
I need to send a bullet
SPECIAL DELIVERY
into your brain.
EXPRESS MAIL
I am so sorry.
RETURN TO SENDER
ADDRESSEE UNKNOWN

—*Erin Orison*

Part 2: Back to Asia

A Calendar

jan. willow *uguisu* (japanese nightingale)
the year begins innocently enough . messages arrive

feb. cherry blossom pheasant
a new dress . magisterial flourish

mar. wisteria skylark
they throw open . her happiness is hard to disguise

april cuckoo *unohana* (flower of denzia)
under his hands . intoxicating fragrance

may *tachibana* (wild oranges) *kuina* (water rail)
wind-scattered rinds . his daring

june *nadeshiko* (pinks) cormorant
the fullness of her lips . silver fish

july *omina eshi* (patrina) *kasasagi* (magpie)
a hundred fans . tattlers

aug. *hagi* (bush clover) wild goose
disappointment . a sad parting

sept. *hana susuki* (pampas grass) quail
rush windows . hiding

oct. chrysanthemums crane
courtiers . sweep of sleeves

nov. loquat plover
tiny presents . his letter

dec. prunus *mizudori* (mandarin duck)
she has wrapped all her belongings in purple silk .
such a rich gift

Her Luck

She dreamed each night
of sushi,
designed tissue, colored-paper
clothes,
disrobed under the pale glow
of Japanese lanterns,
set the table, always, with two pairs
of chopsticks,
believing in feng shui,
in omens.

The Dojo – Lesson 1

Just beyond her reach
the movement hung
precise as a Kanji character,
as meticulous in execution.

Every day she labored toward it,
arms reaching,
traced its reflection.

Sometimes she'd touch a lower corner.
She could fly.
The movement when she caught it,
effortless.

The instructor mutters, "higher."
The redness in her face betrayed
"wrong-thinking."
Her desire only made her thirsty.

Bamboo Basket

For this *ukiyo-ye* (passing world picture)
I do not have a *fude* (brush) wide enough
to catch the coot's call,
fine enough to trace the pigeon's understanding,
sharp enough to hasten my illumination.
Block-like, I stumble along the path.
Master, grant me the strength to hold the paradox—
rainwater in a bamboo basket.

Shanghaied by the Past

(travel essay)

Some call Shanghai the Pearl of the Orient. And, in many ways, it is—organic, iridescent, a nacreous gemstone wrapped around a suffering center stuffed into the belly button of China. Behind it, China's umbilicus, the great Yangtze, crawls through the fat middle of the country all the way from Tibet. Shanghai is young as great cities go. A murky backwater for centuries, its origins as a cosmopolitan center are rooted in the 1843 Treaty of Nanjing and trade concessions won by the British in the ignominious Opium Wars which allowed British merchants to continue to pollute the Chinese populace with opium imported from India in the name of balancing trade. Shanghai, like Xiamen, Canton, Fuzhou, and Ningbo, became a "treaty port" where foreign powers (the British and later the French and the Americans) were granted autonomous, self-governing settlements. Extraterritoriality—freedom from Chinese law and a great distance from their own—came with a license and licentiousness that lent Shanghai all the gravity of a frat party thrown in someone else's house.

Fortunes were made there, and in the late nineteenth and early twentieth centuries, as the Manchu dynasty breathed its last, money poured into the city. It was the place for youngest sons to go to make a fortune; for adventuresome women to find freedom and a leg up, so to speak; for anyone fleeing from an unjust history or a sordid past to hide; for teachers and preachers in search of a flock. Righteous, avaricious, British, French, American, Russian, Indian, Japanese—the world, it seemed—swarmed to the muddy mouth of the Yangtze to mingle and mix with abandon in a wild feeding frenzy. And while Chinese revolutionaries plotted and uprisings rose and fell, Shanghai real estate shot upwards in a rash of high-rise edifices with sky-high prices.

In 1925 when my mother, Genie, a.k.a. Georgiana Mildred Hughes, moved to Shanghai at age four, the city was booming, divided up into a singsong of settlements belonging to multinational communities that had over the past eighty years developed their identities and expanded their reach. At the center of this universe was the Bund, a classy cummerbund of banks and trading houses situated at a bend in the Huangpu River on what was once a muddy towpath. Gateway to China via the sticky fingers of the British and American concessions known collectively as the International Settlement, it was an imperious one-mile strip bounded in the north by Suzhou Creek and the Garden Bridge and in the south by Avenue Edward VII.

Symbols of status and wealth abounded on the Bund. Here rose the port city's all-important Customs House with its grand clock, a replica of Big Ben sarcastically dubbed Big Ching; the Hong Kong and Shanghai Banking Corporation building, home of the second-largest banking institution in the world at the time; and the opulent art deco Cathay Hotel, erected by millionaire trader Sir Victor Sassoon, a testament to the rewards of international drug sales. Beyond this impressive sweep of powerhouses stretched an elitist world of private clubs, expensive shops, and hotels where wealth was flaunted and the city's first park was closed to dogs, bicycles, and the Chinese.

This is the Shanghai my mother remembered—the Shanghai she called home until 1937. It was a dazzling world to child and adult alike, a world filled with chauffeurs, dressmakers, pastries, parties, movies, movie stars, and electrifying sporting events; but there was also poverty and a prejudice to which my mother, daughter of a Welsh professor of English literature and a Japanese actress, was hardly immune.

Mother lived on Avenue de Roi Albert in the French

Concession. At the time, the French Concession was the place to be. Even the wealthy Taipans, flush from their business dealings in the banks and *hongs*—the trading companies on Nanjing Road—made their homes in the French Concession, surrounding themselves with thick walls, ample gardens, and armies of servants. A bohemian center that drew artists, entertainers, and their well-heeled patrons, the French Concession also supported a refugee population that included White Russians, European Jews, and others down on their luck or quite literally at the end of their rope. To the north, in the International Settlement, activity centered around Nanjing and Bubbling Well Roads, the large east-west artery that extended from the Bund to Bubbling Well Cemetery with the fashionable and much-frequented racetrack in between. But it was Avenue Joffre, sometimes called "Little Russia" because of its large Slavic population, that was the city's emotional center. Just south of Avenue Edward VII, it was a welter of mom-and-pop businesses where elegant but impoverished immigrants harnessed their courtly credentials by serving up fashion to the local hoi polloi in a struggle to make ends meet. The public schools were crowded with the children of these parents in distress. Edith, a Czechoslovakian girl and contemporary of my mother's, whose family were among the twenty-five thousand European Jews who found asylum in Shanghai, remembers the bakery her parents opened on Edinburgh Road. Edith's family was relocated in 1943, when the Japanese took over Shanghai, to the Jewish ghetto in Hongkou, in the old American Settlement, where they were confined along with thousands of other Jews until 1945 when Chiang Kai-shek and the Kuomintang took back the city.

Dire as these circumstances were, they weren't as bad as the situation for the indigenous population and for the thousands of Chinese refugees who had flocked to Shanghai's well-fortified western enclaves in search of protection from a merry-go-round of political skirmishes and rebellions. They lived in abject poverty, supplying the city's colonial keepers and their Chinese partners with an exploitable, expendable, and seemingly endless source of manual labor and a market for their drugs. At one time there were close to fifteen hundred opium dens in Shanghai and over fifty shops that peddled it openly. Gangsters like "Big-Eared" Du Yuesheng capitalized on this depravity, making financial killings in opium, prostitution, and labor racketeering and finding acceptance and even respectability in a governing body with similar values. Shanghai was a desperate place.

Children, like many of my mother's cousins and friends, fell prey to illnesses and epidemics: malaria, influenza, pleurisy, leukemia. Adults fell prey to other maladies like profligacy and the temptations of alcohol, drugs, and gambling. Factory workers died of lead and mercury poisoning; porters and rickshaw drivers dropped dead in the streets; beggars starved; and brothels filled up with young women with no other means of support. The destitute were ignored. It's no wonder that the push for a new order took hold and that when the occupying Japanese were finally ousted in 1945, it was the Red Chinese who eventually took control.

Today, after decades of social penance under the scouring influence of communism, Shanghai has resumed its capitalistic course, this time with Beijing's blessing. The French Concession is again the place to be—hallowed, in a way, by its significance as a cradle of communism. Radical young intellectuals were part of the scene in the twenties, and today you can visit the site of the first National Congress of the Chinese Communist Party at 76 Xingye Lu, as well as the former residences of early revolutionary Sun Yat-sen and Zhou Enlai, first premier of the People's Republic of China.

In an irony that is impossible to miss, Huaihai Lu (it used to be Avenue Joffre) has re-emerged as a key commercial strip, though the Old World gentility has been all but expunged and replaced with super-sized fashion franchises brokering brands to the terminally trendy. Side streets like Shaanxi Nanlu (old Avenue de Roi Albert), and neighboring Maoming Nanlu and Changshu Lu feature, as they did so many years ago, a host of little shoe stores and dress shops. New cafés, restaurants, and nightclubs beckon. The often tree-lined streets still sport a continental color, and the concession-era ambiance of backstreets dotted with small businesses, boutiques, and art galleries attracts tourists and serves as an oddly welcome reminder that Shanghai, once the Paris of the East, is back in business.

Other old habits have resurfaced. Western visitors again gravitate toward the Bund with its antique symbols of European dominance, and savvy developers have been happy to comply, dusting off colonial haunts and reframing them for a new generation of devotees. The Peace Hotel, which in its former Cathay Hotel incarnation was home away from home to such notables as Charlie Chaplin, George Bernard Shaw, and Noel Coward, still draws sentimental admirers with romantic notions of Shanghai in its decadent heyday and Nanjing Lu and Nanjing Xilu (once Nanjing and Bubbling Well Roads) with their big department stores, museums, top-of-the-line hotels, and high-end shopping are as popular as ever with the local and international set.

But for a look at old Shanghai, the crowded lanes and alleys of Nan Shi are the traveler's best bet. This is the Old Town, where the Chinese first settled in a walled encampment constructed to deter Japanese pirates. Cramped quarters, crowded lanes, back alleys strung with laundry and a cacophonous and odiferous tangle of sights, sounds, and smells suggest the heady combination of sensory stimulation that surrounded residents of old Shanghai. Here you'll find recently restored neighborhoods like the area around Fangang Zhonglu and temples and tenements and street vendors selling the same snacks—dumplings (*xiaolongbao*), baked sweet potatoes, shaved ice and syrup (*bingsha*), and roasted chestnuts (in winter)—that tempted children back in the twenties and thirties when my mother was a girl.

But Shanghai also has a new face. Developed by the Chinese government in an attempt to make the port city the financial capital of Asia, the Pudong New Area on the eastern bank of the Huangpu River has sprouted from the bog that in the past served alternately as a farmland supplying pigs and vegetables to Shanghai and a storage area where the port's *godowns* (warehouses) and *compradors* (buyers) shifted and sorted the sources of trading house fortunes. In 1990, when Shanghai became an autonomous municipality, Pudong was identified as a special economic zone. Today, clearly the result of a great deal of attention and investment by the central government, it has evolved into a kind of Buck Rogers–George Jetson City of the Future complete with a two-billion-dollar airport, super-long suspension bridges, MagLev train service, and soaring superstructures that vie with other Asian skyscrapers for the title of tallest. At eighty-eight stories, the observation deck of the Jinmao Tower, the fifth tallest building in the world, offers the best views of modern Shanghai. The Shanghai Municipal Historical Museum in the basement of the shocking-pink, sci-fi-style Oriental Pearl Tower—the world's third tallest tower—provides an interesting glimpse of Shanghai's past. Both structures are located in the Liujiazui Finance and Trade Zone, home to China's stock market and headquarters for foreign banks. Pudong, which is actually larger than urban Shanghai, is mainly a place for business, though it is also home to the city's most modern hotels. The Park Hyatt, which occupies the fifty-third to eighty-seventh floors of the edifice, is certainly one of the most spectacular places to stay in the city. With its international investors, tax-free foreign trade zone, high-tech zone, export and processing zone, Pudong is a celebration of capitalism that puts other centers of commerce to shame.

In fact, the new Shanghai has a great deal in common with the old. The communist regime was particularly hard on Shanghai, believing the Western loyalties and bourgeois values it promoted were especially pernicious. Maybe they were on to something. The beggars are back. So are the expats, the drugs, the sex, the shopping, and the real estate boom. The Chinese would say that places have personality, an energy and a spirit that is the product of their geography. If this is the case, Shanghai will always be the head of the Yangtze dragon: powerful, irrepressible, optimistic, wealthy, ambitious, dangerous. Oh yes, and a little vain.

China-jin

(China people)

"China-jin,"
my mother hisses the word
as they pass by, faces like yellow pears.
She shakes her gray head,
now grown wobbly as theirs—
the old ones,
the ones she whispers about.

At times the neighborhood I live in
is Shanghai or Canton,
and she, a child again, a half-caste
Japanese-English girl with black hair
shiny as a myna's wing, an alien
in a sea of similar-seeming ivory and almond.

She straightens, pulls a long face,
like a lady walking past a fish market
tightens the nostrils of that hooked patrician nose.
Her Anglo-Asian lids fold downward.

Sometimes I hear her rattling away in rusty Mandarin,
then Cantonese, her dry voice rising and catching,
an uppity settling on her audience:
a Chinese woman at the local market,
where she has found daikon,
the long white radish that she loves.

The desperate scattering of language—
hoping it meets with smiles and deferential nods
like the "oohs" and "aahs" of the Chinese kids she gave her
    toys to—
she counts these memories as her only worthwhile heirlooms.

An old Chinese man winks at her.
She stiffens, mutters "China-jin,"
this time a clucking deep inside
around the secret pleasure
of being mistaken for one of them.

Relics

The peevish merchant, with her long red nails,
counts coup, counts santos,
piles them on the altar of accomplishments,
but not enough to satisfy
her big-handed hunger.

She wears a ring from Hong Kong, City of Merchants.
She wants your pretty face, your peace.
To get, she sells. Tight-fisted,
her monkey-grip is palmless.
She tastes abacus beads in everything,
dreams she is standing on the fat man's shoulders.

Brown sparrow, why do you return to her windowsill?
She doesn't see you.
Why do you sing for her, too?

Legacy

I.

In the first act, remember her madness—
her wide gash of sorrow, her *obi* of blood?
The tragic Kabuki heroine,
she committed *seppuku*,
hid the cross-wise cut
under mulberry robes.

We walked like *obakes*, like unsettled ghosts.
She cut my long hair. It frightened her.
It stole the first scene of the play.
She made me wear wooden clogs.
She plucked out my eyebrows,
so that people would mistake me for the moon.

II.

In the second act, she unwound her *obi* of blood
and wrapped it around me,
tied my hands and my ankles.
Not even my weeping could wipe it away,
could bring her back from the realm of the dead
where she's wandered as long as I've know her.
She said "We should all have died at once.
We should lie in a common grave."

III.

In the third act, she made and unmade me,
told me again of her deep, bitter wound,
said, "This is your legacy, daughter.
Let the anger boil up inside you,
let the red pour from your ears and your eyes."
She drained me of color and sutured my heart.
I rang like a bell. "Sorrow. Sorrow."

IV.

In the fourth act, the psychiatrist entered.
I thanked him and gave him black stones.
I added them to the scales on his desk.
I discovered that none of his patients survived.
"Look," I said, "I'm better"
"Yes," he said. "Let's pretend."

Epilogue

In the epilogue, I am walking along a seashore.
I'm pretending that beauty can reach me.
I've thrown out the kimonos, the costumes and robes.
I've made a new self out of flowers and surgical steel,
a shiny new self that blooms every spring.
And I've cast all the ancestors
back over the sea,
like pearls.
They are pain.
They are sand.

Selections from Namako: Sea Cucumber

naisho/secrets

The childhood I remember was full of secrets. Really, they were lies.

For example, it was a lie that we went to Japan because my grandmother was ill. The real reason was that my father, Gene, was having an affair, and my mother, Sara, had threatened to leave him. Sara's laughing red mouth and her courage were also a lie. She was always afraid that someone would die—something that happened to her again and again.

For a while, almost every word that came out of my mouth was a lie. Perhaps this was because that is what I saw all around me. But I lied so well that nobody knew. So my lies became secrets, too.

shinnen/new year

It was New Year's Day. A lion had come to our door.

Click. Click. Click.

His fanged jaw snapped open and shut.

Click. Click. Click.

He was dancing to the music of four musicians. His large, red body undulated. His golden beard and whiskers wagged. His big eyes bulged under his bushy brows, and his head bobbed this way and that.

I saw Peganne, Ryan, Claire, and the twins gathered in

the carport behind him. He'd already made an appearance at each of their homes, and they'd followed him here. Like cobra-charmed creatures or rats pursuing a piper, they were mesmerized by his dance.

Ineko-san filled Mimi's arms with oranges.

"Give them to the lion and the musicians," Sara said. "They'll bring you good luck."

"Wow, he really looks real, even though it's only two men in a costume," Samuel observed. Mimi cast a condemning look his way. Just last month Samuel had explained to Mimi that Santa was only a myth. Mimi still hadn't forgiven him for that. I couldn't fault Samuel, since I was the one who, years ago, had done the same thing to him.

"Why is the lion here, Sara?" Gray asked, ignoring Samuel's revelation that the lion wasn't real.

"He's here to drive out the evil spirits," Sara answered. "He'll go to every house. You don't want to miss him. The year will be bad."

I ran to the back of the house.

"Obaachan," I said breathlessly, entering Grandmother's room. As usual, I was shocked by the cold. It was like walking into a freezer. "Grandmother, the lion, you must come and see."

Grandmother was lying in bed. She put one hand over her heart and held up the other, palm toward me, in a gesture of warning and closed her eyes.

"But Grandmother, if you don't come, the year won't be lucky."

She opened her lidless black eyes and stared at me, angrily pushing her open palm toward me. Her gesture was loaded with meaning, more eloquent than words could have been. "Enough," she said simply. "Enough."

"I just wanted..." I started to say, but I saw the samurai set in her mouth and jaw. It would be like arguing with a sword. "I just wanted you to have a good year," I mumbled, backing my way out of the room. *She's going to die*, I thought. Then with a rising fury, *She wants to die.*

I felt frustrated and angry. I was confused. I didn't know what to do. "I'll show her," I said aloud, going to the fruit bowl in the kitchen and grabbing the fattest orange I could.

When I got to the door, the drums were still pounding and the cymbals crashing. No evil spirit would hang around in that racket. Mimi, Samuel, and Gray were dancing around with the lion. Sara had tipped the musicians and the lion men well, so the beast was cavorting mightily. The other children were watching with hungry eyes, wishing their turns were not over. The lion, I'm sure, had not danced so well or so long for them. I ran up to the lion and thrust my orange into its mouth.

"This is for my Obaachan," I said. "She can't be here. Make her lucky."

The dragon held the fat fruit in its mouth. Its head cocked from one side to another. Its pop-eyes seemed full of surprise.

"Look," Samuel said. "He looks like he is going to choke."

The lion staggered backward. Its back rose and fell like a big wave. Then, the tempo of all the bells and cymbals and drums increased and the lion started moving faster and faster. It was twisting and jumping to the crash of the cymbals. It was writhing and leaping and shaking all over to the maddening beat of the drums.

It made two quick leaps in which both of the men inside were simultaneously in the air. Then it fell to its knees and in a split second, the orange vanished into its maw.

We all stood there in silence, mouths open. Then we burst into ear-splitting applause.

"Hontoni sugoi!" Ineko-san said, sucking in air in a strange, hissing way when she said it.

"Yes," Sara agreed. "It's the best performance I've ever seen."

"And it was at our house," Samuel and Gray screamed gleefully. "Wasn't that lion fantastic?"

They were leaping around, not unlike the lion. Mimi was overwhelmed, but she too experimented with a few high kicks of her own. Everyone was satisfied. But I watched the departing back of the two men in costume with a sinking feeling, knowing one man was holding an orange, that the whole show was only a sham, sure that the luck wouldn't hold.

As soon as the lion was out of sight, Mimi grabbed Sara's hand. "Sara, Sara," she begged, "can we have *mochi* nooooow?" She whined out the "now" in a long, nasal song.

Sara had promised Mimi that Ineko-san would toast the glutinous rice cakes, a traditional New Year's treat, on the family hibachi, a wood stove with the size and shape of an oil drum, that occupied a tiled space between the parlor and kitchen. It was also our only source of heat in the winter. Sara was always reminding us not to touch it when it got hot. She told us that blisters would rise and bubble if we touched it, and the skin would come off our hands.

Mimi wanted the *mochi* because Ineko-san told her that her rabbit had gone to the moon. The Japanese say there's a hare in the moon and that it has a mortar and pestle with which it makes *mochi* or "mooncakes." Ineko-san told Samuel, Mimi, and Gray that the rabbit had gone to the moon and was making *mochi* for Mimi. That's why Mimi wanted the *mochi*. She thought it was a gift from her rabbit. Every night, Mimi stood at the window and studied the moon, trying to see her rabbit. When the moon got full, she thought she could see it making the *mochi* for her. I didn't see any sign of a rabbit in the silvery orb overhead. It looked like a mirror to me, a round one with an old woman imprisoned inside it. I imagined my grandmother trapped in the moon.

The *mochi* looked like small blocks of white tallow. Ineko-san put the translucent rectangles on top of the stove. The white surface bubbled and popped on the glowing red metal. She turned each gummy block over. Molasses-brown blisters rose from the part that had been on the stove. Mimi, Samuel, and Gray exchanged cautious glances. It was just as Sara had described it. That was how they imagined their hands would look if they put them on top of the stove.

"Remember, children, this is a typical New Year's food," Sara was saying. "First we toast the *mochi*, then when it's finished, we dip it in soy sauce. Taste it. You can have more if you like it."

The *mochi* really did look like small pieces of the moon. It was faintly sweet, very subtle. It was just as we thought the moon should taste. Dipped in the soy sauce, the ghostly white cake quickly soaked up the brown liquid. It absorbed the flavor like a sponge, the salty taste seeping into its rubbery center. With it, we also ate roasted chestnuts, golden *ozoni* broth, stars of lotus, and chrysanthemum blossoms. We each had to eat a bit of raw daikon radish, although none of us liked it. It was bitter. Sara said it made the *mochi* digestible. But Mimi loved the *mochi* in its *soyu* bath. She ate it until Sara said she couldn't have any more, and even though her belly swelled and she was painfully full, she made sure that Ineko-san saved some for her for dinner.

Later that day, I was summoned to Grandmother's bedroom. I thought I was in trouble for trying to make her see the lion.

"Ellen," Sara said when I entered, "your grandmother has a gift for you, a very generous gift."

I could see in the dim light of Grandmother's room that one of her tea chests was open. The chair that I usually sat in was stacked with white, tissue-wrapped packages. Ineko-san opened one carefully, but not carefully enough. A long slip of white silk slid in a quick liquid motion onto the floor. "Aaah," Sara and Ineko-san sighed, as it puddled at their feet. The packages were full of Chinese silks and brocades, of alabaster satin and ivory charmeuse. They were full of slips, chemises, tap pants, and camisoles, of handmade nightgowns and embroidered shawls.

Ineko-san and Sara opened a few of the packages. "Grandmother wants you to have this trousseau of beautiful things," Sara said. They were made for her, and they're heirlooms."

Sara looked sad. She was worried about her mother. I didn't want those old things. They seemed freighted with sorrow. They had strings attached. They were trouble. I wasn't the right person for Grandmother's stuff. But I knew I shouldn't express this.

"Thank you, Grandmother," I said, feeling miserable.

"Here, Ellen," Sara said, handing me an armful of the tissue-wrapped parcels. I sensed she was trying to brush them aside the way one tries to brush off a troublesome spirit. "Take them to your room. Your grandmother and I want to talk."

They were lovely things, but I didn't want them; I didn't want what came with them. I didn't want the responsibility. I didn't want Grandmother's legacy. But I dutifully gathered up the packages and took them to my room.

Mimi, on the other hand, loved them.

"Put this on, Ellen," she said, holding up a pair of tap pants. "Put this on, too," she said, holding up a shawl. I could see that Mimi was terribly fond of the shawl. It must have reminded her of her blanket.

"That shawl is yours, Mimi," I said. "I can't just give it to you outright, because they'd probably get angry, but I'm letting you know it's unofficially yours. In fact, Mimi, all these things are. I'm giving them all to you. You just have to grow into them. Go ahead, Mimi, put on the shawl."

"Oh," Mimi said, standing on the bed with the shawl on. "Ellen, it's beautiful." Then she looked at me hard. "No one's ever given me anything like this before."

"It's our secret," I said.

"I love you, Ellen," Mimi whispered hotly, pressing her simian-like body against mine. "I love you more than anyone else."

Mimi's love scared me. All her loneliness and neglect rushed toward me. It was so much. I couldn't explain to her that I felt the same way. That there was no one there for me, either, to be vulnerable with.

"I love you, Mimi," I said, feeling her hot, damp body and breathing in the sweaty smell of her hair. *She needs a bath*, I thought, seeing myself in the bathroom with her, telling her a story, the steam curling around us.

"Let's dress up and sneak *mochi*," Mimi suggested.

That's just what we did. We sat in the bedroom, eating *mochi* in Grandmother's underwear, and I spilled soy sauce on the spotless, embroidered white. I stood up quickly. Too quickly—my heel caught the hem of the garment and the tissue-thin silk of the slip I was wearing tore straight up the back.

"Oh, oh," Mimi said, her mouth full of *mochi*. "Whoops!"

"This, they won't like," I responded. "But they're not going to know. We'll just wrap this stuff up, and they'll never find out, and when we open it, I'll be old and you'll be old, and we'll just look at this silly old rip and laugh. Look, Mimi," I said, "it's just like a hospital gown. You can see my whole backside." I turned my rear end toward her and mooned her. Mimi laughed and I laughed. Then Mimi grabbed her shawl and started dancing around. I joined her. We finished the *mochi*, and Mimi fell into bed, exhausted. I tucked her in, then went to the bedroom window and stared at the moon.

The old woman trapped in the moon stared down at me coldly.

"I want Mimi to always be protected," I said to the moon, "to never know what it's like to be exposed and defenseless. I don't want her to be sad. I don't want her ever to suffer." Of course, that was impossible, and I knew it.

In Tokyo, Finding the Kami Way

(travel essay)

Rainfall and the raw complaint of crows threaded through the silence that filled the tiny *haiden* or hall of worship at Ueno Toshogu Shrine. From somewhere on the tree-canopied walkways that circled the shrine grove, the chatter of women and laughter of children wafted in on the mist. More faintly still—almost inaudibly—autos made their whispery way over wet city streets. In the quiet of that Shinto shrine in the heart of Tokyo, the nearly twelve million people who inhabit the metropolis (San Francisco's population is around 740,000) seemed to be little more than a dream.

No dream, my arrival in Tokyo had been very much a reality and a pleasant one—the gentle ministrations of the Japan Airlines staff, the clockwork arrival and efficiency of the airport shuttle that whisked me from Narita along the expressway, over the Rainbow Bridge, and deposited me in what looked like Tomorrowland, the silvery sky-rise complex next to Odaiba Beach overlooking Tokyo Bay. I'd returned to Tokyo after decades of absence to see if I could find something that had eluded me in my childhood, some secret about this huge city in which I'd once felt so lost. That evening, lingering over a cocktail in the Sky Lounge of the elegant Meridien Grand Pacific Hotel, I unfolded my city map to reveal the large splatters of green that indicate the city's many parks and gardens, squinting through the flicker of candlelight to find the little goalpost icons that mark the Shinto shrines. In these shrines, or *jinja*, Japan's folk deities, the *kami* (both natural forces and humans are counted among their number), are believed to reside. It is said of the Japanese that they are Buddhist by belief, but Shinto by virtue of being, so in many ways these Shinto shrines house the spirit of Japan. I circled several, two of them in the Ginza, and refolded the map. On the other side of the moonlit waters, across Tokyo Bay, the sceptered shape of Tokyo Tower twinkled, the huge metropolis spread around it like an extravagant and glittering train.

The city of Tokyo covers more than eight hundred square miles, but on its vast system of interlocking train and subway lines, getting anywhere is only a matter of minutes and a couple of dollars. The next morning, 310 yen or around two dollars and twenty-five cents at today's fluctuating exchange rate, took me from Daiba Station (across the skywalk from the Meridien Grand Pacific) to Shimbashi Station on the monorail, a dove- and mauve-plush ten-minute ride past towers of glass and concrete. From there, another 130 yen and a few more minutes got me to the Ginza, one of Tokyo's trendiest and most popular shopping districts.

The Café Odiri—a lovely European-style watering hole at the foot of the Printemps Department store, was a great place to get my bearings. Next thing I knew I was one of the butterfly crowd, flitting from kimono shop to gallery to designer boutique as I made my way down Sotobori-dori Avenue. Carried away by material enticements, I almost drifted right past Ginza Hachiman Shrine. Situated on the first floor of an eight-story office building and not much larger than a closet, its diminutive dimensions came as something of a surprise. Missing were the cypress and pine that usually surround Shinto shrines. Nature's sanctity and man's harmonious coexistence with it are such an important part of the Shinto belief structure that its places of worship almost always incorporate some homage to this relationship. I wondered if the abstract paintings that filled the vitrines on one of the walls were supposed to fill that purpose.

Other features typical of Shinto shrines were compactly represented. A white- and gray-clad Shinto priest, chanting solemnly to himself, manned a counter upon which wooden prayer tablets and other types of offerings for purchase were displayed. I bowed respectfully, and watched as a young working woman in a cream-colored suit stepped in from the street, cleansed hands and mouth at a small stone fountain, and positioned herself in front of the sanctuary. Looking very much like the raised entrance to a fine Japanese home with a place for offerings in front of it, this sanctuary, or *honden*, is where the *kami* is believed to reside. The young woman cast her coins into the offering box, rang the large bell rope to get the *kami*'s attention, clapped her hands three times, bowed, and clapped again. The ritual seemed perfunctory, a matter of habit. A few steps away the city rushed by.

Only a few of the shrines that I planned to visit were in the southeastern part of Tokyo. To visit Meiji-jingu, the capital's greatest shrine, I decided to take up residence toward the west, at the juncture of what were once Tokyo's most important roads. Even after Odaiba Beach and the Ginza, the fast-paced Shinjuku district, with its skyscrapers and towers, came as a bit of a shock. Entire cities exist within the walls of some of its forty- and fifty-story edifices. Shinjuku Station, right across from the Keio Plaza Intercontinental, my home for the next few days, is easily the busiest station in Tokyo. Approximately two million people pass through it each day. My dazed walks between business towers and fountains and past sex and cinema entertainments took me to Shinjuku Park and to beautiful Hanazono Shrine. Not far from Shinjuku, a short train ride on the Yamanote Line—is Meiji Shrine, Tokyo's grandest, completed in 1920 in memory of Emperor Meiji, the ruler credited with the modernization of Japan, and his empress. Only a two-minute walk from Harajuku Station, Meiji-jingu is impossible to miss, the thirty-three-foot single cypress pillars and the fifty-six-foot cross-beam of its monumental *torii* gate dwarfing everything around it. People streamed, looking small as ants, through it and down the wide walkways. Right behind the shrine complex, 133-acre Yoyogi Park was the perfect spot to sit and ponder the experience. Clouds of hydrangea floated in the patches of shade that framed stone picnic tables.

Groups of students—young and old—practiced everything from violin to tai chi.

In spite of the shrines, in spite of the superlative service and uptown charm of my hotel, Shinjuku was wearing on me. I craved a quieter atmosphere. I knew just where to go. Packing my bag and taking subway and train once again, I headed northeast, toward Taito-ku, to a simple, but much-recommended, *ryokan*, or traditional Japanese inn. Visitors unfamiliar with Japan often have the misconception that Japanese *ryokan* are expensive places to stay. They needn't be. At Sawanoya Ryokan, a comfortable room with shared toilet and Japanese bath costs only forty-seven hundred yen or thirty-four dollars a day. Mr. Isao Sawa, the establishment's amiable proprietor, greeted me warmly upon my arrival and took me upstairs to my room. Morning sun filtered in through the creamy rice-paper panes that screened the windows. On my bedding, a Japanese summer kimono, or *yukata*, waited, folded and pressed. On a low round table, or *ozen*, teacups, tea pot, hot water, and green tea leaves promised a soothing respite. When I closed the door, the smell of freshly woven green *tatami* mats rose up around me. I studied the hand-drawn, hand-lettered map that Mr. Sawa had given me. Umbrella shops, bookstores, bakeries, bathhouses, *tatami* makers, noodle shops, florists, and a host of temples and shrines crowded the page. I'd found just what I wanted—a folksy, old-fashioned Tokyo neighborhood.

It was easy to rise early every morning, to drink my green tea and head out into the close-quartered maze of little businesses that made up my new environment. Nearby Nezu Shrine proved the perfect place to spend a sunny morning before lunching on *zaru soba*—cool, tricolored buckwheat noodles—tempura, and ice cold sake. Another day, my backpack stuffed with goodies—little cakes with delicate swirls of sweet bean paste and golden *sembei* crackers in their *sere*, seaweed wrappers—from the neighborhood shops, I occupied long hours visiting shrines in the Asakusa district. The cramped streets of Asakusa, dense with merchants, are typical of Shitamachi, or the old downtown, when Edo—as nineteenth-century Tokyo was called—was the Shōgun's power seat and the Shōgun, not the Emperor, ruled Japan. I strolled along the Sumida River, watching the ferries cruise down toward Odaiba Beach, toward the "river gate" that had given Edo its name. In the evenings, I sampled the tasty and quite inexpensive fare of local restaurants and pubs and followed my gregarious landlord through the labyrinth of alleys, as he guided me past private shrines and cemeteries, telling me ghost stories, his wooden *geta* or sandals clicking before me as he led the way in the lamplight.

One rainy morning, I headed south along Shinobazu-dori Avenue, toward Shinobazu Pond, the Shitamachi Museum, and the nest of temples shrines and museums that dot Ueno Park. When I'd visited the park as a child, it was only to go to the zoo. I remembered it as a great place for children, but it is a fine destination for people of any age. There, I stopped at Ueno Toshogu Shrine, stepped into the *haiden* and hesitated, stocking-footed, beneath the gold and cobalt portraits of warriors, princes, and philosophers and listened to the rain.

I had been in Tokyo for nearly two weeks. A few days before leaving, I moved back to its center, to the Capitol Tokyu Hotel in Chiyoda-ku close to the Diet, the Japanese ministries, and the parks and gardens that surround the Imperial Palace. A grand location and an entertaining one—Eric Clapton, Michael Jackson, Diana Ross, and the Three Italian Tenors are just of few of the celebrity tenants who stayed there when in Tokyo. Its ample rooms were quite a switch from my previous residence, and they carried a much higher price tag. Still, high prices seem in keeping with a Presidential Suite with a kitchen installed so that Pavarotti can make pasta or an Imperial Suite with an unobstructed master bedroom view of Hie Shrine. My room, which was considerably smaller, also had a magnificent view. I looked straight down upon the koi pond where the fish, enormous torpedoes of silver and flame that looked huge even from my sixth-story perch, swam about in their languid circles.

Hie Shrine was right out in front of the hotel, separated from the street like most holy places in Tokyo, by a steep flight of stairs. Inside its *torii* gate, it was peaceful, sunlight bouncing off of the small gray stones of the courtyard. A couple of princely roosters, all amber and emerald, strutted about the grounds. I washed my hands and rinsed my mouth at the fountain, walked up to the sanctuary, rang the rope bell, and clapped to get the *kami*'s attention. No longer hesitant, I gave my prayer of thanks, realizing at last, as I hadn't when I was a child, that the presence of the *kami* is delicate, like most things of value in this world. It is found within a quiet heart, one that moves effortlessly from the frenzy of daily life to the silence of a Shinto shrine, in tranquility and a profound sense of balance even in the midst of chaos.

Shinkichi's Tale

Shinkichi-san
dipped his bucket into the water
at the Yunoichi Bathhouse.
All around him — other bathers —
the slow din grew rounder, rose to the ceiling.
In the water before him, his body floated,
large.
He'd had too much to drink
last night in the Akasaka district.
Sweat and flesh about him in the steam,
big men unwinding,
wanting to weep, Shinkichi-san,
dipping his bucket,
lost them,
drifted, quite simply, away.
He was alone.
He did not think at this time,
"Ah, I have attained *satori*."
That had happened to him once before
on a crowded Tokyo street.
He awoke off the curb,
and a bus had nearly killed him.
This time he was quiet,
alone.
Only the water was still there.
He had no clothes left.
He went about his business.
Some say they saw him that day in Tokyo Ginza.
Some say as far as Nara.

Many say that he appeared to them,
but, strangely, nude—
a visitation.
Shinkichi-san says nothing,
keeping his own counsel.
All agree, they did not see him leave
the bathhouse.

Selection from Namako: Sea Cucumber

amaterasu-omikami/the sun goddess

Amaterasu, Amaterasu-omi-kami, the Sun Goddess—her name sounds like a song. She and her brother, Susano-wo, who dominates the earth, and their sister, Tsuki-yome, the Moon Goddess, are the last three children of Izanagi, one of the two Creator gods.

Amaterasu and Susano-wo, the heaven and the earth, are the most significant of the Japanese *kami*—the Imperial line traces its origins to them—but it is Amaterasu to whom all hearts aspire. She is the most radiant, the most serene. She rises like the sun at the end of the long winter. She gladdens hearts. She makes the rice seedlings shoot heavenward.

According to the *Kojiki*, said Sara, Izanagi-no-mikoto, His Augustness the Male Who Invites, and Izanami-no-mikoto, Her Augustness the Female Who Invites, stood upon the Floating Bridge of Heaven and stirred the seas with a jeweled spear. The brine went *koworo-koworo* (curdle, curdle), and when they drew up the spear, the brine that dripped down from its tip made the islands of Japan. And they said, "Good, now there is a country." Then these two Creator gods, brother and younger sister, descended from the sky and settled on earth, and began to create a host of *kami*. The first *kami* they made was set adrift in a reed boat. This *kami*'s name was Hiruko—Sara said that Hiruko was the same as the god Ebisu, who was one of the eight scary statues at the Daimyō. The second *kami* they produced was the island of Ahaji.

Then Izanagi and Izanami made fourteen more islands.

After that, they created a long list of *kami* including Inatsuchi-biko-no-kami (*kami* rock-earth prince) Ō-wada-tsumi-no-kami (*kami* great ocean-possessor) Haya-aki-tsuhime-no-kami (*kami* princess swift autumn) and so on, until Izanami gave birth to the fire *kami*, Kayu-tsuchi. Kayu-tsuchi burned Izanami badly when she gave birth to him. Then Izanami, who was injured, adjourned to the underworld where, even with a decaying body, she gave birth to more *kami*. And Izanagi, who followed her, grieving, was horrified when he saw that she was no longer perfect and divorced her, creating more gods on his own, until he created three great *kami*—Tsuki-yome, Susano-wo, and Amaterasu.

But from the beginning there was strife between Susano-wo, the *kami* of earthly tendencies, and Amaterasu, the *kami* of heavenly virtues. Susano-wo was disrespectful and destructive. He destroyed the neat boundaries of his sister's rice paddies and sent tortured animals to her serving maids to disturb them. In fact, Susano-wo so offended his older sister that she hid from him, locking herself up in the Heavenly Rock-dwelling. Then the whole Plain of High Heaven and the Central Land of Reed Plains fell into darkness, and the result was so horrible that the eight myriads of heavenly *kami* conspired to lure her out.

Ame-no Uzume performed a provocative dance. Birds were made to sing. Jewels and a mirror were tied to a *sasaki* tree, and Amaterasu heard all the song and laughter and gaiety and peeked out. She was most intrigued by the sight of her beautiful face in the mirror. Then the *kami* drew her out into the world, hurriedly barring her retreat back into the cave. Then the heavens and the earth rejoiced:

Ana omoshiro-shi / How good to see one another's faces!
Ana tanoshi / What a joy to dance with outstretched hands!
Ana subarashi / How revitalizing the music of nature!

Sara told me the story, and looking around at the shiny green grass and deep brown earth pushing its way past the last thin retreating remnant of snow, I could see that Amaterasu-o-mi-kami, the Sun Goddess, was back. I turned my face up into the sun, enjoying its heat on my lips, cheeks, and on the thin skin of my eyelids.

"So that is the story of Amaterasu," I concluded, turning to Anne who walked next to me on the road to the bus stop.

Anne kicked at a rock with her boot, sending up a shower of slush.

"How can you remember all of those names?" she asked.

"I don't remember them all," I reported honestly. "I only remember those few. There are bunches more. There are hundreds of *kami*. Almost everything is a *kami*."

"Is that rock I just kicked a *kami*?" Anne asked.

"Yes, probably," I said.

"Is the slush a *kami*?"

"I don't know," I answered, considering the question carefully. "I'm not really sure."

"Well, if everything is a *kami*, how can you do anything without doing something wrong to a *kami*?"

"You can't. You have to be very careful," I said. "That's the point—do something wrong and some *kami*, somewhere, is bound to be upset."

"Well, I don't think I like that," Anne mumbled. "Are people *kamis* too?"

"Yes, kind of," I said. "I think so. At least they turn into *kami* when they die."

"Is a *kami* a ghost?"

"That's a good question, Anne. I asked Sara that."

"What did she say?"

"She said a *kami* was more like a soul."

"Nature has a soul?"

"Yes, according to Sara, it does."

"Hmmm..." Anne responded, sinking into silence.

We walked along without speaking for some time.

"It was a pretty weird winter," Anne said suddenly. "Mr. Graham being kicked out as a teacher; I missed seeing you; and what happened to David Vintner? He just disappeared."

"Yeah, pretty strange," I agreed, sidestepping the last question.

I hadn't seen Anne much at all. It was as if our enforced separation and the events that had taken place had created in me some barrier—like a river—and I was on one side, and Anne was on the other, and we watched one another from across the swift current. School wasn't the same with Mr. Graham gone. There were no more games about David Vintner. I was left with a collection of secrets—secrets I couldn't share with anyone, not even Anne.

"I think my grandmother's going to die soon," I announced, reaching out toward Anne from across the fast-moving stream that divided us. "She wants to go back to Akishima. I think she wants to go there to die."

I didn't tell Anne about the lion and the oranges, about the old woman in the moon, about Deshi and the peaches, or about the notebook I'd lost and claimed was hers. I didn't tell her about my grandmother's trousseau, the half shell of an igloo under the moonlight, or the feeling of David Vintner's mouth on mine. And Anne, without these pieces of information to help her understand, could only say, "Wow." And I watched the river between us widen as if swollen with melting snow, watched it become a torrent—wide, wild, and unbreachable—between my life and hers.

"I wish it were April," I said suddenly. "I wish all of this snow would go away."

Anne nodded, kicking up more chunks of gravel. Then her boot hit something matted and broad, sandwiched between the rocks and the mud.

"Hey, look at that," she said, digging it up with the toe of her boot. "It's a glove."

"Hey, that's Samuel's glove," I exclaimed, recognizing it from the double white stripe around the wrist. Samuel had lost the glove in November. It must have lain there under the snow all winter long.

"Not anymore," said Anne, sending it flying from the tip of her boot.

"No, not anymore," I thought, watching it turn from glove to projectile. Samuel had grown quite a bit that winter and the glove looked shrunken and pitifully small. "It's too small now, anyway," I agreed with Anne. "Samuel's grown up. It won't fit anymore."

"So much," Anne said carelessly, "for the glove *kami. Au revoir, mon amour!*"

"Yep," I agreed, admiring her soft, straight, brown hair and the way her thin chin pointed into the cold. *Au revoir. Au revoir.* Farewell winter. Farewell childhood. Farewell my dear, sweet friend.

Selections from Dead Love

Ashes to Ashes

Narita Airport is located around sixty-six clicks east of Tokyo. To get to the city you have to race through a quasi-industrial wasteland blighted with giant apartment blocks composed of thousands of cramped little dwellings occupied by Tokyo workers and their families. Laundry draped like prayer flags festoons the narrow iron balconies that climb up the faces of tower after tower, and on a hot August day the seamy tableau swelters under a thick mask of grit.

Alone, in the backseat of the air-conditioned sedan, I hunched by the door, my face pressed to the window, at once excited and apprehensive about the upcoming meeting with my dad. Would I be able to forgive him for abandoning us, for my mother's drift into madness and death?

Ryu sat in the front seat with the driver. He was on his cell phone again, arguing with someone named Mura. "Fool," he snarled into the phone. "It is business."

Yakuza business, I suspected, which had to be nothing worthwhile. I had to remind myself that, handsome as he was, this was no knight in armor, but a *yakuza* in tattoos. Why in the world would my father send a gangster to fetch me? An uneasy feeling made me squirm in my seat. I tapped Ryu's broad, suited shoulder. He turned to me, his black eyes narrow and, for a moment, almost cruel.

"Ryu," I asked warily, "why did my father send you to meet me?"

"Bodyguard," he said, lips stretching over his teeth in a long gondola of a smile, dark eyes turning squinty with pleasure.

His smile was ominous, but disarming. A flutter of excitement kicked its way into my chest and drifted down into my lap. "Mmmm," I nodded, still wary, more distracted than appeased.

He turned back to his phone, speaking quietly now. I leaned back in the seat and resumed surveying the scenery. By the time we reached the Rainbow Bridge, the magnificent span that arcs from Odaiba Beach to Tokyo, the dirty haze had thinned. Sunlight did a spangled dance on the waters of Tokyo Bay. I was Dorothy first setting foot in Oz.

Soon enough we were crawling through the crowded Tokyo streets where pedestrians and vehicles vie for purchase. Large signs looming far overhead promised colorful nights ablaze in a neon extravaganza. Intersections bustled with life. Ancient, modern, wooded, high-tech—Tokyo was a city of contrasts. Ryu seemed to draw energy from the surroundings. I watched his body react physically to them, his movements quickening, his neck and jaw muscles tightening in a way that was almost electric.

My father's apartment was in the Roppongi district of Tokyo. If the city has a foreign heart, this is it. It's an international compound, the home of many an expat, a neighborhood full of Japanese antique stores, Western-style restaurants, swank hotels, and fabulous Roppongi Hills, a high-end, sky-high "village" for the terminally trendy. Dad's place was on a tree-lined residential street with a park nearby in which a handful of noisy Western kids were scooting around on their Razors.

"We are here," announced Ryu, easing out of the car. He held the front door for me and we stepped from the sidewalk into the cool, marble lobby. We took the elevator to the third floor. The chauffeur brought up my bags. The walls on the third floor were covered in ash-colored silk. At #3 Homat Higashi, Ryu pulled out a platinum key ring with two keys upon it. He took off one of the keys and handed me the ring with only one key upon it.

"There," he said. "Go ahead. Open it."

"My father is here?"

Ryu nodded toward the door.

The apartment, grand by any standards, was enormous for Tokyo, where space is at a premium. From the vestibule, three steps led down into a sweeping double chamber. Two huge windows, through which sunlight streamed, stretched across the living room and dining room walls. The carpet was white, the furniture dark, the sofas a rough bronze silk. Door-sized abstract canvases by well-known painters covered vast expanses of wall. I recognized Pollock, de Kooning, Diebenkorn. To the left of the entrance, on higher ground, a long hall reached past a guestroom and bath toward a cavernous master bedroom. To the right of the vestibule was the kitchen entrance through which I could see a room full of gleaming black granite counters and stainless steel. Perfectly appointed, spotlessly clean. Just the kind of soulless environment I'd expect from my father. I stepped down into the living room, examined the books that had been so carefully placed on the tables. My father, framed and caught under the glass in a series of photos, looked very much like the man in my mother's old pictures. There he stood with heads of state, with presidents past, present, and possibly future. Much heavier now, his hair not blond but gray, he still had the arrogant look, though time had hardened his smirk.

Ryu watched me coolly. He took out a cigarette, lit it, and leaned back against the front door. "Put the bags in the first room," he instructed the chauffeur.

I stood by the window, gazing down at the children racing around in the park below. "Ryu," I asked cautiously, "where is my dad?"

"Oh," said Ryu. "He's not here. He told me to give you this." He reached into his suit jacket and held out an envelope with my name on it. The note inside was handwritten in the same scrawl that appeared on my father's checks.

> Erin,
>
> This will cover your needs for as long as you are in Tokyo. I leave you to Ryu. He will take care of you. Just do as he says.
>
> Christian

There was, of course, a check. That, at least, I could count on. I glanced at the photos of my father again. His face had the pinched look of a man with a mean little heart.

Ryu sensed my mood.

"Look," he said, taking the note and holding his cigarette to it until the corner caught fire. I watched as it writhed under the lash of heat, curled into flaky gray cinders. Ryu laughed as the note fell apart, the bits of ash fluttering toward the floor. "Look," he began again, "you can't just sit here." He looked at his watch. "Come with me. I'm going to introduce you to Tokyo."

Blame It on the *Fugu*

> Those who eat *fugu* soup are stupid.
> But those who don't eat *fugu* soup are also stupid.
>
> —old Japanese proverb

Ryu was back and I, stupidly, was excited. He'd been gone for a little less than a week, but to me it seemed like forever. Tokyo is a bizarrely beautiful city where every step seems to take you deeper and deeper into a rabbit hole of adventure, but I was so lonely. I felt as if I'd been set adrift like the little shrines that the Japanese carry to the sea and launch. I missed my bodyguard, but when he returned I knew that something had changed. His careless, exquisitely intimate, and possessive manner had disappeared to be replaced by something slick, detached, and extremely professional. He was still attentive and protective, but I sensed that a great and insurmountable wall had risen unaccountably between us. It was evident at once. I tried hard not to feel hurt by it, and when he asked me to dinner the night after he returned, I was certain I had been mistaken. I wore a yellow silk dress, silk stockings, orange lipstick, and, because I wasn't sure how he felt about me, very high heels. The extra height made me feel more secure. We were going to have *fugu* in the one restaurant in Tokyo that Ryu believed truly understood how to prepare it.* The restaurant was in the Ginza, Tokyo's elegant, though somewhat old-fashioned "downtown." Ryu had on a dark teal-blue suit and a silver-gray tie, the French cuffs of his shirt fastened by small ivory castles reminiscent of the pieces one uses in chess.

"Ryu-san, this fish, this *fugu*, is poison, isn't it?" I asked in Japanese.

Ryu laughed awkwardly and answered in less-than-perfect English. "No, Elin" (he could never seem to say "Erin"). "It is only poisonous if it is prepared incorrectly. Yamada-san knows exactly what to do with this fish. *Honto*."

All right. I believed him. I nodded and put my hand on his chest, right over his heart. I let it rest there, unmoving. Ryu smiled tightly, took my hand from his breast, and let it go. If he'd looked into my eyes, he would have seen the questions flickering in them, perhaps the unhappiness and doubt. But he didn't. We entered the restaurant.

---

* Fugu is the Japanese name for all fish of the family Tetraodontidae, class osteichthyes, order Tetraodontiformes, known in English as the blowfish or globefish. Highly poisonous, and at the same time very tasty, it has been the cause of many deaths over the centuries, including that of the famous Kabuki actor Mitsugoro Bando VIII in 1975. Japan consumes approximately twenty thousand tons of blowfish yearly. The safest time to eat fugu is in the winter months. This scene takes place in August. Blowfish toxins, which block sodium channels in nerve tissues, paralyze muscles, and induce respiratory arrest, have been identified as an ingredient in zombie powders.

The restaurant was one of those places that you'd never find unless you were looking for it, unless you were Japanese. When Ryu entered, heads turned. Of course, Ryu had been to Yamada's restaurant many times, though never with me, and I certainly had little in common with the usual clientele. Mrs. Yamada, the owner's wife, rushed up to greet us.

"Matsuda-san, good evening," she said, glancing sideways at me. "We are so honored to have you here tonight."

Ryu's narrow, dark-lashed eyes darted sideways. He grunted a response.

"We're here for *fugu*," I whispered to the matron, conspiratorially.

"Oh, yes-u," she said in English and smiled. Our eyes met, and I think she understood my excitement, the thrill of having *fugu* for the very first time. "This way. *Dozo*," she said kindly, directing us to a small blue booth.

"Yamada's wife loves to dance," observed Ryu. "If she knew you were going to perform in one of Nakamura's productions, she'd ask for your autograph."

"Mmmm, and you? Would you like my autograph, too?" I put my hand over his, unfastened a cufflink, and pushed the stiff white fabric of his sleeve up, revealing the snaking tattoos. The starched cotton folded, almost like paper, over the dark markings on his skin. Ryu's name means dragon, and I liked the way the tail end of this particular dragon had wrapped itself around his arm. With an index finger, I traced the coiling serpent up under his sleeve. We are like famous lovers, I thought—star-crossed, of course. Then I pushed the thought aside.

Ryu sighed. His white teeth flashed for an instant, then the smile disappeared.

"Ahhh, so we're in a mood tonight, are we? What's wrong Ryu? Are you sad?"

Ryu did look sad. True, I hadn't known him long, but I had never seen him that way.

"What are you doing to me?" he laughed ruefully. "You want to leave your mark on me? There's no room on my body. This flesh belongs to the *yakuza*."

"Surely, there's a place for me somewhere."

"Like the Americans? A heart with your name: 'Erin Orison, My Girl.'"

"Yes, something like that. And I know just the spot." I tossed my dark hair and leaned back, victorious. His eyes told me that I had left my mark somewhere deep inside him, but he would never admit to this. He laughed instead, roughly and without joy. Then he smiled and looked past me.

Poised for the summons, a waitress hurried over.

Ryu went through the motions. He placed our order. "*Hamachi* with white radish, octopus, *ebi*, then the *fugu* soup, of course, and sake."

The waitress nodded. "*Hai*, Matsuda-san," and rushed to the kitchen.

"They're all so afraid of you," I observed. That is one of the things I liked most about Ryu—that and the absence of sentiment. Without sentiment there is no pain. There was no room for sentiment in my life.

"But not you, eh?" Ryu raised an eyebrow. "You aren't afraid of me?"

"No, but sometimes, Ryu, I am afraid for you. I was worried when you were gone. You run with a dangerous crowd. Men like Mura. Men who, like you, can do great harm."

"And you," he said softly, "you have no reason to be afraid?"

The sake arrived. Ryu seemed relieved. It was cloud-white and cool. He drank deeply.

"I'm not afraid of powerful men," I sighed, thinking of the one man this adjective conjured up, the one with the scalpel that had cut up my heart.

"Like your father?" he asked, replacing the cufflink.

"Like him, of course."

"You should be."

"There's no purpose in fear." My nonchalance was an act, one that I had perfected.

"So Japanese."

"Why, thank you, Ryu." I laughed, raising my glass. "*Kampai*."

"*Kampai*," he responded and drained his cup.

The first of many toasts. Ryu relaxed a bit after that. I felt him thawing. Suddenly it seemed he couldn't take his eyes off me. He watched me eat: watched me as I swallowed the shimmering *hamachi*, as my teeth cut into the coral-pink curl of *ebi*. We drank more sake, chewed on the octopus. Wanting to amuse him, I told him funny stories about my schools and girlfriends. He leaned into the diversion. I wanted to think he was enjoying himself. Then, the *fugu* arrived, small fillets adrift in a big bowl of liquid. Ryu passed a hand over my bowl.

"No poison, you're sure?" I asked with a smile, taking a sip of the steaming mixture, not pausing for his response. "Oh, this is delicious."

Unlike me, Ryu did not drink deeply. He merely dipped his lips in the broth. His mouth was glistening, and I wanted to lean toward him and kiss him. Then the noise in the restaurant began to sound like water, like water running, like a brook or a stream. Musical. Hypnotic. And my heart was suddenly racing. It was beating very fast. How warm it was in the restaurant, and all of the lights were twinkling like stars: starry, starry night all around me as I floated on a river of sound.

"Oh, I think I've had too much sake," I whispered, hand to my brow as the first little inkling of danger began to tie down my limbs. What was going on? Not the *fugu*? Surely, not that.

Ryu still watched me intently, his dark eyes never straying from mine. I tried to say his name, "Ryu," but though my lips puckered slightly, no sound came forth. I felt the room slide sideways. Ryu stood swiftly and caught me before I crumpled forward. I felt my chin come to rest on his shoulder.

The owner's wife noticed, looked worried. Ryu apologized, tried to simplify matters. "Too much to drink, *neh*?" I heard him say.

Mrs. Yamada's smile was strained. She nodded and glanced toward the kitchen.

Ryu gathered me up in his arms. He is very strong. He carried me to the street. A cab was waiting at the curb. The door opened automatically, as cab doors do in Japan. Ryu deposited me in the cab, muttered something to the driver, and the cab whisked me away. Ryu stood there, at the curb, and watched the cab disappear. Then he turned and walked back into the restaurant to finish his dinner so that Yamada-san would not worry, so that he'd know everything was okay.

"To throw away life, eat blowfish." That is what the Japanese say. *Fugu*, blowfish, puffer fish, globefish, swellfish, river pig, *Sphoeroides testudineus*—whatever you call it—it contains in its skin, liver, ovaries, and intestine a neurotoxin that is 160,000 times more powerful than cocaine. One of the most poisonous nonprotein substances known to man, tetrodoxin packs a lethal wallop that is five hundred times that of cyanide, and yet the water-swallowing, passive-aggressive fish that is infused with it has long been considered a delicacy. That's because *fugu* is also a powerful stimulant. If properly prepared, and that means in a manner that does not induce death, it provides quite a rush: a warming, a tingling, a sense of euphoria. With luck—and if the chef has been exceedingly careful about his preparations—death will not ensue. But blowfish and nature are capricious. The toxicity of this sea creature depends upon the season, the fish and, most important, the physiology of the individual who consumes it. It is a very dangerous fish. In Japan, only licensed chefs are allowed to prepare it. Still, every year there are deaths caused by blowfish. But people continue to eat it. Why? Because flirting with death is a thrill.

Ryu was especially fond of *fugu*. He loved the flush that suffused his body as his heart went into overdrive, the slight mist of perspiration that formed on his upper lip and brow, the gentle numbing of his extremities, and the way the world around him seemed to soften and bend as he drifted up and above it. Yamada had prepared a dish called *chiri*, in which the delicate fillets of the puffer fish have been simmered in a broth that contains the skin, the liver, and the intestines of the creature. To Ryu, *fugu* was a beautiful weapon, more like a fine blade than a gun. It gave death or delight; he liked that. It bothered him a little that it was Clément who had suggested the blowfish and given him a powder to add to my portion; that in this, as in other things, he had become Clément's pawn;

but no matter. The powder would work with the natural toxins in the *fugu* to effect the necessary results. To Yamada, his wife, and their scrupulous clientele, I would appear to be nothing more than inebriated. To those who mattered, the aim was achieved. I'd been dispatched, and all involved would be happy.

I had never eaten *fugu*, but I did like to follow Ryu's lead. It was fun doing things with the *yakuza*. He was dangerous, too, like the *fugu*. That excited me. But this particular blowfish dinner had it in for me, and I passed out as I sipped at my cool, milk-colored sake, as I prepared to skewer a small Japanese pickle in my Mingei-style bowl. The cab ferried me through the dark streets of the city to my father's apartment. The driver took my key, carried me upstairs—you can't trace a man who must wear white gloves—and deposited me in the bedroom. He positioned me on the bed, placed the key in my bag, and pawed at and smoothed out the wrinkles in my dress. Then he did a curious thing. He leaned over me and kissed me. I could feel the cold lips grazing mine, vaguely recognized the sickly sweet smell that wreathed them—a smell like flowers dying. I knew the smell. Familiar and frightening, he had come back.

"Sleep well, princess," he said, and removing one of his gloves, slid it into my handbag. Then he looked for the phone, found it in the kitchen, and placed three anonymous calls.

By this time my temperature was subnormal. My corneal reflexes had disappeared. Aphonia, dysphagia, and aphagia had set in, and although I still seemed to be conscious, I couldn't speak or swallow or really understand anything that was going on around me. Medics arrived at that point and I was taken to the hospital where I was pronounced dead.

And then I was born again.

His Stalking Feet

It doesn't take long to disappear in a city like Tokyo. Exiting the building, I turned left, heading up Roppongi-dori away from the crossroads. I continued along Roppongi-dori until I came to a series of multistory towers that caught the glint of the setting sun in their steel and glass ramparts and flashed it back to the ant-like pedestrians like some great, indecipherable semaphore. Tokyo gleamed all around me. I was seeing it as though for the first time, and as before, its shimmer was entrancing. I stopped in my tracks, heart pounding, head back, spinning slowly. I believe, for a moment, surrounded by that glory, I was happy. It couldn't last. That's when I felt it: something, something very close... something sly and slippery...something I'd encountered before, something I needed to flee.

I took off, weaving through the side streets, then backtracked to Roppongi-dori and turned left on Gaien Higashi-dori. Twilight had unobtrusively draped itself over the city. Lights began to wink on. My pace slowed to a walk as darkness crept over the town. But the darkness offered no cover. I could still feel something following me in the gathering gloom. And I recognized it. Bad, ominous, so unpleasantly familiar: It was Takashita, the cabbie, Mura, Carlyle; it was him.

I scooted around a corner, crossed the street, moving quickly past closed shops, skirting the western perimeter of giant Aoyama Cemetery. Things became deadly quiet, the gentle purr of the twilit city gobbled up by a black hole of silence, my panting trail through the ink-webbed streets devoured breath by breath by the death-dealing creature that stalked me. I looked back over my shoulder. My eye caught swift movement—shadows bumping into each other, colliding—that vanished. Murky stillness swam into the breach.

Then it was back: my pursuer, heavy, suffocating, and certain. And there were others! I could feel them, three maybe four others, just like the first. A low growl rose involuntarily in my throat. No response, not even the sound of footsteps on the sidewalk—I was alone. I picked up my pace. Again, the phantoms fell in behind me. I heard a feverish tittering.

A sick feeling uncurled in my gut. It rose from my abdomen and crawled into my throat where it lodged and threatened to choke me. My disgust had a smell: the smell from the hospital, from the apartment—the telltale odor of death. My heart raced. I could feel them behind me: a thirsty pack, their hunger a thick tongue of horror, snatching at my back, creeping greedily up my spine.

I was back on the main thoroughfare, sprinting, afraid to look behind me. I pushed my way past the pedestrians streaming down Aoyama-dori and into the Tokyo subway. Step, step, step, step, step—I raced down into the luminous underground: crowds, noise, people pushing and shoving, their faces fluorescent, a bruisy yellow-green.

I stepped into the current, slipping in past the turnstile, let it sweep me along as the next train rushed up, doors sliding open, blank-faced people falling out, blank-faced people crowding in. It was an underground full of zombies! I winced at the irony. Huddled in a corner by the silver seats, I stood with my back to the door, electrified, every hair on my body at attention. A girl with bad skin and long bangs that curtained her eyes looked sheepishly up at me. I glared down at her and around the train, trying to spot my pursuers. Everywhere I looked I thought I saw them, but the characters around me looked innocuous, tired and uncomfortable, maybe even a little afraid. Still, I felt they were on the train.

Omotesando Station. Meiji-Jingumae. I switched lines from Chiyoda to Yamanote. Harajuku Station, Yoyogi—the crowd shrank and expanded at every stop like an enormous amoeba. We were nearing Shinjuku Station, and that is where I knew I'd alight. Somehow Shinjuku Station signaled safety.

When we pulled up to the platform, the crowd spat me from the train. I reeled into the river of three million souls that flows daily through Tokyo's biggest station. No ticket, I pushed my way through one of the turnstiles, a surprised commuter stranded in my wake. Up stairs, through corridors, past crowded shops, down passageways greased in noise and food smells: quickly, quickly, until the fast-moving stream of humanity burped me up and into the high-rise glitter of the roiling Shinjuku district. The crowd thinned as I jogged away from the station. Quiet night closed in around me. I had lost them, lost them somewhere in the teeming subterranean city. A feeling of joy rippled through me. I slowed to a walk, breathing deeply, and let myself be dazzled by sparkling Shinjuku...

One Thousand Cranes

(for Sadako Sasaki 1943–1955)

One thousand cranes bring health.
She folds them silently
although already she
is slipping from the radiation illness,
falling from
the pinnacle of her childhood,
ten years after
the bombing of Hiroshima,
back toward that land of shadows and singed souls
from which she thought
she'd climbed.

Gold, pink, persimmon—
the purple ones
are prettiest.
How many had she folded?
Not one thousand, surely,
not one thousand or
she never would have died.

The little hands
like butterflies,
schoolchildren
disbelieving in
sad endings
helped her (too late)
constructing

the Tower of One Thousand Cranes,

thinking, in that way,
to bring back the dead.

Selections from The Hand of Buddha

Amphibians

The difficulty stemmed from the fact that she had married a fish. "A fish," that's what they called him—his sister, Daphne; his mother, Alice; his father, Clay. He was long-limbed and white, with slender paddle-like feet like natural fins. He was fond of pointing out swimmers' feet.

"Look," he'd say admiringly. "Feet like paddles. He'll probably win."

And he was right. A fish from a family of fish.

They swam. The whole darn family swam. Their lives revolved around the big 165-foot water-filled rectangle that was their pool. They ate there and drank there. They fought and made up there. When Alice had each of her babies, there was no need to study Leboyer or have them in bathtubs. The water was always with her. She floated through life. She nursed them through sunburns and ear infections, plucked them from the water when they started to fight, and toweled them dry when they started to shiver, their teeth chattering like baby castanets.

Melanie couldn't swim. She was afraid of the water, but she learned to live by the pool. When you marry a fish, the water is always a few feet away. Her complexion turned golden, then brown. Red highlights darted down the dark fall of her hair. A light scattering of freckles cast itself over the bridge of her nose. To fit in, a nonswimmer among fish, she mastered certain deceptions. She learned to look languid, under the harsh sunlight, her book tented over her, while the boisterous family voices rose over the water. She learned to captivate Jake's father, Clay, the least zealous swimmer, and trap him in long conversations. She learned to smile and shake her head demurely when her fish would glance over, raise his eyebrows, and suggest the watery pleasures of his domain. Sometimes she would sit at the edge of the pool and dangle a sylphlike leg in the water. Then her fish would swim over. He'd leap up from the water to kiss her, pleased with himself, with the ease and facility of the movement. And Melanie would laugh, shake off the splash, and retreat from the pool. And he'd follow her, landed, transformed again into a gravity-governed creature. Melanie rarely slipped into the pool when the others were there. It was too risky. They were too careless, too casual about the water.

Her memory was of the pool in Medicine Bow. Children swarmed it like flies. She was one more fly in the heat. Her mother had said, distastefully, that the children peed in the pool, and that had quelled Melanie's ardor, so that she hung back when her father was teaching the boys how to swim. In school, she heard that polio came from the water. She thought of this every year, when they lined up for the sugar cubes in small paper cups, as the bitterness of the medicine crept down her throat and into her body. She thought about this when she saw the children with leg braces or anyone in a wheelchair. She thought of Franklin Delano Roosevelt swimming, as a child, through his long summers. And pools were linked, in her mind, with disease.

Still, the water wormed its way into her life, threaded its way through her childhood. Swimming holes in Wyoming—the Milk River, the Snake—the boys' splashing dives into the murky green. They were beautiful memories. It was true that all of the moments in her life that approached perfection, were somehow linked with the water, that carefree, fluid dimension. But, inextricably tangled with these, were the pains—warnings about the slipperiness of serpentine when it is wet (she pictured snakes in the mottled underwater green), a fall and a cut on sharp, hidden rocks, the fear of infection, later her own lumpish adolescent form in a swimsuit, and ultimately and most frightening of all, her big brother's drowning in the cold waters of the Trinity Alps.

Fate has a way of dealing strange cards. She didn't know, when she met him, that Jake was a fish. When she found out, she was a little afraid, her eyes widening as Jake's mother, Alice, proudly pulled forth medal after medal. Jake was a North Coast Champion. He'd set records in the hundred-meter IM. But that might have been part of the attraction—his mastery of a substance that made her flesh quake.

So, in an incredible irony, her most perfect moments were still bound to the water and peppered with a generous helping of her fears. She could never move inland. She would always be a girl clinging desperately to flotsam, watching helplessly from the shore.

For their honeymoon, she and Jake had gone to Puerto Vallarta. The trip was a gift from Alice and Clay. The fine sand filtered into all of their clothing. Jake and the water were nearly inseparable. When Melanie looked into his blue eyes, she saw the sea. She combed the shoreline, growing sun-warmed and brown. Jake's fair skin, charmed by the latitude, turned rosy, then burned. His nose became bright as a strawberry. His lips swelled and blistered. His eyelids, sun-damaged, were difficult to open. He squinted through the gold fringe of his lashes. The sunglasses hurt the tender bridge of his nose. His sun-bleached hair was stiff and unkempt. It was painful to run a comb through it. His scalp was flame-colored. Melanie bought him a Panama hat. She wrapped his long legs in the white gauze of her Indian cotton skirt. She remembered Alice's tales of her children's summers. How, ill-suited for sunshine, they would burn, and she would wrap them in Crisco and wax paper—the only thing to relieve the pain. Melanie pictured Alice's children lying like cookies on their thin twin beds. She dubbed Jake her "darling albino." Swathed in his white shirt and the filmy lap rug, he would sit like an invalid in the shade of the palms, sipping daiquiris and waiting for nightfall. At night, he swam in the dark waters of the hotel pool or in the black, starlit waters of the sea.

And Melanie watched and thought of a poem that her mother read to her when she was a child, "...we've gone to search for the herring fish that live in this beautiful sea./Nets of silver and gold have we..." Still she was afraid. When she took her eyes, momentarily, from the lone swimmer in the black sea to look down at her hands, she saw that she was wringing them, and that her knuckles were white.

Jake coached water polo and managed a pool. He taught life-saving to crazy little kids. Every day he would swim his laps. Melanie went to the pool to watch him. She loved to see him move through the water—effortless, fluid, like a magical thing—a seahorse, a porpoise, something half-man, half-fish. He was fast in the water, and powerful, flicking here and there like an eel. And when he rose, water streaming from him, in the humid indoor natatorium, she would catch her breath quickly, grateful that, once more, he'd come back to her, and she could relax again.

Jake's skin smelled faintly of chlorine. He looked like a madman, his eyes rabbit-red. Melanie bought him new goggles. In the meantime, she was trying to learn how to swim. She took lessons at the college, after the library closed. But she never did more than tiptoe around in the shallows. She never progressed. Her fear held her back.

When Jake started working for Clay, he gave up coaching, but he never gave up the pool. He kept looking for new ones, testing them out for chlorine levels, temperatures, hours, indoors and out. He'd come back to her and report.

"Melanie, I found a great pool."

But ultimately, he'd swim anywhere, wherever he could. It was that important to him. They would spend weekends on Mission Bay, in Santa Cruz or Carmel. They had the whole California coast. They even went down to Baja. On the East Coast, they stayed on Hilton Head Island; on South Padre Island on the Gulf Coast. Always, there was water, water sports, play. Melanie felt lonely most of the time. Her deceptions were beginning to wear very thin. She felt like a handicapped child, injured and afraid, one of the ones with polio.

When Clay moved part of his business to Asia, Jake managed the startup. Melanie and Jake lived for a month in Singapore. Melanie ran with Jake's friend through the Malaysian forests. She played cards and video games late at night with his business associates. On the weekends they'd board the rattle-trap bum boats and head for the islands to snorkel. There were always more people on the boats than there were life jackets. The Malaysians had to make money. Melanie would shudder. Then she'd push the dread from her mind.

It was monsoon season. They were scouting an island. The humidity could bury you. The rain came down in a curtain. Soaking wet, they took to the boat. The rain stopped as fast as it had come on. They anchored off a small cove. The boat was full of beers and snorkeling gear, and everyone, women and men, suited up and plunged over the side. They looked like strange neon alien creatures bobbing about in the water. For hours they seemed to circle like that. Melanie sat and read from a book that one of the girls, Annelisa, had given her, *Emily of Emerald Hill*. She drank thick, sweet Malaysian coffee. Then she drank beer. The book was short, and she finished it. All around, the sea was bobbing with heads. She began to count them. She counted everyone except Jake. Every so often, a snorkeler would swim up to the boat.

"Hey, Melanie, how about a swallow of beer? Oh, great, thanks. You're a gem."

Melanie had to go to the bathroom.

"If I were in the water, I could go," she thought. "They are probably all peeing away."

Jake was the only one who hadn't swum up to the boat.

When Kenneth came by, she asked, "Where's Jake?"

"Hasn't he been here?"

Melanie shook her head no.

"Gee, Melanie," Ken said, "I don't know. I haven't seen him." He could see something desperate in Melanie's eyes, the first gleam of panic.

His eyes quickly scanned the water's surface. "Don't worry," he counseled, "I'll try to find him." Kenneth swam off.

When Mark swam up to the boat, Melanie said, "I can't find Jake," and her voice and her eyes rang with an urgency. Mark said he'd tell Jake to swim back by the boat if he saw him. Melanie checked her watch. Too much time, too much time had passed since she last saw him. No one knew where he was. No one was rushing to find him.

She wanted to scream his name out over the water. "Jake, Jake, where are you? Come back. I'm afraid." But she clenched her jaw and knotted her fists. She was unreasonable. He was fine. She was overreacting. Jake would be embarrassed. But how much time was a reasonable time? A sickness enveloped her. Her stomach was upset. Her legs were shaking. She sat, frozen, counting seconds, silently begging Jake to come back to the boat.

When Jake swam up to the boat, she was angry. She tried to hide this, as well. But Jake saw it in her eyes. He saw her anger. And he saw her fear.

"I'm sorry, Melanie," he said meekly.

He climbed out of the water. He wrapped his towel around her and sat next to her, holding her hand for a long time. He knew all about Melanie's brother, how he had drowned. The tightness of her grip on his hand was startling. It made him want to cry. When everyone was back to the boat, they headed to Tiamon Island, laughing and joking. Melanie didn't feel well. She and Jake went to their hut. That evening they lay on their beds, not speaking, listening to the ghostly sounds of the karaoke music wafting from the bar in the tepid island night. It got caught up and tangled in the drone of the waves as it drifted toward them.

The summer before their tenth anniversary, Jake and Melanie went to Italy. They were lucky. They stayed in a fourth-century castle with five other friends. They'd selected it from a brochure filled with gleaming mansions and villas. They'd picked this one because it was seven kilometers from the coast. They'd picked it because of the beautiful pool. The gorgeous Tuscan sunlight cascaded down castle walls. Every day, they would lie in that sunlight, letting it bake them golden, the color of Tuscan bread. In the mornings, Juliana, the housekeeper, would set out the lounge chairs and drape them with fleecy blue towels. They'd read by the pool, play cards, drink chianti, eat olives and cheese and rich pasta salads. There were rafts of various sizes stacked by the pool. The men were all swimmers, but only one of the women was comfortable in the water. Melanie sat all morning at the side of the pool, her legs dangling in the cool water. When Monica hopped in and started to goof around on a float, Melanie followed. Monica wore her sun hat in the water and all her gold jewelry. She didn't want to get her hair wet. She was worried the burgundy dye would run off. Melanie paddled about in the pool. She ducked under the water and opened her eyes. Monica's chubby legs waved before her. Melanie grabbed for them. She watched them run off to the deep end of the pool. Melanie surfaced, laughing. Monica was laughing, too, her broad lipstick grin flashing over perfect white teeth, her elbows and torso propped provocatively up on the raft.

"I'm going to catch you," Melanie said.

"I'll hide out on the deep end," Monica crooned slyly.

"You'll see," Melanie said and kicked away on her raft.

Melanie floated on her stomach and back in the shallow end of the pool—the one thing she'd learn in all of those classes.

Jake said, "Melanie, do you want me to teach you to stroke?" He got up from the card table and stood at the edge of the pool. Melanie looked at his ten swimmer's toes. She examined them closely. They were long toes. They were twenty percent of his long, paddle feet. She'd already been in the water for a long time. She had started to shiver. She nodded warily.

"Okay," she said, teeth chattering, "Okay, what do I do?"

Jake showed Melanie how to push through the water. He taught her to lift her elbows, relax, draw figure eights, work less to get farther, but he wouldn't teach her to breathe.

"That's your reward when you master the stroke."

Melanie practiced the stroke every day for a week.

"Want to see me stroke?" she asked each of the friends.

"Sure, Melanie," they'd say, and they'd watch her.

Melanie swam back and forth many times across the width of the pool. She still couldn't breathe, but she wasn't afraid. The water wrapped around her like a cool blue gel. She felt it envelop and buoy her. It ran through her hair. It ran over her body. She could float on it, glide through it, immerse herself in it. She just couldn't swim underwater. The water would push her back up.

"See, Melanie, you're sink-proof," Jake kidded.

Melanie was surprised. She saw it was true. If she liked the water, relaxed in it, it would gather and lift her, the way Jake lifted her sometimes. These were perfect moments. The sunlight, shimmering on the water's surface, entranced her. She was hypnotized by myriad ribbons of light. She made peace with the water. She felt like a fish. She was breathtakingly happy.

It was Melanie's favorite vacation, but when she came back, she wouldn't get into the water again. It was a dream, far, far away. Jake didn't push her. He'd look at her quizzically when she'd sit by the pool at the club and watch him swim laps, her book tented over her eyes. But he said not a word. Melanie watched Jake swim back and forth in his lane—free-style, backstroke, butterfly; butterfly was her favorite. In the lanes next to him, the other swimmers kicked and crawled back and forth. Some even wore their snorkels and fins. But none of them swam as quickly as Jake or had the same beautiful form.

One day, when the sun was high—it must have been noon—and the lap pool was empty and quiet, Melanie picked up a kickboard and slid into the water in the lane next to Jake's. She kicked furiously, but the Styrofoam board and her body angle increased the resistance.

"Kick harder," Jake said.

Melanie made it a quarter-way down the lane. Then she buried her face in the water and kicked harder and covered half of the length. She kept kicking like crazy, but she didn't get far.

"How's it feel?" Jake asked.

"I can't breathe," she gasped.

"Keep kicking," Jake encouraged. "You just have to practice. Your legs aren't strong enough yet."

Melanie struggled the length of the pool. She thrashed about with her arms for a while. The lap pool was shallow. When she ran out of breath, she'd stand up. It was not like it was at the castle. The water fought her. The lap lanes were long. Everyone else knew how to swim.

Exhausted, Melanie climbed from the pool and dried off. She sat on a chair at the pool's farthest corner and resumed her reading. Jake walked over, shaking water out of his ears.

"You okay?" he asked, sitting down next to her.

Melanie couldn't answer at first. She felt her vision grow blurry. The print in her book swam before her. She felt as if she were underwater. She was crying.

"I thought it would be easy, if I loved it," she said. "It's not. I'm weak and ridiculous and I look like a geek. Does it have to be so hard?"

Jake wrapped a muscular arm around her shoulders, a big swimmer's arm, one that worked laps.

He looked down at her weepy, tear-puckered face. At that moment, she was five years old, a funny girl from Medicine Bow. She looked like the wacky kids that he'd taught at the pool.

"Poor, Melanie," he said, laughing. "Don't worry, you'll get there."

Melanie felt his large arm tighten and lift her ever so slightly. "Not this time," she thought, and wriggled free of his embrace.

"Melanie," Jake implored, arms closing around her again. He pressed her to his chest. She felt herself drowning. She couldn't breathe. She struggled free one more time. She pushed him away, pushing him hard. Melanie pursed her lips and narrowed her eyes into mean little slits.

"Jake," she said hotly, sniffling now, her fists clenched into two trembling knots, "Jake, nothing is hard for you, is it? I can't stand it anymore."

"What do you mean?" Jake asked warily. He'd never seen Melanie like this before, her face scrunched and angry. She was furious.

"Jake," she said fiercely. "Nothing. Nothing fazes you, does it?"

Jake sensed somehow that this was a monumental issue. One that he could not address with the buoyancy with which he handled everything in his life.

"You're wrong, Melanie," he said simply.

"Water scares you. Sometimes you scare me. You are unfathomable. There all these hidden currents with you. I never know what to expect. But I don't give up. You're too important to me."

Melanie looked up at Jake, at the startled blink-blink of his eyes, the way they clouded and cleared. That's all she saw because at that moment the dam broke; the frustration of years poured through the floodgates. Relief rolled over her. She shut her eyes tightly and let herself be carried away by the seas that continually swirled around them, the sea of Jake's laughter, the sea of her tears.

Rubber Time

"How about Guam? I think that could be erotic. Why don't you write about Guam?"

He's got to be kidding, Tamara thought. *What could possibly be erotic about Guam?* Besides, she'd never been there.

"Okay," she said, "sure, I'll give it a try." She would give him Malaysia and disguise it as Guam. They must be similar. *Were there rubber trees in Guam?*

THE GIRL WALKED ALONG THE embankment, not three feet from the Jeep. Kenneth could almost reach out an arm and touch her. They were moving forward in inches—traffic jam up the road and people on foot. Minutes stretched into hours. "Rubber time," he thought, "Guam."

Last night he had run the Lion City Hash with Norm and his harriers—twelve miles through jungle and cemetery. Then they got drunk. Rubber time in his head. Rubber time in his body. He was tired and hung over. Coconuts split by the side of the road, rotting fruit, heat, a fetid smell, like graves turned over—he was feeling nauseated. But he was acutely aware of the girl, her thin arms a smooth chestnut-brown. She was soon out of reach, striding past him, still independent like the other young girls; not like the infant-carrying Indian women with the red smudges between their brows, the layers of dress, flower garlands, dragged down by the weight of breasts and bellies, the heavy lacquer upon their toenails. So many people walking along; it was like a river running past on the road—Chinese, Indian, Japanese, Malay. A break in the traffic—he caught up with the girl. Moving slowly, with purpose, so close he could smell her—musky, a mixture of sandalwood, jasmine, curry spices. Kenneth started to salivate.

"Old lech," he thought.

On the distant horizon—billowing green forest, red earth, clouds pregnant with rain. Closer in—lines of rubber trees, frail as wraiths or ghosts, long forked trunks leaning into one another, like women with their hands to their foreheads, bleeding the milky latex from their newly opened veins. In Kota Tinggi, the girls had been swathed in scarves and veils. Anonymous. The young ones in blue and white; the older ones in bright fuchsias, pinks, oranges—female colors like jungle blossoms—also scarfed and draped; also anonymous. Their smiles broke out and faded quickly. These people blossomed early, wilted swiftly. No shelter beneath the anemic rubber trees.

Again, the girl had outdistanced him. Kenneth Cormack McGinnis watched her skirt past the other pedestrians, her narrow hips hypnotic under blue and white silk. Her movement slid, like a penknife, down through his gut, up through his penis. His foot slipped on the gas pedal. The Jeep lurched forward. The driver in front of him stuck his head out the window and let out a string of abuse...

STORY NUMBER TWELVE—DONE. THIS WAS her gig. She was making money. There was client demand. She worked on referral. It occurred to her that it was, in some ways, an unsavory enterprise. Someone, a man—as yet, she had no female clientele—would call her on a friend's recommendation. He would call her business number. He would say, "Hello, my name is so and so. Mark (or Mitchell or Daniel or someone) told me about you. I'd like a story about the New Hebrides. Let's say, I was stranded there..."

Tamara would think for a moment. New Hebrides, huh? She'd have to do research...

Then Tamara would bat out an erotic story, no holds barred, all stops out. And when the check came in the mail, she'd drop it into its plain brown wrapper and post it. Sometimes she'd get calls—lascivious calls—but, hell, she could handle that too. She'd say, "Look, there's plenty more where that came from."...

After she finished the Guam story, Tamara headed for Colors, her favorite lunch spot. She met Jerry there. Jerry looked awful...

When she got back to her flat, the phone was ringing. She noticed the queue of messages—six on the counter. She did not want to answer the phone. She let the machine do its job. She was moving toward some crisis and she didn't like it. She opened the bottom drawer of the file cabinet and pulled out a bottle of Jack Daniels and a Dixie cup. *Good old Dad*, she thought warmly, *my bad habits.*

The liquor stung its way down her esophagus, fell with a plop into her stomach, and began to glow there—a small pool of incandescence. *Ah, much better*, she thought, calmer, the furies once more at bay. The warmth began to spread to her limbs. "Ambrosia," she sighed, pouring another Dixie cup's worth of nectar, and opened the top desk drawer. Tamara put her boots up on the desk and flipped through her story.

HE WAS SO FUNNY, THIS man, and he had a nice smell like tea leaves and bay rum. Nikki hoped he would not go away. He'd offered her a ride to town, and she had accepted. But then they had inched along and laughed about how futile it was to try to get anywhere quickly by car. He pointed out how the monkeys were mocking them, noisy, as they dangled from trailers of vine that draped the scarred trunks of the rubber trees. One of them, busily farming the thatch of fronds that roofed the forest, plucked some of the fat yellow and green fruit from its nest in the branches of the coconut palms and threw it at them. A slow-moving target is easy to hit. It glanced off the windshield. "You are not entirely safe," the man had forewarned.

She knew that she wasn't safe. Especially now. They sat on the crusty lip of a stream clogged with scabrous logs, having carelessly abandoned the Jeep at the roadside. They had both taken off their shoes and thrust bare feet into the lizard-green water. Nearby the earth was a snaggle of palm stumps. A few kinky, caramel-colored sheep grazed on what little they could find. The man was laughing and talking and pointing out this tree and that. She was thoughtfully studying his legs. He was wearing shorts and must wear them most of the time because his legs were a light mahogany brown under their vapor of golden hair. They were strong-looking legs, lean and hard-muscled, and his thighs, which were revealed to the joint by the very short shorts, were taut and rod-like, even at rest. His feet, by contrast, now submerged in the murky shallows, were white, almost blue. Like pale fish, they stirred under the water's algae-furred surface, closeted creatures of darkness.

"Look." The man pointed high overhead. "Those clouds look like temples." Above them gray peaks of cloud, thick with monsoons, rose in great columns, in layer upon layer of wall.

Nikki nodded and threw back her head, her dark brows raised, her mouth open in an expression of innocent awe. Her legs, too, were exposed to the thigh. She had drawn up her skirt and tucked it beneath her so that her legs hung bare over the banquette of hard ground. Kenneth wanted to slide a hand up the smooth sweep of her thigh. The hot humid afternoon seemed to gather itself about him. He was perspiring slightly. He wanted to lean toward her, explore her mouth with his tongue, the pliant chamber between her legs with his hands.

"One quick move and you'll scare her," he thought, with an experienced hunter's patience. "Take it easy, old man."

TAMARA'S REVERIE WAS INTERRUPTED AGAIN by the insistent ringing of the phone. The message machine clicked on.

"Hello, is this Tamara? This is Ted Wilson, again. I am a friend of Jason Newby. Jason recommended..."

That guy again, Tamara thought. She remembered his voice from an earlier message. *What the hell, a client*, she reminded herself. She picked up the phone. "Hi, this is Tamara."

"Oh, hello there." The caller sounded surprised and a little nervous. "My name's Theodore. Ted. You know Jason Newby?"

Yes, Jason Newby—adventure erotica: cliffhangers, escape scenarios. "Ah, yes, Jason," she said.

"Right. Well, I liked Jason's story."

"Voyeur? Homosexual?" Tamara queried tartly.

Laughter. "Well, no. I hope that isn't a problem. Let me explain. I'd like a story, a story for my magazine."

"Do you have something in mind?"

"Well, no, not really. Just something along the lines of what you wrote for Jason."

"So, no other specs?" Tamara was feeling distrustful and cranky. A magazine. Yeah, right. She was tired of these men and their games. "Well," she said airily. "I happen to have something already written—a piece set in Guam. Since you aren't particularly selective, I could send that story to you."

"Sure. Sure, that would be great."

"How much does your 'magazine' pay?"

"How much are you used to getting?"

"Fifty dollars a page. This story's seventeen pages."

"Well, that's a little high."

"Nothing less."

"All right, fine. Eight hundred and fifty dollars. I need it right away."

"No problem," Tamara said. "Here's how it works. You send me a check, I'll send you the story."

"Okay, Tamara. Where do I send the check?"

What a waste, Tamara thought as she hung up the phone. She picked up her story, the one she'd just finished, and thumbed through it again. Well, if someone was willing to pay money for a story she cared about, she was certainly ready to sell her heart down the river. It was sad to her, though, to think of this particular story thrust into the top drawer of somebody's bedside table or the locked drawer at work. It was a damn good story. It deserved a better fate.

So Tamara was more than a little surprised when a check arrived, via messenger, from Ted Wilson, Editor, *Compendium: A Journal for Men*.

"Hell's bells," Tamara whispered and let out a low whistle. "That guy was for real."

She posted the story with real pleasure. Posted it and waited for the response. She thought about Ted, Ted Editor, as she'd mentally baptized him, opening the envelope. She could see him now, sitting at his desk reading it, turning the pages slowly, becoming aroused, getting up to close the door...

Ted Editor didn't call. A week passed by, then another. No word. Tamara couldn't stand it. Was he going to use the story? Did he like it? Had he even read it? Surely if he'd read it, he would have telephoned. She decided she'd wait one more day. She checked her answering machine almost every hour, scrolling through messages. Nothing from him. Frustration was not a feeling she liked. She rang him up at his office.

"Hi, yes, Tamara, I got the story. I read it. It was a little... well...unexpected. I can't use it in the magazine."

"Uuuh," Tamara said, stunned. "You editors sure know how to reject. So," she said, regaining her aplomb, "Do you want your money back?"

"Nooo." Tentative. "I liked it. I liked it a lot."

"Do you want another one?"

"Well, I'm afraid I've just about blown my personal story budget," he said with a laugh.

"Well okay," Tamara said weakly. "Sorry you couldn't use it." She hung up, feeling depressed.

It's funny the way people insinuate themselves into your life. All Tamara could think about for the next couple of months was Ted Editor's voice. He'd been so nice to her on the phone. A big fat rejection wrapped up in a kind male voice. It made her feel sick. What did she have? A couple of "likes." *I liked it. I liked it a lot.* It bothered her. He didn't love it. He wasn't even going to use it. But he "liked" it, and he had paid her eight hundred and fifty dollars out of his own pocket for it.

So what was the big deal? Other guys paid. Yes, but they had gotten just what they'd asked for. This time she had sent a little piece of herself, and it was not what this man had expected, but he had liked it anyway. *Damn,* she thought. *I should never have sent that to him.* Now, she was feeling some kind of personal connection, some weird obligation...

SHE STRUGGLED THROUGH THE NEXT couple of days, falling back into bad habits, drinking and hung over, until she could no longer stand it. Tamara yanked up the phone and quickly punched in the number of Ted Editor as she had done a number of times, hanging up when his answering machine responded. This time, to her surprise, she got the real guy. A mellow male voice answered.

"Ted here."

"Uh, hello," she said, off-balance. "This is Tamara." She didn't like the way her voice sounded—girlish, mousy shy.

"Tamara? Tamara!" The recognition was nearly instantaneous. "Well, hi, Tamara." He seemed pleasantly surprised.

"Look, Ted," Tamara said, "I'm going to send you another story. I'm going to try again, okay?"

"Tamara," he said, "Don't. Really, it's all right."

"No," she insisted, "It's not. No charge. I *want* to do it."

"Tamara," he asked suddenly, "are you okay?"

"Yeah," she said, "yeah, I'm okay. I think I'm okay. No, hell, I'm not okay. And it has something to do with you and that stupid story and your rejection of it."

"Tamara, I liked your story. I told you I liked it."

"Yeah," she said, "well, what exactly did you like about it?"

"Well, let's see, I liked the girl, Nikki. I liked the way you pulled me deliciously along from page to page. And I liked it when you wrote," he paused, 'His mouth moved expertly up her thigh, his tongue hard, leaving a trail of warmth. Her legs parted reflexively. Hands on her hips, he pressed her up toward him. She felt as if she were ascending, rising up to the towers of cloud, high overhead.'"

Tamara felt herself melt. She had to sit down. "You remember what I wrote?" she asked, incredulous.

"I have the story right here on my desk," he answered. "Listen, Tamara," he added, "I'm a little worried about you. Why don't you come over? Meet me here at the office. We can have a drink together. Talk."

"I usually don't meet my clients," Tamara said warily.

"Well, this is different, isn't it? Come over. I have some time. You have the address."...

TED EDITOR'S OFFICE WAS IN downtown Oakland. It was on the eighth floor. The elevator climbed slowly. Tamara was nervous. Her palms were sweating. By the time she got to the door, she was hoping he'd left for some reason, that he wouldn't be there. She knocked. No one answered. She cracked open the door. It was a gray and white office, the furniture black leather and chrome. She noticed the slick magazines neatly fanned on the tables. Obscure literary ones, in volumes, lined the shelves. Tamara stepped inside.

The office was dark, deserted. On the wall behind the front desk hung a large lithograph of a voluptuous blue woman. Bisected on the vertical axis, half her body was naked. The other half was further exposed, her internal organs, blue-tinted, visible in perfect detail. Beneath her, a band of Times Classic type read: *Compendium: A Journal for Men.*

Well, this is it, Tamara thought, as she drew in her breath.

A thin slice of light cut the floor behind the right side of the lithographed wall. Tamara tiptoed toward it. It came from a door just around the corner. Tamara rapped on the door and opened it.

"Excuse me, Ted?"

She caught him completely off guard. "Oh, Tamara," he said, surprised, looking up from his work. "I didn't hear you come in."

He rose and walked around the desk toward her, nearly tripping on one of several piles of manuscripts stacked on the floor in front of an adjacent credenza. Not a graceful maneuver. He lurched forward, nearly falling against her.

"Sorry," he said, smiling.

"No problem," Tamara responded, looking up at him. He was tall, over six three. She realized that he did not look the way she'd expected, only because she had not pictured him in her mind's eye. He was a little on the heavy side. He had dark brown hair, shot with gray, and wore wire-rimmed spectacles. He extended a hand and guided her, through a mine field of books and submissions, to a chair. Then he sat at his desk. He swept aside the manuscripts stacked in front of him. He leaned forward. The light hit his glasses and bounced off, leaving an impenetrable glare. All Tamara could see were the mirrorlike surfaces of the lenses. She couldn't see his eyes. He seemed distant, remote, a passionless intellectual. She had a cottony taste in her mouth, the way she always felt on small boats at sea.

Ted didn't say a word. He stared at her for what seemed like a long time through the opacity of his glasses. Then, as if reading her mind, he removed them.

"So, Tamara," he said. "How are you?"

Tamara liked his eyes. They were straightforward brown eyes with a twinkle of confidence.

"Nice office, Ted," she said, ignoring the question.

"You know," he said, "you are not at all as I pictured you."

"Really?" Tamara responded, intrigued. "And how was that?"

"Well, you look so, well, wholesome."

"Wholesome? Like I drink milk or something?"

"Kind of," he said. "Kind of healthy."

"Thanks," Tamara said tersely. "My daddy always told me, with his brains and my body, I could write my own ticket."

"Nice guy," Ted said. "Rocket scientist?"

"Journalist."

"Hah," he laughed. "Lucky you."

"Yeah, only one thing more screwed up than a writer—a writer's brat. See, Ted," she added, suddenly serious, "I don't need an editor. I need a shrink. Will you be my shrink?"

"Tamara," he laughed, "I'm not a psychiatrist."

"I don't care," Tamara said. "I like you. I want to talk to you. I'd even pay you."

He raised his eyebrows.

"You don't have to pay me, Tamara," he said quietly. "I enjoy listening to you. I think you're fascinating."

"Really? Why's that?" Tamara urged desperately.

"Need you ask?" Ted replied, holding up a gray folder, presumably containing her story, and raising an eyebrow.

Tamara found herself breathing more quickly. The paper-filled room was rising around her, spinning. Flattery always hit her like that. It was like Jack Daniels, only better. She felt high. She sat back for a moment, getting her bearings.

TED'S OFFICE WAS PREGNANT WITH the ensuing silence. Tamara felt herself surrounded by it, comforted. She could hear the shallow pattern of her own quick breathing, the long slow pattern of his. She squeezed her eyes tightly shut and opened them quickly. Ted was watching her, a smile tugging at the muscular edges of his mouth.

"Tamara," he said, "you're quite an extraordinary person. I'm really glad that I've met you."

He got up, walked around the desk, and sat on the edge of it, right in front of her. Her face was eye level with his lap. "Hey," he said, looking down at her, hands on his knees, his gaze direct, empathetic, penetrating. Tamara felt dizzy. His loins were a few inches away from her face. They were large and compelling—an all-powerful masculine vortex. In another few moments she was going to collapse toward them. "Save me, Jesus," she thought. She needed a drink or something.

"Want to go for that drink now?" Ted asked innocently, reading her mind. "You talk. I listen. How does that sound?"

"Fine. It sounds fine," Tamara croaked huskily.

"Great!" Ted pulled her up from the chair. "Let's go sweetheart," he said with a Bogie-like whistle of S's, and grabbed his jacket.

"Watch your step, here, Tamara," he directed, as he steered her through the archipelago of manuscripts that littered the floor. "It's not entirely safe."

"That's for sure," Tamara said looking over at him, drunk with proximity and desire.

He pivoted quickly in the carpeted hall. "Stairs or elevator?" he demanded. "Your choice."

"Oh, I don't care," Tamara said, back in rubber time again, "whichever's slower."

Ikebana: Woman with Flowers

pink anthereum: we hope that the baby will be a son.
curly green willow: tough and resilient, the boy will have humor.

In a tall glass vase
she arranges the stems,
the encoded languages of flowers.
She wonders, will Westerners know?
Note on rice paper—a gossamer shield.
Gold is the color of sorrow:
"We have gained much. We have lost so much more."
The afternoon hours tent around her—
kimono of patterned emptiness—
the way green tea brushes porcelain.
Each leaf-blade, a knife, cuts the silence
with thought precisely incised into void.

blue stones: reproof

She is grateful for the red maple,
for the mannered arrangement of color.

She cannot shake the old characters:
three pines and a roof, meaning women
or the wood-bridge over a stream.

Onnagata

Swan-necked,
he glances over the fan of stork wings and the wild peonies
that adorn the shoulder of his Kyoto-silk kimono.
Hyacinth-white,
his face composes itself beneath the harsh, black-lacquered wig;
his lips, a Chou seal—small, red-inked.
The gentlemen in the first and second rows
lean forward,
looking not like inky herons, but tortoises
stretching their thin necks beyond their dark, white-collared shells.
There is the audible hiss
of amphibians sucking in air.

His walk more graceful
than the walk of any woman,
the crafting of each movement like fine paper folded,
a fragile thing.
The audience was reminded of white cranes
or the moonlight over Lake Towada.

In the third act,
when he tore his hair and cheeks,
his fan-like brows forming a tepee of sorrow,
his observers, deep in their own chagrin,
felt the same pang that one felt when Lady Fujiko swallowed
poison,
as though a knife had been thrust into one's side and twisted.
Some bit the inside of their cheeks.
While others crossed and uncrossed their legs.

Naturally, when the curtain fell,
there was nothing left on stage
but the fine Kyoto-silk kimono.

The girl, a tired chrysanthemum,
he has arranged before the mirror in his dressing room.
Her nakedness makes him shiver.

Sakura-no-sono

It was early Spring in your uncle's cherry orchard,
blossoms—pink.
The last time you were there, you
wore high-heels
for the first time—
just sixteen.

This time you were running.
The raw cold, drawn in
with every breath,
a knife blade driving
deep into your chest.
Nose bleeding from the effort,
you tasted salt.

And all around you, the cherry orchard
was ablaze,
a maze of black-trunked trees
like torches dipped in rags and oil
and lit.

American bombers whined overhead,
fat insects swarming.
Your arms, like skinny leather wings,
cranked at your sides.
You ran, earth-tethered, knees shaking.

And you saw the man beside you running, headless,
thirty yards before
he fell as you
were running
on and on
toward an invisible finish line.

And the branches of the cherry trees were lit
with flames,
the sparks—petals of fire, carried
on the wind.

Containment

(for the Fukushima 50)

Man in white — HazMat Level A —
ghostlike, moving, breathing slowly —
in my horrified dream I hear your ragged
inhalation-exhalation through the
self-contained breathing apparatus (SCBA)
they say will keep you safe
from radiation: particles and gas.

These could choke you, stop your already
laborious progress through a plant men made
to fuel a lust for power.

You are anonymous, face encapsulated
by the hood, voice rattled
by the supplied air respirator, pushed
into the voice-operated channel — your
umbilicus to clean-up operations.

You are my zombie hero, dead man walking,
while the Big Brains meet and find new ways
to slice and dice the acceptable margin
for terror.

If I could shower you in flowers, make whole
the body that you sacrifice, through some
bright communal magic, I would do it.
But you are that magic; you are the white-bright
light of courage that dares to contend with
the murderous pissing poison, the greed, the desire,
and patiently clean
it up.

— Erin Orison

Part 3: Death and Shadow

Night Movement

I had been flayed,
stripped
white as eucalyptus
under moonlight.
Marissa, newly dead,
the curl of her hand
still locked
round my fingers.

That's when the music started,
softly and full of allure.
That is when
the canals
began to fill.
Insistent.
Tympany.
The chanting came much later.
But then,
it was as though
the thin lid of a tin
had been rolled back
and the bristling herring,
thick in their heavy oil,
rolled their eyes
(if they had eyes)
upward to reveal
a black heaven
a-twinkle with the old fish shoals
moving in mysterious arcs.

In Vatika

(travel essay; excerpts)

My first trip to Greece was years ago with my husband, Lawrence. We were traveling around Europe after the death of our newborn daughter, Marissa, our only child. We came towing regret, weighted with sorrow. We came running. Germany, France—we tried to escape the bitter specter of Marissa's mortality and ours. But the world, as we saw it, was grainy and gray, like an old film run way too many times. In Athens, Connie and her husband Wayne helped heal us, their care and their friendship like a pair of hands lifting us up. The small chapel of Saint George at the top of Lykavittos Hill, the towering Acropolis—on those Athenian summits the penetrating, life-affirming light of Greece found its way around and into me. In that cauldron, the damp stranglehold of death and tears and incessant mourning was burned away. There were subsequent trips to Greece: to Madouri with poet and friend Nanos Valaoritis; to Neapoli; to Crete with Thanasis Maskaleris. "Come," he told us, his massive carnelian ring flashing as he took a deep drag from his Dunhill cigarette, "I'll prepare an island for you." Then a long hiatus...

My feet...the water laps up and touches my feet on the rocky beach in Agia Ilia and I am thinking of Iphigenia. The water, which is jazz-blue, slaps the shore with a gentle smack, smack, smack. From my shady spot beneath a cowl of rock, I watch the women splashing about in it, breasts bobbing upon the cobalt surface. We have just dined on calamari at the small taverna above the beach. Calamari, tzatziki, Greek salad, eggplant salad, spanakopita—the meals are invariably similar, consistently delicious. Laughter bubbles up from the bodies playing in the surf. Crab-like, I angle back toward the rock, protecting myself from the sun. I continue to puzzle over Iphigenia, whose story I chose to tell last night as we shared our favorite myths. I can't imagine why I chose this particular myth. Iphigenia, the ill-fated daughter of King Agamemnon and his queen, Clytemnestra, was sacrificed at Aulis so that the winds would blow, so that the Greek fleet could set forth to conquer Troy. It always struck me as so very sad that this poor child—she was a maiden, a *kore*—would become the sacrifice. In one version of the story (Euripides's play, I think) she is carried away by the wind. Yes, of course, there'd be a wind here. Carried off to the Black Sea where she is safe for a while.

> In your bark beside the sleepy sea, close your eyes,
> my darling, wait for me...

There was a wind to carry Marissa off, wasn't there? I like that version of the myth.

Iphigenia. The name haunts me. The women here talk about their daughters. Mary Jean's daughter is a poet and a dancer. Gail's daughter dances as well. She'll be off to a new college this fall. Barbara's daughter, Piper, has just visited Neapoli. Together they hiked to Paradise. Doreen has a beautiful little granddaughter whose name is Kayla, a very wise little girl, according to Doreen, who gives Doreen so much pleasure. Linda Jue's two adopted daughters are from China. She shares their photos and details about their likes and dislikes. They have silky black hair and beautiful cheeks full of roses. I listened to these stories like an impoverished ghost. My girl is an invisible presence who sits silently beside me, follows me wherever I go. I wish I could point her out, share her with others. I am ashamed of my empty arms.

I've told only Virginia about my Iphigenia. "I had no idea why I selected that myth," I say, sitting in the front seat of her tiny car, and my eyes well with tears. This morning, heading off to her house from Connie's, where I'm staying, the cab driver—the drivers dance and sing here—rolled the windows of the car down, and Greece—the berry hills, the eye-blue sky—poured in. He had the radio on and the whine of the bouzouki, the tremolo of pipes, was lifting me from my seat. The breeze had a song in it, too—an old one. The feeling, a melancholy ache fretted with joy, reminded me of my mother. The ghosts walk here. We keep wondering where the entrance to the underworld is. I have looked it up. Some say it is at Cape Tainaron on the Mani peninsula, the next knuckle of land on the Peloponnesian fist, that Odysseus and Heracles found their way into Hades's realm. Others say the entrance is in Ereğli, a city in Zonguldak Province, on the edge of the Black Sea. There are, I think, many entrances to the underworld, and there is surely one of them nearby, because my lost ones visit here. So palpable is their presence in this wind-tousled land. They are everywhere. I hear them in the spindrift whisper of the silver leaves of olives; feel them in the silky webs the spiders cast across the little-traversed mountain paths we walk along; see their dark, mulberry messages written in the earth beneath those sacred trees. They are tied up in the sunlight and the wind and my own frangible carapace, the one that ticked off another birthday just before I left the U.S.

One night Connie and Barbara celebrate for me with a chocolate cake, the filling between the layers thick with honey. There is dancing, laughter. Beautiful women, bejeweled and shawled, drift in and out of the parlor of Connie's home, out onto the terrace where the citronella burns, their laughter echoing down into the streets of Neapoli. "Invite the neighbors," says Connie, "that way you will have your party with no complaints." The neighbors are all there: Sula, Sam, and Lobbi, the editor of the local newspaper. We are eating squash blossoms stuffed with cheese, eggplant, traditional *salata khoriatiki*, drinking wine, and the young girls are dancing.

Connie's nieces, Chrysa and Alexa, on break from college and their whirlwind summer travels, are here to write as well. Chrysa, whose name means "golden flower," looks as if she is dusted with the precious metal. Her hair falls about her shoulders in honey-colored curls; her eyes warm amber, almond shaped. Her younger sister Alexa is like a princess, tall and fair, her dark hair cascading down her back in thick, black waves. "Come on, Linda, dance!" they command.

They are giving a lesson in Greek dancing. Behind them a growing tail of women snakes, weaving back and forth on the terrace between the chairs, the citronella candles, the occasional glass of wine. The moment is hypnotic. The women spread across the space like stars. I see constellations form, disassemble, form again, a tiny Milky Way of faces lit by party lights. And then my feet are moving to the rhythm, to Chrysa and Alexa's patient chant. The boisterous line of women winds around the small terrace. The girls call out the steps. I follow...

I SIT IN THE HOT, hot sun on one of Virginia's many terraces, listening to the stories, each one a beautiful creation. Mythic. Catharine's trip to the cemetery, Ann's interaction with the goddesses, Colleen's kiss, MJ's wild wind, Barbara's love affair with olives, Doreen's doctors and Dionysus, Gail's evil eye, Alexa's church, Chrysa's *yia yia*. Inside me there are stories forming also, but mine are so sad and confining.

When Thanasis comes, I cling to him. He is quick to respond to my e-mail. I know he is in Greece. He is at a poets' and translators' conference in the House of Literature at the European Translation Center in Lefkes on the island of Paros where he is team-translating English texts into Greek and Greek into English. Will he, can he, come here? He can lecture, I write, on Dionysus. Perhaps, he answers me from Naxos where he claims he's gone to greet Ariadne. In the myth about the labyrinth, Theseus abandoned her there. "Another blow to the matriarchy," he says. Yes, he will come. He'll leave from Tegea, in Arkadia, the region of his birth.

It's as though he has some kind of telepathy. Does he know how much I need him? I am mourning, my sorrow deepening. I am drifting further and further away. Thanasis is big and kind and benevolent, and as we sit in the taverna eating okra with tomatoes, Greek salad, and the little grilled fish, *barmbúni*, eating even the heads, I anchor on him. He is stalwart, a rock.

Does he know as I hug him that he is an island in the sea of my despair? Sometimes I can't think. The stories crash around and inside me, wake me. Sometimes they send me into dreams. I am lost in them, and when I surface the wind assails me, grasshoppers surround me, the surf rasps like a snare drum in the back of my mind. We are all, in some way, cast adrift, I think. Together or not, we are always on our very separate voyages, tossed on seas made entirely of our own experience. By day we feel the sun, the breeze, the salt sea. In the evening the *korai* dance and we drink wine and toast our travels...

IN FARAKLO, A SMALL VILLAGE nestled high up in the hills around Neapoli where we are hiking one morning, Barbara shares what she knows about the Greek concept of the *xorio*, the ancestral village. It is the place from which one's family hails, the root, the heart of a lineage, and the place to which future generations often return. I have one, I know, somewhere in Japan. I have not been back, though my brothers and my sister went there once as children, with my mother, a few years before my younger brother, Paul, drowned in the cold waters of the Trinity Alps. I have an ancestral village in Italy as well, and one in Wales where my grandfather was born. I have been to Japan, to Italy, and to Wales, but always as a wanderer, a person without a home, and I have not visited these family fonts. I wonder about them in a vague way, but I cannot bring myself to go. Perhaps one day I will. I don't know. I realize that it is not the familiar that draws me. I feel loose and rootless, roaming and meandering, an Odysseus of sorts, trying to find my Ithaca. Cavafy says Ithaca, the home base we seek, is ultimately within us, and that it is the search for Ithaca that inspires our travels.

> Have Ithaka always in your mind;
> to arrive there is what you are destined for.
> But do not in the least hurry the journey.

Once or twice I thought I had found it—Ithaca. Sometimes, for a little while, I find shelter in some imaginary cove, like here, in Vatika, but I am off again. There was a time when I believed there was a place where I could settle.

> Ithaka gave you the beautiful voyage.
> Without her you would have never set out.

But it's different now. I am on my own, and my daughter is gone, and there is nothing left but for the winds to blow.

Nightfall

I lie on my blanket under a willow.
Its shaky black limbs spread over me,
the little leaves biting my face.
I am a picnic for insects.
The whine of mosquitoes drowns out
the fading roar of a plane.
A chorus of crickets starts up, stops, starts,
in grinding insistence, the same singular note.

The light flickers, dies.
Even green turns to charcoal, to black.
The sky shrinks, recedes with voices and sound.
Objects come forward.
The fig and the birches loom.
The fence has become a shadowy wall,
the sky the top of a tomb.

The heavens, now, are wakening above me,
opening their tiny little eyes.
My pupils dilate, a black wasteland
flat and reflective as pools
into which the stars drop their light
like heavy beads of acid.

Selection from The Hand of Buddha

Los Mariaches del Muerto/ The Musicians of Death

Isabella was contemplating the nature of Death, and incidentally, the meaning of Life. At nineteen, she was pretty and bright—not yet the radiant beauty that she would later become, her luminosity being of the kind that brought to mind the Virgin of Guadalupe, which perhaps accounted for her perennially unmarried status since celestial auras have a way of discouraging ordinary suitors, although it could be argued that her single state had been brought about by the death of the infant and the other significant events that took place in her nineteenth year.

The child was not Isabella's, nor did it belong to the Anglo couple, Señor and Señora Stetson, for whom she worked. The child that died had been in the care of Iñez Felicia Casa-Contide, another of the brown-skinned young women who worked in the Anglo households of Santa Fe and who made up the social community of well-employed Mexican girls that was Isabella's.

That Iñez was in no way responsible for the child's death, and could in no way be held culpable, was a miracle. Sometimes when people—Anglos, anyone—are in grief, they reach out with long fingers of blame to pull others into their misery. So it was a good thing that the baby had died during the night when Iñez was safely home and asleep in her tiny, twin bed in the small house on the outskirts of Santa Fe where she lived with her mother, three sisters, and two brothers. At one time, the family had hoped that Iñez would be asked to move in with the Morrisons, the couple she worked for. Iñez had resisted. Her mother, sisters, and brothers thought she was crazy, but it turned out to be a very good thing that Iñez did not move in with the Morrisons. If she had accepted, she would have been there when the infant died, and the death would have surely been attributed to her negligence. The Anglo doctor's pronouncement was that the Morrison infant had died of SEEDS. That is what Iñez reported to the other maids when they gathered to hang their washing.

"SEEDS?" Isabella asked.

"Yes, *si*, yes, SEEDS. The poor little creature choked in the night." Iñez crossed herself. "Such a precious *hijo*. He must have choked on the seeds."

"Oh, my goodness," Isabella exclaimed. "Did *you* feed the baby the seeds?"

"No, Isabella," reported Iñez. "And the family, they are so fine, they never even accused me."

"That's very strange. *Muy extraña*," said the other maids, knowing that if the children in their care were to choke to death on seeds they would certainly be found at fault.

Isabella thought this was extraordinary, too — not that the baby should die in this manner, but that Iñez had not been blamed. She could not reconcile it with the way she knew things were between maids and their Anglo employers. So, at dinner as she served up the *sopa* for her Señor and Señora, she mentioned the death of the Morrison infant and the manner of the baby's death.

"The doctor, Minton," she reported, "he says that Iñez's baby died of SEEDS."

"Seeds?" Señora Stetson queried, her pale blue eyes fluttering as they did when she was confused.

"Yes, seeds," repeated Isabella. "You know, he choked. Suffocated. He must have eaten too many of them."

"Seeds?" the Señora repeated, considering the word. "Died of seeds? That's very strange." Her blue eyes kept fluttering for a while, then stopped and went very pale. They were looking inward, searching her mind. Isabella had noticed the Señora did this when she was thinking very hard.

Isabella continued. "Such a tiny baby," she said sadly. "Of course, it was very foolish to feed him seeds." The Señor wore a worried expression. His eyes went from Isabella to Lauren, his wife.

"SEEDS," Lauren, the Señora repeated, "Hmmm...seeds." Then, all at once, the light went on. The clouds parted; her eyes brightened; the blue rushed back into them.

"Oh, Isabella," she corrected. "I think you mean SIDS. Yes, I believe that's what Doctor Minton must have said—SIDS. Sudden Infant Death Syndrome. Many infants die this way. No one knows why. They just seem to stop breathing. Yes, yes, the doctor must have said SIDS. Don't you think so, Rob?"

"Sounds logical," said the Señor, his brows unknitting, glad to see the confusion leaving the face of his wife. The Señor didn't like confusion. He would be upset if he felt that Isabella was generating a little pool of confusion in their otherwise organized world.

Isabella's coffee complexion flushed burgundy. She was embarrassed now about the seeds. She knew that the Señor and Señora were right. An Anglo doctor would make an Anglo diagnosis.

Lauren placed her soup spoon precisely upon the china charger beneath her soup bowl. "Yes, yes," she said happily, glad to have cleared up the confusion, "the doctor must have said SIDS."

"SIDS," Isabella repeated as she cleared the soup course, angry at herself for her foolish mistake. She was mad at the other maids for their ignorance, but a part of her mind also backed away from the pat explanation of the Señor and Señora Stetson. Sudden Infant Death Syndrome. That still didn't explain it. Why did the baby die?

Isabella knew better than to pursue the subject that evening. She served the fish course, then the salad. She finished this all with dessert, which the Señor ate with relish and the Señora declined. The latter part of the meal progressed without incident, and when it was finished, the Señor and Señora retired to their separate corners to read. From the window of her pleasant garden cottage, Isabella could see the light on by the Señora's bedside. It glowed eerily in the upstairs window of the adobe-style home until late that evening when the shadow that was the Señor bent over the shadow that was the lamp and put it out.

The next day, Isabella informed the other maids about how mistaken they were.

"But, what does that mean?" asked LaRosa, the oldest and fattest of them all. LaRosa was thirty-eight years old. She had raised two young boys to manhood in the household she worked for. She had single-handedly raised four children of her own at the same time. All six children loved LaRosa. She was more a mother to the two Anglo boys than their own. LaRosa had great authority. She would not accept an Anglo fact without examining it very, very closely.

"It means nothing," LaRosa declared, throwing all of her weight and authority against the rationale of the Señor and Señora Stetson, against the Anglo doctor. "The little boy suffocated," she summarized, "that we all know. But we still do not know the cause." LaRosa sounded extraordinarily wise and powerful when she spoke in this manner. She was almost a shamaness. If she were in Mexico, she would have a house paid for by the village and the people would bring her gifts.

"Iñez," she said, addressing the pretty young maid, "Iñez, I think you have the answer. Why don't you tell the others about the Smurfs?"

"The Smurfs?" Iñez repeated, hypnotically, eyes on LaRosa. "Oh, girlfriends, they are terrible!" Iñez was recollecting the little pink and blue creatures that had been scattered about the blessed baby's nursery. They were scrawny, pin-headed dolls with long noses and evil grins. They were very bad objects for sure. Very wicked.

"The baby, he liked them," she recalled sorrowfully, referring to the terrible Smurfs. "If I took them away, he cried. But, they were jealous of the *hijo*," she reported. "They are dreadful and nasty, those Smurfs."

"Tell us how the infant died," LaRosa demanded.

"Yes, yes I will tell you," Iñez said softly. "The Smurfs—they suffocated him."

A group gasp escaped from the ample and lovely bosoms of all the maids. This, they could believe. Iñez had, on occasion, shared stories with them of her battle over the Smurfs. She had suspected their evil intentions. She had tried to keep them out of the nursery, but the baby had fussed, his parents had become concerned, and the Smurfs had remained in the Morrison infant's bed.

"Have you mentioned this to the Señor and Señora Morrison?" Isabella asked warily.

"Oh, no," said Inez. "I wouldn't do that. They get very angry when I say things like that. They are very upset now. I don't want them to get mad at me."

"Iñez is right, of course," LaRosa announced firmly. "It was the Smurfs that killed the baby. They sucked the life from his little chest."

"Yes, the Smurfs, the Smurfs," the other maids nodded. "They killed Iñez's charge."

That evening it was Thursday, and Señor Stetson was running. He ran every Thursday night all along the Paseo de Peralta and up Artist Road, past Ten Thousand Waves, the spa on the hill. He ran ten miles every Thursday without fail. Isabella thought it was very strange that he ran so hard and so long. "Just like a horse," she thought to herself. "Why would a man do that?" Isabella made him a cold plate on those nights and set it aside for his dinner. If Señor Stetson had been in the house, she would not have mentioned the Smurfs. But he wasn't. So, when Lauren—Señora Stetson—sat down to her dinner at the long dinner table, Isabella mentioned the Smurfs and Iñez and LaRosa's conclusions about how they had smothered the baby.

"Yes, it was strange for them to think this," Isabella hedged, "but Iñez and LaRosa are certain that the evil deed was performed by those horrible blue and pink creatures."

Señora Stetson's face registered a quick succession of emotions. First, her blue eyes gave a small flutter of confusion; then, they widened in disbelief; then, her rose-colored mouth opened in a small oval of awareness; then, her pleasant, small-featured face rearranged itself in a smile.

"Isabella," she said, brushing a stray wisp of ash-blonde hair from her forehead. "Isabella, don't you realize Smurfs are only toys? Toys cannot kill an infant."

Isabella looked down at her black slip-on shoes. Señora Stetson's feet, visible just under the table, looked neat in their beige suede, perfectly groomed boots.

"I didn't believe it anyway," Isabella insisted. "Iñez and LaRosa are too superstitious."

"Yes," said Señora Stetson. "That's right, Isabella. Now," she asked, lifting her napkin and placing it carefully upon her lap, "what have you made us for dinner?"

The next day, Señor Stetson called Isabella into the library. "Isabella," he said, "you have me somewhat disturbed." Isabella knew what he was planning to say.

"This business about the baby that died—the seeds and the Smurfs—you realize, don't you, that this is all nonsense?"

Isabella nodded, glumly. It had been a mistake to confide in the Señora.

"I hope," Señor Stetson concluded, "that you are simply reporting what you have heard. You do not believe these things. Superstition is a very dangerous thing," he continued. "It comes of ignorance. It breeds misapprehension. I don't want to think that you support or display this behavior."

"Señor," Isabella mumbled, "you know I was just repeating what Iñez and LaRosa had told me."

"Then you know that this is just ignorance talking. Good, Isabella," the Señor said kindly, "I'm glad that we had this talk."

Isabella did not go back that Friday to the little Plaza de las Glorias where the maids gathered to hang and fold washing. She had decided to withdraw from the group project. The environment of the maids was once her whole world, but the baby's death had changed all of that. It was funny, she thought, how something seemingly unrelated to something else could cause such a great deal of change. Suddenly, she no longer wanted to see Iñez and LaRosa and the other maids. Their large brown eyes and smooth simple faces reflected back an image of herself that embarrassed her. She did not want to see them and say, "It wasn't the Smurfs at all!" They would argue with her, of course. They were stubborn and insistent. Their world wouldn't change. But the Señor and Señora, Isabella sighed, all the Anglos—they were stubborn and insistent too. Much more stubborn, in fact, than her own people. Still, theirs was a way that she hadn't yet tried. She must look into it further. She must give it a chance.

So, Isabella quite consciously turned her back on her old friends. She enrolled in the local community college. She signed up for math and history and science in a single semester.

The Señor and Señora Stetson were amazed. They were also visibly pleased. Once again Señor Stetson called Isabella into his library. This time he said, "Isabella, my friend, who teaches at the community college, says you have signed up for his class. Is this true?"

"Yes," Isabella nodded, looking down at her feet. "Yes, I am going to history class with Señor Betterly, and I am taking math and science, too, Señor.

"Well, that's fantastic, Isabella," he boomed. "Why didn't you tell us?"

Isabella had learned her lesson; she had not confided in the Señora. But the teacher, Betterly, he had told the Señor. Anglos, she concluded, cannot keep secrets.

Señor Stetson was pacing the carpet in his excitement. He was running his hand through his hair.

"This is wonderful, Isabella," he said. "The future will open up for you. Opportunities will be yours. Of course, selfishly, I worry that it means that we'll lose you."

Isabella blanched when he said this. The last thing she wanted was to lose her job. "No, Señor," she started to say, but he stopped her.

"No matter," he continued, "that will come later. In the meantime, you will study. You will learn. I like to think, that in some way, I influenced this decision," he said soberly, stopping his pacing, turning to her, and looking into her eyes with great meaning.

Isabella couldn't return his gaze. "Yes, Señor Stetson, you did," she mumbled. She was becoming convinced that she might not have done the right thing. She looked down at the carpet with its thunderbird design. She saw a great big pool of confusion spreading out and filling the library.

The next day at dinner, the strange magic started. The Señor and Señora Stetson presented Isabella with a very large check. A bonus, they said, to help with her education. Isabella stared at it in disbelief—she couldn't believe her good fortune. She wanted to share this marvelous news, so in a cinnamon-colored skirt, a fresh white blouse, and well-polished black shoes, she headed for the Plaza to see her old friends.

"Isabella, Isabella," they started to say, as she walked in the door, "we have missed you. Have you been ill?" But they saw, almost immediately, the bright color of her skirt, the starched crispness of her blouse, and the shine on her shoes, and they knew that there was more to it than this.

"Oh," gasped Iñez, "Isabella, you are in love."

Isabella looked out through the window. She didn't want to lie to her friends.

"No," said LaRosa, "Isabella isn't in love—love looks much softer than this."

"Isabella," she asked her voice husky and rough so that it sounded like a man's, almost like the voice of Señor Stetson. "Isabella, what is this about?"

"School," Isabella managed to squeak, feeling like a traitor. She no longer wanted to share the news of her good fortune. Somehow her good fortune felt like a very bad thing. "I am going to go to school."

LaRosa arched one eyebrow, then the other. "Aha," she said with a dark smile. "Our ways are no longer enough."

Isabella shrugged her shoulders helplessly.

"You will see," said LaRosa in a deep and prophetic voice. "You will see, Isabella, that the Anglo ways are also not enough.

But," she added portentously. "I may have the answers you seek. Remember our revelation about the Smurfs, Isabella. Things are not always as they seem."

Isabella left feeling uncomfortable. She did not see LaRosa again.

All spring and summer Isabella took courses at the community college. She learned about theorems and constants. She learned about gravity, chaos, and centrifugal force. She learned about tyrants, Western imperialism, and Manifest Destiny. Her brain sometimes felt as if it would explode with all of the things she learned. Other times it felt like a sieve or a colander—something full of holes, and all the knowledge was running out of it as fast as she put it in. Mostly, she felt like an impostor, especially when Señor Stetson would quiz her about her studies, and she would answer him, hearing herself saying the words and wondering what in the world she was talking about. But she would see Señor Stetson nodding with a grave expression on his face. And she would hear him say, "Yes, yes, that is right, Isabella. You are certainly right about that." Señora Stetson also seemed pleased with Isabella's progress.

"You know, Isabella," she said, "there is a logic to the way you do everything these days. Like the way you serve dinner and the way you put the clothes in the drawers—long-sleeved shirts on the bottom, short-sleeved shirts on the top."

Isabella used to put all the Señora's favorite clothes on the top so that they would be easy to get to. With the new arrangement, Señora Stetson began to wear clothes that she used to wear rarely, largely because they didn't look good on her. These days the Señora didn't look as handsome and perfectly dressed as she used to. But the Señora was happy. Only Isabella felt that things were really not right.

Isabella knew that all the intelligence that she was feeding her brain was not falling quite into place. She had piles of facts, but they didn't really explain anything. The more she learned, the more understanding eluded her. Her quest for answers brought only more questions. Her logic led her down some interesting paths, but actually, it led nowhere. And she seemed, always, to be going back in by the same door through which she came out. But she had to admit, she was doing quite well in her studies. She was in the top two percent of all her classes, and her teachers were urging her to transfer to a four-year college. Her classmates asked her opinion on everything, and the Anglo boys were in awe of her brilliance. This was really the beginning of this tendency of Isabella's to inspire awe in the opposite sex, a trait that persisted for most of her life. So, in spite of a fundamental disconnect between Isabella's mind and the knowledge that filled it, everything about Isabella's shift in perspective seemed designed to propel her toward greater and greater success. Now, three lights were on at night in the Stetson household—one in the library, one in Señora Stetson's bedroom, and one in the cottage behind the big house. Three lights. Three readers. Three trains of thoughts.

As for the other maids, Isabella rarely saw them anymore. Once or twice she ran into Iñez at the market or one or more of the others downtown, but the meetings were always somewhat awkward. They were embarrassed by the changes in Isabella, and she was embarrassed, too.

It was at just such a chance meeting, early in October, some weeks into her third semester in college, that Isabella ran into Iñez on the busy sidewalk where the Native Americans sell their wares in front of the Palace of the Governors. Iñez looked terrible. Her eyes were all puffy and red. She looked as if she'd been crying for days.

"Iñez, what's wrong?" Isabella asked, grabbing her friend's arms. Her love for Iñez rushed into her heart. Her friend's sadness almost overwhelmed her.

Iñez's face registered nothing but shock. "Oh, Isabella," she gasped, "you mean you don't know?"

"Don't know? Don't know what?" Isabella asked, genuinely surprised.

"LaRosa," Iñez blurted out with *gran fuerza*, great force, in her speech. "LaRosa is dead."

Isabella stood for a moment, dumbfounded by the news. LaRosa was dead. Impossible. She felt as if she were standing, alone, in the middle of a vast mesquite- and cottonwood-dotted plain. It was just like the one near Santa Clara Pueblo where she'd gotten lost as a child. It was noon, very hot, and the vultures, *zopilotes*, were circling overhead. She thought they were circling for her, but it turned out that they were circling for a cow with a big, swollen stomach. It lay on its side, its legs like four clothespins sticking straight out. Isabella approached the cow cautiously. It was still alive, but the flies were already crawling all over its face. Isabella had found a long branch and brushed them away. They came back. The buzzards continued to circle. Isabella had kept walking, trying to find her way back to her parents. She succeeded only in putting more distance between them. When they finally found her, having mobilized the whole pueblo, everyone was unhappy. Isabella was not hugged and kissed. She was scolded.

Iñez's sweet round face appeared suddenly, looking concerned, from behind an imaginary cottonwood tree.

"Isabella," she asked, "Isabella, are you all right?"

"*Si*," Isabella said quickly. "How? How did LaRosa die?"

"It was very strange, Isabella," Iñez replied in a whisper, as if she worried that someone might overhear. "LaRosa had a small mole on her stomach, and it got larger and larger until it was the size of a hand—the size of a tarantula spider. And it looked like a spider, too—furry and dark and of an irregular shape. LaRosa showed it to us one day. She said the shadows were growing inside her. They were turning her inside out. The mole, it grew very fast, and the next thing we knew, LaRosa was dead. Of course, we never told Father Quito what LaRosa had said. He might not have given her the sacraments."

"It was good that you didn't tell Father Quito," Isabella nodded approvingly. Father Quito had not always agreed with LaRosa. An ongoing war, that was defined by a repetitive series of skirmishes during which the young women usually sided with LaRosa, marked their relationship. In spite of this, LaRosa's faith was never debated. She was very religious. But it irked Father Quito that she and the other young Mexican women were more drawn to the tales of the miraculous, the ceremony and pomp of the Catholic Church, than its rules and its dogma. LaRosa would want the last sacrament. It was good that she wasn't denied it.

"When did LaRosa die?" Isabella asked, trying to place this disaster in the sensible framework of time.

"Over a month ago," Iñez replied sheepishly. "I'm sorry we didn't tell you, Isabella, but we never saw you to tell you. We thought you were angry with us. We knew you were upset with LaRosa. LaRosa kept saying you would be back, but you didn't come back, so we figured you'd abandoned us for your school and your studies."

Isabella swallowed hard and nodded. She could see how they would all think that. Still, it distressed her to have missed LaRosa's funeral, to have never offered a prayer, and she was greatly disturbed by LaRosa's death. What had caused the sudden growth of the mole? How had it killed LaRosa? She went to her books for the answers. She read about melanoma and cancer. She read about chemotherapy, radiation, and bone marrow transplant. She read about macrobiotic diets and peach pits and papaya enzymes. She didn't come up with one answer—not one—and she found herself back at a door through which she had previously entered, back at the death of the Morrison infant with the big, dark blot of LaRosa's mole growing between her and her understanding.

Isabella decided to see Father Quito. She made an appointment and spoke with him face to face. It was hard to ask this man all her questions, to expose the confusion that puddled about her without the dark grillwork that protected her in the confessional. She sat stiffly on one of the leather-covered Spanish-style chairs in Father Quito's office. A two-foot statue of the Virgin of Guadalupe, hands outstretched, clad in blue and lit from below, looked down peacefully upon her from a small ledge built into the stucco wall upon which it had been ensconced. Isabella noted, with some surprise, how much she resembled this particular rendition of the Virgin of Guadalupe. Father Quito noticed, with a febrile little twinge of pleasure, exactly the same thing.

"Isabella," he said, "LaRosa has gone to a better place."

The puddle of confusion around Isabella ceased its amoeba-like maturation. Her agitation instantly disappeared. Her face rearranged itself, becoming as impassive as the face of the plaster Virgin on the wall above her. What was Father Quito saying? What in the world did that mean? Nothing. He was telling her exactly nothing.

Father Quito could see that the nacreous pearl of wisdom that he had presented to Isabella as his answer, and that generally met with profound success when offered to the other members of his flock, was not having the desired effect. She had shut every window of her shimmering, silvery little soul and retreated to the depths of her own personal ruminations. Her brown eyes became as dark and guarded as the grillwork of the confessional.

"Isabella," he squeaked, trying again, desperately wanting to win her back, "remember, we are having service for the Feast of All Saints, the Día de los Muertos, in a few weeks. Come to the service, spend the day in contemplation; make your peace with LaRosa then."

He knew, in his heart, that this would appeal to Isabella. The church would be filled with incense and the smoke of candles lit for the departed. Bright flowers would festoon the crosses in the little graveyard next to the church. There would be small sugar skulls stacked like bricks on every gravesite and the ants would march merrily back and forth, giddy with sugar, in their long processionals over the mounds. "Heavenly Father," he prayed, "I know that I am playing right into their hands, but really what else can I do?" *Beyond the grave*, he whispered to himself.

It was one more of LaRosa's skirmishes and, once again, she had won. The Virgin of Guadalupe seemed to smile down on him, too, her face luminous, her carnelian mouth gently mocking.

But it worked.

"Yes, yes, Father Quito," Isabella was saying. "You are right. That would be a good time to offer my prayers." It still wasn't the answer, but maybe she would find one in the sanctuary of the church on that very significant day. Yes. Yes, the Día de los Muertos—surely if she were ever to find the answers she sought, that would be the time and the way.

"Thank you, Father Quito," Isabella said, executing a spontaneous curtsy.

"Of course, my child," Father Quito said humbly, taking her small hand, quite proud of himself for doing the expedient thing. It had worked after all. He felt guiltless and strangely elated.

All Saints Eve arrived at the appointed time, to be celebrated by each culture in the appropriate ways. There were cats, witches, and ghosts in some of the neighborhood windows. The Señora Stetson wouldn't dream of decorating her home in that manner, but she had arranged several large and beautiful gourds in hefty Native American baskets on either side of the entrance, and she had three big bowls of candy ready for Isabella to hand out to the children that invariably came to the door. Greeting Halloween trick-or-treaters was Isabella's job, so she went to church early that day and stayed until almost twilight.

She walked home in the dusky, late afternoon, still dizzy from the incense, the candle smoke, the murmur of prayers; her knees red and bruised from repeated genuflections. She had no time to reflect upon the effect of the prayer or to sort out the tumble of emotions and images that rolled through her heart and mind.

The first little children were already on the walk when she arrived, and she had to hurry to intercept them at the door.

"Trick or treat," said a tiny red devil, barely breathing behind his mask. "Trick or treat," said a midget gypsy and a messy teenage boy with eyeliner around his eyes and two pillow-sacks, both filled with candy. Isabella kept dropping the candy bars into their pumpkin buckets and bags, and they kept coming—witches, goblins, dinosaurs, Smurfs. (Yes, Smurfs. At least, she thought one of them was a Smurf, or was he?) genies, dancing girls, gangsters, ghouls, cowboys, vaqueros, skeletons—lots of skeletons—and fairies. Isabella was exhausted by the time they quit coming, and the hour was late. It was almost eleven p.m. The Señor and Señora had already retired to their separate corners to read.

When she stepped out into the garden, Isabella realized why the children had kept coming. It was a perfectly beautiful night out. In the Stetsons' backyard, the adobe wall that surrounded the garden screened out all but the loftiest breezes. These faintly stirred the trellised roses, threading the cool night air with the most delicate strands of fragrance. Under the moonlight, on the dark carpet of grass, the bell-shaped flowers of ramps sparkled like miniature galaxies of stars, and the smell of grass and wild onion rose up and dissolved like the smoke of small votive candles. Tiptoeing along the flagstones, Isabella made her way to her cottage. She glanced back at the house. Every light was off except the one in Señor Stetson's library and one in the Señora Stetson's bedroom. Isabella turned her light on and prepared for bed. She slipped out of her black shoes and out of her dress and into her white cotton nightgown. She folded back the floral coverlet of her bed—she wouldn't need the extra blanket; it was a warm night. She turned out the light and lay there in the dark and the silence for a moment. Then she turned the light on again, quickly, stepped to the window, and opened it, letting its two halves swing outward toward the garden. She could still see the lights on. Señor and Señora Stetson were still reading. Seeing the lights reminded Isabella of her studies, so she went to the closet, took her big history book out of her book bag and opened it to the section about the Overland Trail. What did she expect to find on those pages? Reasons for things? Order? The stagecoach and mail carriers did not hold her interest, so she found herself nodding off now and again, the point of her chin hitting her sternum and jarring her back into a muddled consciousness.

It was on one of those quick jerks back out of slumber that she heard the music. Soft at first, as she fought her way back from her dreams. Then louder, and soon she was wide awake and amazed by the loud caterwaul in the garden just outside her window. *The Señor and Señora will be very upset,* she decided as she stuck her head out of the window to see where the noise was coming from.

Isabella almost couldn't believe her eyes. Arranged in a half circle facing her window, in the middle of the grassy lawn, were six mariachis. Four had guitars, one had a xylophone, and one had a fiddle. All wore enormous sombreros, but the strangest thing of all was that these mariachis were skeletons.

"Shoo, go away," hissed Isabella, like an angry goose. These children in skeleton costumes were playing a noisy trick on the household. The Señor would be furious, she surmised. But when she looked at the bright square that was the library window, she noticed no flicker of movement. In shock, Isabella looked at the mariachis. It was impossible that the Señor hadn't heard them. They were really wailing away, strumming their guitars and singing in high nasal singsong. She noticed that each one was wearing some kind of weapon. One wore a machete at his waist. One wore a pair of big pistols. One had a couple of ammunition belts over each shoulder, crisscrossing over his chest. Another had a lariat tied at his waist. One had a rifle, and one had a bull whip strapped to his back.

Isabella could see right through them, too. She could see through the narrow slats of their ribs, through the long, skinny ladders of vertebrae, to the house where the two windows glowed like the lopsided eyes of a jack-o'-lantern. The skeletons strummed away, clicking their teeth together like castanets, and began to sing louder. They advanced toward the window rattling and clanking with every step. Oh, what a din they created! The crook of each finger made a sharp snap like a twig. The tilt of each head made a sound like a string of firecrackers exploding. And the music—the keys of the xylophone, which the xylophonist would lift and carry whenever the others took even two steps, were made of bones arranged on a metal frame rotten with rust. The strings of the guitars, which were certainly made of catgut, produced a sound like twelve cats being pulled by their tails. The maracas threatened like rattlesnakes, and the violin yelped and squealed as if it were being tortured. And the song—no sirocco had ever whined its way through a ghost town with a more wretched moan, no Mexican poet ever more plaintively lamented lost love.

All in all, between art and their antics, the mariachis produced a dissonant but delightfully lively music, and Isabella felt it entering through her ears, massaging her mind, and rocking her insides with laughter. And, as she listened, she realized they were singing about LaRosa.

"Where, oh where did my beloved LaRosa go, oh, oh, oh," one of the skeletons moaned.

The others responded in a chorus of howls. "Ow, ow, ow," they yelped.

"Oh, I don't think man or woman will ever know, oh, oh, oh," the morbid mariachi continued. And, again, the others howled back their agreement.

"Do I care what the priest and the doctor said, ed, ed?"

"Noooooo," the skeleton chorus moaned.

"All I can say is my darling is dead dead dead dead."

They had wailed themselves into a frenzy, and every bone in their bodies was by this time clicking away in a fabulous percussive finale. Isabella found herself humming and repeating the last lines of the song to herself. "All I can say is my darling is dead dead dead dead." It seemed so conclusive, so certain. "LaRosa," she thought, "I think this is your answer." Isabella felt her whole body relax. The skeletons nodded—clatter, snap, clatter; swept their sombreros from their heads—rattle, creak, pop; and bowed. Isabella applauded softly. The light went off in the library, and a few moments later the one in the bedroom went out.

Dark Parent

The ninja knows
that the shadows provide
the shelter you seek
but recoil from,
being beige,
perhaps pastel,
a target, actually...

knows
that you will break cover
because "sneak"
and "lurk" are
bad words
to you.

You will streak
into the sunlight
where the brilliance
will halo your
dark form

because you are heavy and slow
and human
and do not love the void—
your dark parent—
the only one
that can shield you.

—Erin Orison

Selection from Namako: Sea Cucumber

yurei yashiki/ghost house

(excerpts)

My family took its leave of Grandmother with the same confusion with which we did everything. Sara and Gene smiled wanly, apologetic for the mad scramble of children collecting their things. Samuel, Mimi, and Gray had a way of accumulating objects — rocks, old junk, street dust — whatever happened to be in their vicinity. Separation from their surroundings was always an arduous process.

"Leave that here, that's your grandmother's," Sara snapped at Mimi, who had just pocketed a handful of nuts and a tiny ceramic tortoise.

"Oh, sorry," Mimi said perfunctorily. She opened her hand, and the loosened booty rolled noisily in all directions over the lacquer surface of Grandmother's table. Gray and Samuel gathered their coats. Part of a cookie that had found its way into one of their pockets was stepped on and ground into the *tatami*. The neat rows of slippers that lined the *genkan* doorway had deteriorated into a jumble. They were no longer properly mated, but paired, instead, with this gardening tool or that half-opened umbrella. Mimi could not find both of her socks. The one she did find was a small, grayish ball. Sara took it from her with an admonishing look and slid it quickly into her purse. By the time the children were lined up at the *genkan* door to kiss Grandmother good-bye, Gene had started to scowl. Sara looked worried. Grandmother and her maid, scandalized by the chaos, remained coolly aloof. Each child marched up as Sara had instructed and dutifully kissed the cheek that Grandmother proffered. I waited politely until the others were done. Then I walked up to Grandmother to give her what I thought was a granddaughterly kiss. She drew back, surprised. She seemed more offended than pleased. The maid's brows raised to form a small teepee of chagrin.

"Oh, no, dear," Sara whispered, "You will be staying with Grandma."

I couldn't believe what I'd heard. I turned to Mimi, Samuel, and Gray. They were quarreling over some rub-on tattoos that they'd bought at a Japanese store. Gene was watching them glumly, probably thinking of Tokyo traffic or dinner reservations. He wanted to leave.

"Oh," I responded, a knot, like paste, in my throat. "Oh. Well, I guess I'll see you tomorrow."

"You'll have a wonderful time," Sara said, smiling and hugging me falsely. Sara knew that this was far from the truth. I felt I had been betrayed.

"Good-bye, Ellen," Gene added, kissing me on the forehead right through my bangs.

"'Bye," I mumbled. I stepped back up to the porch with Grandmother and her maid to watch my parents battle their way down the slender garden path with their children, as if herding three furious little pygmies through high and impassable brush.

At first I was angry. I thought of Samuel, Mimi, and Gray in the dark ballroom. I imagined them exploring the recesses of the hotel. I pictured Sara and Gene suffering through another dinner with them, alert to the possible catastrophes, dismayed by the inadequate table manners of their children and exhausted by their endless exuberance. Then all my things arrived by messenger from the hotel, and I realized with a pang that I would not be going back to them the next morning. I watched with horror as the maid expertly unpacked my few travel clothes from my suitcase and placed them in the drawers of a cherry wood dresser in one of the bedrooms. She moved expertly. Within minutes, my clothes vanished into that deceptively blank façade and the suitcase disappeared. My mouth grew dryer as she pushed each of the small drawers shut. She looked at me cheerily, brisk as a nurse opening sickroom curtains, her mind on other things. It was clear by her manner that she had no idea as to the depth of my despair.

"I reeve you," she attempted, in English, with a very deep bow.

I nodded, unable to speak. And I was left alone...

I SAT BACK ON THE futons and stared at the photos through half-closed eyes. I flipped through a black photo album that I'd found in one of the tea chests. The names of the people, the places and dates, were written underneath each picture in English. The white crayon captions made the pages look like a boneyard. Sara had already introduced us to some of the ghosts—to Aunt Sally, the missionary, and to the tragic twins, Katsuko and Karl. Karl died of leukemia at twelve. Katsuko died a year later of the same disease. Sara had shared all of these stories. She told us about China, where she was raised. She told us about fires and wars. Sara did not edit her stories for children. I wished she hadn't told us as much as she had. She had clouded our world with the dark history of her family, with stories of death, flights, and lovers. Canton. Tiger Mountain. Algiers. Bombay. Footless beggars in Shanghai. Houses on fire. A man without a head running beside her. Furs traded for cabbages.

In the bedroom that I had been given, the maid had left a terry cloth kimono striped in pale pink and lavender that I think was Grandmother's, and a large white bath towel. She returned to the room to fetch me, smiling, her teeth wet and shiny as pearls. She nodded, the way she had nodded at Samuel and Gray and indicated by gestures that I was to put on the kimono. I was certain the robe and a towel meant a bath. I followed her out of the house, clomping along in *geta*, the awkward wooden clogs she'd given me to wear. We crossed the small patio at the back of the house. We came to a wooden building. It looked like a large dollhouse. It was walled on one side by sliding *shoji* doors, panels framing opaque panes of milky white glass.

"Dozo," the maid said, smiling. She moved politely aside.

I stepped out of the *geta* and up to the raised entrance. The door slid open easily. Hot steam rushed through the doorway to greet me.

"Dozo," the maid said again.

I nodded, and stooping a little and continuing to bob my head, backed my way in. Sliding the door shut, I sighed. All of my misery surfaced. Everything was too strange. It was unbearable. I took a deep gulp of the comforting steam. I was ready, almost, to cry.

Behind me I heard the quick fall of water, the scrape of a wooden stool, and a voice.

"Koko-ni osuwari."

I wheeled, startled, to see Grandmother standing, pale as marble, a glistening apparition in a halo of steam. Her gray hair was pulled up in a hard, tight bun on top of her head. She was naked. Lanky and thin, the sheen of her whiteness was like death. A faint triangle shadowed the joint of her lower limbs. Her face, implacable, seemed carved out of stone. In her right hand she held a big wooden dipper. A look of impatience moved quickly across her face.

I stood also as though I were frozen, shrouded in curling steam, the kimono still wrapped about me. I did not know quite what to do. Grandmother motioned toward the blue-tiled wall where a couple of empty hooks jutted. I looked sadly down at my pink and lavender robe. With the glum resolution of one condemned, I walked to the wall, took it off, and hung it on the hook, my fingers lingering over its folds.

Grandmother regarded me critically. She handed me the dipper. In the corner of the room was a round wooden tub, full of water, with a fire burning under it—the source of the steam. It looked like a cannibal's stewpot.

"Oyu otoringisai," Grandmother said, demonstrating how to scoop the water out of the hot tub and pour it over you. I did as her gesturing indicated, taking a large dipperful of water and pouring it over my body, afraid to make a mistake. It was scalding. I squeezed my eyes shut, trying hard not to flinch.

"Koyatte, yoku karada yusugu-no desu-yo."

I watched as she pantomimed washing and rinsing, and pointed me toward the tub. She handed me a tiny white cake of soap and turned, bending to pick up her own, her lean buttocks pointing toward me. Standing outside the tub, she began to wash herself carefully, caressingly, with the rectangle of soap, her hands sliding along her limbs, slipping down her neck, around her thin breasts. She took a handful of rock salt from a ceramic crock and rubbed it into her shins, her calves, and her thighs, until her lower extremities, buttocks to toes, were streaked a furious red. All of this she did with complete disregard of my close observation. I played with the white cake of soap and rubbed it haphazardly here and there; my focus entirely on Grandmother. She punctuated every procedure with a dipperful of the scalding water. Her head flung back, I watched her inhale deeply and groan, her eyes half-shut, unaware of me, unconcerned with my child body, my self-consciousness, and my surprise.

My body looked nothing like hers. It was not porcelain white. It was nut-brown from days in Montana and Wyoming, from days in the desert. I didn't have breasts, just two pink buttons on a flat chest that was beginning to puff out in a couple of hump-shaped mounds. I tried not to pay much attention to them. Once, years ago, my friend Alison and I had painted our nipples a flashing Mercurochrome orange, using what we'd found in the medicine cabinet. The Mercurochrome bled through our blouses, making two round stains on the laundered white of our chests. Our mothers were scandalized. They separated us. We could not play together for weeks. I realized then that nipples were off limits. It really was best to ignore them.

Grandmother did not seem to regard things in this manner. She climbed the steps up to the tub, stepped over the rim, and immersed herself in the water. She closed her eyes. The sweat beaded up like dew on her upper lip, on her brow. Her face flushed rosy under the steel-gray helmet of her tightly combed hair. She seemed to rest that way for a long time. Every so often a purr-like groan would rumble deep in her throat. Fascinated, I now stared blatantly, having completely forgotten my dwindling bar of soap and my idle dabbing of this spot and that.

Climbing finally from the tub, she tossed a comment over her shoulder, offhandedly, in Japanese, "*Hayaku shinasai.*" "Hurry up, child, or you will dry out," or something like that. She dressed quickly and left.

I was alone with the hot tub. I climbed into it, trying to imitate her, wanting to feel as she felt. I threw back my head and inhaled. It was hot. I thought of the giant king crabs that Gene had brought home one winter, how they bobbed around blushing crimson in a large cooking pot. We had cracked open the bodies with hammers, pulling and sucking the sweet white meat from the legs. I felt like one of those crabs. My body floated beneath me like an alien thing. It was turning bright red. I was getting so hot, I thought that I was going to explode. I was dizzy and becoming confused. *I'm going to be cooked*, I worried.

That scared me. I scrambled clumsily from the tub. I felt like crying again. The terry towel was horribly harsh on my flesh. It felt rough as sandpaper. All I could think of was how much I wanted to go home. I wanted everything to go back to normal. I thought of the red-haired woman, of my comment to Sara. That red-haired woman was the reason for this. She must have been an *oni*. I wished I had never spoken of her.

I put on the robe and stepped from the bathhouse. I nearly twisted my ankle trying to slip my feet into the *geta*. It was dark and quiet outside. Overhead, the sky was studded with stars. The night air was cool. The high bamboo-lined fence of Grandmother's garden screened out the city noise. I heard none of the Roppongi street traffic. But I could hear the cicadas' tremulous whine and the repetitive *liin-liin-liin* of the bell crickets suspended in their small bamboo cages up under the eaves and on Grandmother's windowsill. I could also hear television sounds drifting from the open window of an apartment next door. The suggestion of voices seemed to become entangled above me in the bamboo's dagger-like leaves. Japanese words and phrases, half-formed and unintelligible, wrestled overhead in the foliage, trying to reach me. Images from the black pages of Grandmother's photo albums filled my mind. I made Chinese eyes, pulling up on the corners of my eyelids, and threw back my head to look at the stars. They swam in a blurry twinkle, shivered and slid like sprites of light. They looked strange, as strange as the world I was trapped in. Their weird stretches and shifts made me giddy. I felt a box open inside me. The sides flapped down and the bottom fell out. Everything became silent and empty. I rocked back under the shock. I felt raw, exposed, and full of a horrible grief or loss. I waited, breath held, for something to happen. Nothing. The night air became suddenly bitter and painful, harsh like the rough terry towels. I walked very quickly back to the house...

THAT NIGHT, IN BETWEEN THE cicadas' cry and the bell-crickets' *liin-liin-liin*, I heard the long, ragged sound of Grandmother's coughing sawing through the velvet darkness. One, two, three, four, on and on, on and on like sheep plunging fearfully over the dream-haunted precipice.

For weeks I lived like a ghost, speaking to almost no one. I went to the store, alone, to buy Grandmother's bread. I found a park nearby with a well and shrine where I could sit by myself for hours. I found a library full of Japanese books, none of which I could read. The texts were like hieroglyphics, a wall that I still couldn't climb over...

SOMETIMES I WOULD SIT AND stare at the Japanese characters and the bland, smiling faces in Grandmother's magazines which, curiously, one must read from back to front. Though it didn't matter; I didn't know what I read. I went with Grandmother to the bank or with the maid to the market.

I stood in the garden and watched them at work, their bonneted heads bent over flowerbeds. Haruka, Grandmother's maid, said:

"Heaven and earth are flowers—
God, as well as Buddha, are flowers.
The heart of man is also the soul of flowers."

I was surely disappointing my grandmother in just about every way. I knew nothing about bulbs or perennials; about bonsai, the pines and cedars that they purposefully dwarfed; or *ikebana*, flowers arranged—yin/yang, sun/moon—in a manner that supposedly mirrors the world.

GENE HAD LEFT THE CITY for a while on business. I stayed on, my grandmother's hostage, while Sara, having sacrificed me for her freedom from Grandmother, played house in a Japanese hotel and shepherded her children across town in a series of taxis and buses. Most of my days were passed in solitude. Grandmother could only handle children two at a time, having only two hands to drag them about, and she wasn't fond of misbehaving children.

The days seemed to creep by. Then, suddenly, it was early August. All around us the city was celebrating: O-Bon (the Festival of the Dead), Mamemaki (the bean-strewing), and the myriad tiny regional festivals—Shinto, Buddhist, and Zen—that are observed in all quarters in a metropolis as varied as Tokyo. We got used to the click of dragon's teeth, to the evil grimaces of little ivory devil heads with ruby-colored glass eyes. Phosphorescent paper *obake*, female ghosts with long dark hair, footless, their kimonos disappearing into smoky whiffs, dangled in all of the ten-yen shops. Because they glowed eerily in the dark, Samuel, Mimi, and Gray loved these and bought them by the score. They scared one another moaning, "Obaaakeeee," in deep, spooky voices and told each other progressively more frightening stories.

We lived in the shadow of the Kabuki-za—the classical Japanese theater. Grandmother loved the stage. She'd once been an actress in the Takarazuka, an all-female theater. Ghost stories were a part of both traditions, and she and Sara loved to tell them.

In the spirit of O-Bon, Grandmother, forgetting her ban against English, told us *Yotsuya Kaidan*, a particularly grisly tale.

We were in Grandmother's parlor, sitting on some silk futons and *zabutons* that Sara's tailor had just delivered. It was humid that day. Everything smelled faintly of mildew. Unlike Sara, Grandmother had a thick Japanese accent, so even though she told it in English, the story had a strange, foreign sound.

"Iyemon was an evil man," she began, "a ronin, a maverick samurai, forced by the great economic grindstone to earn his living as a maker of oil-paper umbrellas."

Grandmother spoke with savage certainty. A fierce gleam came into her eye. "The samurai were once a powerful class. When the reformation took away their masters, a dreadful force was unleashed. We are a samurai family," she said, looking directly at me. "Our code is one of honor and strength. This you mustn't forget."

She continued in a colder and quieter tone. "Iyemon had fallen so low that his only redeeming virtue was his lovely wife, Oiwa. So selfless and pure was Oiwa that she had given this bad man a child. Just as a lotus opens in mud, grace can descend and flower even among demons. But in this world, wickedness often rules. Unbeknownst to the delicate Oiwa, her husband had murdered her father, his father-in-law, because the old man was privy to his darker past.

"Were these crimes enough? Not at all. Tempted further by passion, Iyemon was seduced by the youth of his neighbor's granddaughter. She, foolish girl, was in love with him, too, and wanted nothing more than to marry him. So, at the urging of the girl's grandfather (Iyemon needed little convincing), Iyemon administered a 'blood-road-medicine' to his ailing wife. Oiwa thought this was a potion to strengthen her after the birth of her child. In reality, it was a poison. Its purpose was to put an end to her life!

"Poor Oiwa," Grandmother keened. "She had no idea why she grew weaker and weaker. She was so ashamed that she did not quickly recover to perform her service as wife. And her baby died, because when it drank the milk from her breast, it drank poison, too. Imagine the mother's sorrow. Her own milk, she thought, had sealed her child's doom. She sank into deepest despair.

"An old masseur took pity on Oiwa. Taking her to a mirror, the good servant showed her the truth. But the truth is not always a pretty thing. Oiwa's beautiful face and figure had been deformed by the poison. The black waterfall of her hair had vanished. In its place was baldness and a few stringy wisps. She had lost her teeth to the terrible drugs. One eye was so swollen that it couldn't be opened. Iyemon had turned her into a monster!"

Grandmother paused dramatically, lips pursed. Mimi whimpered and grabbed for my hand, her fingers locking on mine. The rest of us sat in horrified silence. Reassured that the performance was having the proper results, Grandmother went on. "How often we find that sentiments reflect the vessel that holds them. Iyemon had tainted Oiwa with his evil. Her emotions took on the hideous shape of her disfigurement. She was filled with hatred and the desire for revenge. But a spirit as sweet as Oiwa's could not inhabit the same frame as these ugly emotions. So the gentle Oiwa died at last. However, her brutal resentment remained.

"Iyemon's crime did not go unwitnessed. His servant, Kobotokei Kohei, knew of his wicked act. But a guilty man buries the truth, so Iyemon murdered him too, on the trumped-up excuse of theft. The servants of terrible masters are doomed.

"Iyemon nailed the body of Oiwa to one side of a board, Kohei to the other, and set it adrift on a river. He was free, at last, to satisfy his desires and marry the young girl next door.

"How very surprised Iyemon was," Grandmother said in her best Kabuki-style singsong, "when he raised the veil of his beautiful bride and saw, instead of the girl, the disfigured face of Oiwa. With a samurai's lightning speed, he drew his sword and severed the head.

"How shocked he was, when the ghost of his servant, Kohei, blocked his flight. He thought not a minute, but cut that head off as well.

"And then, oh, it was the worst surprise of all! For Iyemon had not killed the ghosts of Oiwa and Kohei. No, in reality, he had slain his neighbor and his new child bride!

"Where can a man like Iyemon escape from these terrible deeds? Oiwa's tortured face, the proof of his vile work, appeared to him everywhere—in the river where he had thrown the bodies, in the lantern trailing hair-like tresses of smoke that swayed over his head. He could not even hide on Hebiyama, Snake Mountain, far from all men. All of nature abhorred him and rose up to accuse him.

"Isn't it, finally, an act of kindness that his brother-in-law found him and killed him, thus ending the cycle of terror? Perhaps not. Perhaps Iyemon's horror continues with this story. But the spirits of the dead are avenged when we tell it, and the natural order restored."

Inspired by Grandmother's narrative, Sara told us the story of Takata-sama and the Terrible Mask. Mr. Takata was Grandmother's second husband.

"Hanabe Furigawa, your grandmother," Sara began in her best bedtime-story voice, "was, in her youth, a great beauty. Having run away at an early age from the imprisoning responsibilities of a powerful family, she became an actress, forsaking the world of duty for one of pleasure. Men loved her and she loved them, finding in the sensual world her supreme satisfaction. But being of an old and honorable family, she could never forsake her disciplines. These came to center around her appearance. Milk baths, oatmeal scrubs, salt rubs, and rosewater were all part of her arsenal. Her beauty was maintained through a regime so exacting that it went from the realm of art to that of religion."

Sara looked over at Grandmother and cleverly arched an eyebrow. Grandmother gave the slightest of nods, bidding Sara to continue her tale.

"Hanabe-san was really so lovely that she got all the leads in the plays. Conquering hearts in the same way, she also got all the leading men and had plenty of ardent fans. Thus, she had her pick of fine husbands, selecting and marrying three men in the course of her flamboyant career. All three were men of style and great wealth—one Japanese and two European—but no man was more dazzled by Hanabe-san's beauty than Mr. Takata, her second husband. He knew nothing of her maintenance program, being generally away on endless business that added to his already monumental wealth and to the stress that he was continually under. His health, as a result, was not good. His only relaxation was in returning to the arms of his elegant wife, to the effortless radiance that was his greatest inspiration.

"Coming home one night, a few days early from a business trip, Takata-san breathed his usual sigh of relief. Thinking it late and not wanting to disturb Hanabe-san's slumbers, he crept through the house. He entered the darkened bedroom with his hat still on and his briefcase still in his hands. Hanabe-san was not sleeping at all. She was in the middle of her secret beauty routine. Thinking she'd heard a burglar, she bolted out of her bed. That is where she was when Mr. Takata saw her, a tall figure in her ghost-white pajamas. Her face was completely covered in a mixture of pressed tomatoes and clotted cream. The cucumber slices that covered her eyes had started a ghoulish slide down her cheeks. She recognized her husband and screamed, probably more so than she would have had he been a burglar. Expecting his lovely wife and faced, instead, with this frightening apparition, Takata-san also let out a scream. It was said that this shock nailed the lid on his coffin. The "unmasking" as Hanabe-san came to call it, seemed to weaken Takata-san's constitution. He was never the same again. Nor, for that matter, was the marriage, for your grandmother never forgave him."

Grandmother's maid, Haruka, appeared with refreshments. I could tell that she had been listening, too, maybe hiding behind the sliding door to the parlor. Grandmother and Sara sipped dark green tea, studying the way the leaves fell and rose and fell again, swirling once, twice, on their perfect journey through the cup. Mimi, Samuel, Gray, and I drank milky brown tea sweetened with plenty of sugar. Refreshed by the tea and inspired by the contemplative spirit that had settled upon our circle, Sara told us the story of Senjin-san's ghost.

Senjin-san was our youngest uncle. He lived, as he always had, in northern Japan on the family lands in Akishima. Known for his gambling, carousing, and fondness for women, he always seemed to find the best parties, even in that pastoral part of the world. Coming home late one rainy night from just such an affair, with a burp on his lips and a belly full of rice wine, he stopped at the side of the deserted country road to relieve himself and was filling a ditch with a powerful sake-laced stream when a beautiful woman came out of nowhere. She begged him to help her, claiming that someone was trying to kill her. In an uncharacteristically ungentlemanly fashion, perhaps brought on by his boisterous nature, perhaps by the wine, Senjin-san ignored her plea and lunged at her instead. He fought hard to win her, but she was unyielding. The next morning, two neighborhood boys found him on that muddy path complaining loudly, wet and disruptive, with his head firmly stuck in the fork of a tree.

He said he'd been tricked by a *kami*, or spirit. No one believed him. But Senjin-san stuck to his story, even going so far as to dig up from the local *shimbun-sha*, the newspaper office, a surprising old story about a young woman of fine birth who'd been dragged to the very spot and murdered by robbers. He was convinced that the ghost of this lady, in quest for revenge against the abuses of men, had appeared to him and misled him, turning herself into a tree, compromising him, and cluttering this transformation and his entrapment with innuendo. He insisted that his humiliating discovery was her form of punishment. Other times, he changed his story completely and claimed that *kitsune*, the shape-shifting fox, had changed itself into a woman and teamed up with a badger, another magical animal, to trick him. He was fondest of telling this tale when he had been drinking awhile.

Mimi, Samuel, and Gray were still living in the children's dormitory of the Daimyō Hotel. The constant presence of goblins, demons, and gods seemed to have had an affect on them. I wondered if the demons weren't winning. Transformed by these stories and by our surroundings, drunk with mystery and with their fear, Samuel, Mimi, and Gray hid behind curtains when they could find them, jumped out from behind tables and screens, did Frankenstein imitations, and ran yelling through the treasured vegetable garden of one of Grandmother's unfortunate neighbors. The woman would run from her house brandishing her gardening shears, crying helplessly, "*Warui, warui, wampaku-na, kodomo-tachi-me!* Wicked, wicked, naughty devil-children!" She would take her stand, a ferocious guardian, next to her trampled eggplant. The ground around her feet was littered with the delicate purple blossoms.

"Yes, you had better run, you evil things, because when I catch you, I will cut off your ears and make them into pickle pots."

We danced around in the streets whenever anyone else in the city did, buying festival foods or candies with clear rice-paper wrappers that had to be sucked off, standing in huge crowds, stretching high on our toes, hoping for dragons, drums, or priests in white or priests in bright orange or half-clad young men with sticks and dances; singing, chanting with a breathless crowd, yearning for golden shrines, colored paper, the ritual scattering of rice or salt or blood-red beans.

I was also reeling under the influence of the confusing, multilayered world around me. I struggled without direction through a landscape mined with disturbing surprises and few explanations against a backdrop of Ukiyoye, floating world pictures—woodcuts of geisha and Kabuki actors plying their trade—the very real vision of pale women dressed only in steam in the great Tokyo bathhouses that I visited with Sara and Grandmother or of the park-like shrines tended by silent, white-shrouded priests.

One afternoon, I followed a procession on its sinuous journey through the labyrinth of Tokyo streets. The Shinto priests were moving a shrine through their parishes. The shrine was the chosen home of a *kami*, or spirit. The *kami* was represented only by this golden abode and its talisman, a wooden paddle, upon which was written a mysterious Japanese character. The shrine was balanced on a glittering palanquin that rested on the specially chosen shoulders of six of the district's most handsome young men. They were dressed only in loincloths. White headbands circled their foreheads. Their dark hair rose over their headbands like spiky cockscombs.

In this way, the shrine spirit visited all of its worshippers, spreading blessings. And, in this way, the celebrants honored the *kami.*

"Wasshoi! Wasshoi! Wasshoi!" chanted the young men as they ran through the neighborhoods with the precious palanquin on their shoulders. They had a lot of ground to cover.

"Wasshoi! Wasshoi! Wasshoi!" the wild throng screamed back.

"Wasshoi! Wasshoi! Wasshoi!" I heard myself yelling as I tried to hang onto the dragon's tail, the end of a parade that zigzagged through every lane and alleyway in the district.

I wanted to look into the shrine. I wanted to see the *kami.*

What does this kami *look like?* I wondered. Was it male or female? Beautiful or scary? I tried to get closer, but it was unapproachable. It bobbed on before me on the shoulders of the six young men threading their way through an ecstatic crowd.

Hands waved in the air. People jostled and pushed. It was too confusing. The dragon was moving too quickly. I lost hold of its tail. I got tangled up in the mob that milled about in the streets. The voices of the young men moved further and further away, and I found myself in an unfamiliar part of the city, much dingier than the places to which I was accustomed.

Suddenly, I was alone. I trotted along a sidewalk bordered by a ditch in which raw sewage flowed. Cheap *nawa-noren,* rope blinds, covered the entrances of the dirty *soba-ya* stalls, *taishu-shoku-do,* and sushi stalls. I passed derelict ten-yen stores and closed restaurants with chipped *maneki-neko,* good luck cats, beckoning in their grimy windows. The air smelled like sour milk and garbage. A baby wailed. It might have been a cat. It was a long, twisting cry. I wondered where it had come from.

A very muscular Japanese woman in a thigh-high pink dress leaned in one of the doorways. Her long, yellow-shinned legs were bare. To her left was a mountain of empty beer bottles, brown and long-necked, their labels a flashy Sapporo-red. She nudged the pile with the toe of her pink, high-heeled shoe as I passed. The bottles tumbled and clattered, rolling in all directions. Swaying on her high heels, the woman moved in on my flank.

"*Michi-ni-mayottano?* Are you lost?" she asked in a curious way.

She had a young, well-formed face, but her skin wasn't good and she wore too much makeup.

I nodded.

Then her red lips pulled back in a leer and she lifted her skirt. She had nothing on underneath, and I saw that she wasn't a woman at all, but a man. She puckered her lips up in a monkey-like grimace that was meant to parody a kiss. Then she laughed. I turned and fled. I heard her laughter ringing behind me in the empty streets as I ran.

I tried to retrace my steps, circling back and back. Finally finding a landmark, a familiar shop, I slowly reconstructed the path I'd followed, but it did not seem that I was heading home at all. The vision of the woman pulling the short pink dress up over a penis swam before me. I followed that image as it receded in the dusk toward a darkened lintel, the portal of Grandmother's house.

Selections from Dead Love

Hide and Seek

(excerpts)

Ryu was a member of the Japanese underworld, but nothing had prepared him for Haiti—for the poverty and the inconvenience, for the dark faces shut tight against inquiry. The theft, Mura's flight—all these were embarrassing things. And there was me. Ryu was supposed to kill me that night at the love hotel. He had made a mistake. He had dallied, and Mura had stopped him in his tracks before he'd achieved his purpose. Then Mura had stolen the chip, though Ryu had left him for dead in an alley behind the club. Now he had to find Mura.

They speak French and Creole in Haiti, and Ryu spoke Japanese and some English. When he found a translator, the fellow, who was not at all fluent in Japanese, had trouble understanding him.

"I need to find this man," said Ryu in Japanese after engaging the translator. He handed the translator a photo. The translator nodded furiously and stuck out his hand for more money. Together, they showed the photo to Haitians, who looked at it with glazed eyes and no recognition until they found an old woman in Jacmel in the southernmost part of the island.

"Theese man is dead," said one woman at last as she examined the battered photograph of Mura. "You must look for Arnotine Ferucand. He keeled him."

Then the search began for Arnotine Ferucand.

Arnotine Ferucand was easy to track. They had only to follow the laughter. The mere mention of his name seemed to send people into high-pitched hysterics. Arnotine, the translator explained with some difficulty, was a *bokor*, a Vodoun witch doctor, a sorcerer who knew how to steal a man's body and dispose of his soul. "He is Guedeh," claimed many of the interviewees. "He is Death."

Whatever his real identity, his name opened mouths, loosened tongues.

"What do you know of Arnotine Ferucand?" scoffed a tall young man on the second day of their investigation in the vicinity of Jacmel. He regarded Ryu with suspicion. Then he looked at the photo of Mura and chuckled. "Oh, yes this man is dead. And Arnotine knows it. Arnotine has become very powerful. Today he is Arnotine Ferucand. Tomorrow he could be you. You find a dead man, and this creature will be there.

"Talk to Ronan Duras," he added, looking down with disdain at the rumpled form of the translator. "Ronan will tell you about Arnotine. Tell Ronan I sent you."

There was no laughter in Ronan Duras. He was a wizened old man with pencil-thin limbs and hair like white spun glass. "I hate him," he said simply when asked about Arnotine. "He is not human. He is very bad and he makes a mockery of our sacred rites. That man you call Mura is dead for sure, but I can show you the rock under which you can find Arnotine Ferucand," he said, and he spat. Then he handed the translator a handmade business card. "Come to this *hounfour*," said Ronan Duras. "Come tonight."

What an invitation! It seemed Arnotine's name opened doors as well as mouths. A *hounfour* is a gathering of *Vodou société*, a secret gathering to which strangers are rarely admitted. This one took place the next night in a room in a boarded-up factory, a low-slung concrete bunker of a building with a roof of corrugated tin. Ryu went alone. He almost got into a fight at the door. He had a hand on his knife, a fine Kyoto blade the size and width of a letter opener, and was ready to slit the throats of four angry men who'd put rough hands on him, when Ronan Duras intervened. Ronan was the *houngan*, this *société's* spiritual guide and leader, and he fancied himself Ryu's host.

"Let heem in," said Ronan Duras. "Theese man is my guest." The four men stepped aside.

Old Ronan escorted Ryu into the candlelit den where a gargantuan woman lay on a table in the center of a swaying and shuffling crowd. "She is sick," whispered Ronan, his voice thin and dry. "I will heal her."

Drumbeats and low chanting, almost a crooning, rocked the room. Two men bumped into Ryu hard—he thought on purpose. His hand went to his knife. Then a woman in the crowd, a thin woman in a sheer white cotton blouse and green skirt, began to twirl. She was whirling around and pulling at her blouse as if something were crawling all over her.

The rest of the men and women in the room were also moving faster. They were stamping their feet in a kind of dance, singing and occasionally yelling. The drums got louder, wilder, and the woman continued to spin, colliding with people, staggering, twirling on and on.

Ryu hated it. He hated the dark, close, sticky, smelly mass of humanity that surrounded him. He tried to move out of the woman's way, tried to press himself into the crowd, but the crowd parted so that in the middle of the floor it was only the woman and him. Then the woman threw herself upon him, her skinny breasts mashed up against him, rubbing and pushing in a sickening way, arms flailing, slapping his head and his face, reaching—as he reached—for the knife.

She got to it first. She waved it aloft and squealed. The sharp blade glinted magically in the rheumy quarter-light. White teeth flashed in all the dark faces. Screams broke out, and, brandishing the knife as if it had a will of its own, the woman charged at Ryu and pounced...on the squawking chicken that someone had thrown into the air between them. The blade worked swiftly and severed the chicken's head while the decapitated body continued to flap and fly, flinging blood on the whole congregation. Ryu, who was closest, was completely bespattered. But now the woman dropped the knife and lunged for the chicken and soon enough had stuffed part of it—the squirting part—into her mouth, feathers and all. Now white feathers flew out over the crowd, a snowfall of death in the sweaty room. Then quick hands, Ronan's hands, grabbed the twitching bird and placed it upon the ample breasts of the big woman on the table. The enormous woman writhed as he pressed it into her bosom.

"This sick woman will live," said Ronan Duras. "Arnotine Ferucand will die."

Meanwhile, the skinny woman had thrown herself onto the floor where she squirmed and spasmed, her green skirt thrown over her head. Just an ordinary evening at the old *hounfour*. Ryu recovered his knife and pushed his way out to the door while the rest of the *société* kept up the frenzied dancing. Dancing, drumming, dancing (from the place in the shadows where he waited, Ryu could hear them) long, long into the night.

The next day, advised by Ronan Duras, Ryu went out, alone, to look for the sick woman. She was seated in a shack at a kitchen table upon which was displayed the head of a pig, flies ecstatically spinning around it.

"Come in," she responded gaily to Ryu's knock on the frame of the rag-draped lintel.

"So, you have found me, Ryu," she guffawed when the *yakuza* stepped gingerly inside, careful not to let his clothes brush up against the filth in the kitchen. It stank. It smelled like death. Ryu sniffed and forced himself to look away from the pig.

The big woman was beaming at him. She had short frizzy hair, a broad face peppered with tiny black moles, two missing front teeth, and breath that could, and should, clear a room. Still, there was something disturbingly familiar about her.

"Oooh, you are a smart one," she cooed. "You track me all the way to Arnotine Ferucand. Witch doctor, you see. Arnotine is a *bokor*, a witch doctor, and he helped me. Old Ronan, he wouldn't help me. But Arnotine, he did. He taught me many things, magical things. But he's dead. Old Ronan don't know that. He don't know nothing. Arnotine been dead for a long time. And now I am dead, too. That old fraud couldn't save me. But that's okay. I got Arnotine's secrets, my secrets now...and you, you got me."

She babbled along in Creole. Of course, Ryu did not understand a word she said. He just stared at her, trying to decide what to do, his black brows knitted, his dark-lashed eyes narrow and observant.

She laughed again. "Haw, haw, haw, Ryu-san. You don't recognize me, do you? But I know you, and I know why you're here. You want to take me back. That's your mission. Me and the chip. And I know who sent you. Those *yakuza*, yeah? Okay, I'm ready," she added holding out her arms; hands palm upward, wrists and fat pinkies touching. "Take me home, Ryu-san. I'm all yours." And she said it in Japanese.

How He Fell for You

All roads lead to Shinjuku-ku. 3-7-1-2 Nishi-Shinjuku. Once again I found myself in that high-rise, fast-paced part of town, very close to the station. Why did everything seem to lead back there? Why did it feel so familiar? 3-7-1-2 Nishi-Shinjuku was a hotel—close to fifty stories, one of the tallest in the neighborhood. I walked up the curve of concrete drive that swept up to the front. The entrance was cavernous, a huge lobby of rust-colored marble and wood. On a banquette of creamy oak, a wristwatch sat. Sculpted in brass, it looked meltingly soft and perfectly real where it lay, as if left by someone. Someone. Someone at the entrance. I felt eyes upon me from every direction. Dark squints and scowls. I spun around only to find myself surrounded. They stood and squatted all around me, their heads leaf-shaped, elongated; their haunches thick and powerful; their dark weapons tipped in ivory and gold. Some had long necks and breasts like torpedoes; others had gnashing teeth and fiery raffia hair. All were as black as pitch and filled with fierce power: African fetishes, almost a dozen of them, mounted on five-foot blocks of black marble along the walls of the lobby. I walked up to one of them, reached up a hand to caress wooden knees as sharp as cut glass. "From the collection of Hiroshi Nakamura," read the placard on its marble base.

"Hiroshi must see you." Hiroshi Nakamura. Hiroshi. The name was so very familiar. Hiroshi Nakamura.

"Can I help you with something?" a thin Japanese man in a dark two-piece suit asked in pleasantly accented English.

"Hiroshi," I intoned hypnotically. "Hiroshi Nakamura."

"Ah," he said quickly, sucking in air, subjecting me to a quick inspection. What did he see? A very young woman, carelessly clad in a salmon-colored chemise with mismatched socks and out-of-style shoes. I must have satisfied some secret criteria because he closed his eyes and bowed slightly, led me to a bank of elevators and, addressing a brass panel the size of a light switch, inserted a small brass key. One set of doors slid immediately open.

"Hiroshi Nakamura," he confirmed with a nod. "*Dozo.* Please." Then the doors shushed closed.

There were four buttons in the elevator, two pairs of two. The top two were labeled *Kozue* and *#1*, the bottom two were labeled *Lobby* and *Gym.* Excluding the other buttons was easy. I pushed *#1* and zoomed up fifty floors to be deposited on the level between forty-nine and fifty, between the restaurant, Kozue, and the Park Hyatt's rooftop spa: 3-7-1-2 Nishi-Shinjuku, #1.

The doors shushed open to the baleful music of a *shakuhachi* flute, solo and hoarse, crying into the white-carpeted foyer. The sound emanated from a monolithic sienna-red door (no doorknob, no visible features) that stood open about fifteen feet away. The great finger of sound found its way into my pelvis and snaked up through the upper half of my body, finding a resting place right behind my eyes, which started to water unaccountably. I opened my mouth as if to answer. No sound came out. But I felt as if my own mouth were a great speaker from which the sound of the flute now emanated.

Maybe I was actually moaning when I slipped through the door. I gasped audibly once I was inside.

Before me, black as tar, shiny as oil, the floor stretched like a wide pool of molasses. It was so glassy, so smooth, that I found myself removing first one shoe, then the other, setting my stockinged feet directly upon it. It was cool and slippery, and I slid along the top of it like a saint walking on water. Rising up from it, like giant piers, were a series of columns identical to those in the lobby, except that they were lower, perhaps two feet from the ground, with more of the horrible statues set upon them like a headhunter's trophies on pikes, and arching over that onyx black substrate, a full two stories overhead, was a roof so white it was blinding.

But I had no time to dwell upon any of this. The flute was disappearing into the hiss and spit of smaller woodwinds and the rumble of kettledrums furiously pounding with a force that nearly floored me. In desperation I looked to my right at a huge, wall-sized window where night was reflected, to the distant face of Mount Fuji, obscured by the foreground shadow.

That's when I saw him, sitting rigid as a pharaoh on a brown leather armchair, his eyes wide and boring into me with an almost palpable heat. He seemed as startled as I. Then he threw back his head to the roar of the kettledrums, and I half-expected the room to ring with loud, saturnine laughter. Instead he pushed himself stiffly to his feet, head thrown back, his eyes never leaving my face, and he walked toward me. He was thin and bald and he slid over the floor like a phantom, with supernaturally feline grace. I, in turn, slid toward him, drawn as irresistibly as an iron shard to a magnet.

Hiroshi. Hiroshi Nakamura.

My approach brought a smile to his lips.

"*Naze shitte ta no*? How did you know?" He asked in Japanese first, then in English. He seemed to know me, but seemed to have no knowledge of the summons. His hands flew toward me wrapping around mine like gloves of ice.

"Koan is dead," he said sorrowfully, and I could hear the tone of the *shakuhachi* flute in the ragged break in his voice.

"But I have finished the ballet. Something I couldn't do while he lived. You will dance it," he added. "That is why you are here. Dance it, Erin, as you have never danced before. It is full of my grief, my guilt, and my regret. How could I know of his illness? He never told me. How could I know that it was the reason he ended our relationship? I dealt with him cruelly, and when, in the end, he tried to reconnect, I turned a deaf ear. I was heartless. And now he is dead, and I can't bring him back to ask his forgiveness. How many turnings in the dark of the cave of life are taken through misunderstanding? This ballet is my tribute to him. It is my best work. My only work."

Several *samisens* "oohed" and "aahed" at this, and again I felt the music take hold of me, of Erin, in the strangest way.

"You know this part," said Hiroshi. "Frivolous, vain, like the flower dance, the *hana-odori*."

I felt my head swaying from side to side as Erin's body became absorbed by the music. One foot turned in, I took a delicate little step, then another, eyes down so that I could watch mesmerized by my reflection on the onyx mirror of the floor. Lean like a heavy-headed lily, sway, sigh, step, step, step, lean, sway, sigh, then freeze. The high-pitched twang of a single string cut through the other instruments, full of judgment, full of blame. Now the movements were *butoh*, drawn from the dance that came from the war, from the suffering and shame of Nagasaki and Hiroshima. These were the movements of dying, and I mimicked them with a bitter exaggeration, balanced on one foot, one hand reaching in an eternity of pain toward Hiroshi.

He staggered backward. He had not yet choreographed this part of the dance. Erin was improvising. I could feel it. Her being was reading his mind and inscribing upon the space that surrounded us the exact line of his misery. Twisting sideways now, still balanced, crane-like, on a single stem, chin over my shoulder, I raised my other hand to my face, touching my eyes and mouth, aping the gestures of lovers. Then I turned toward Hiroshi, opened my mouth, and snarled. I was an *oni* now, a devil with no remorse. Hiroshi's hand flew to his heart. I slid slowly to the floor in a Chinese split and, bending from the waist, touched my forehead to the floor. The music ended in whispers—whispers, bits of woodwinds and strings and snare drums, then silence.

It was powerful, potent enough to raise the dead, and indeed, Hiroshi looked as though he had seen a ghost, but this was not a reaction to savor smugly, because I saw at once that Hiroshi was actually looking beyond me, beyond the T that I'd settled into on the floor. His eyes were looking out over the expanse of polished black wood to the door, which was now completely ajar. Standing in front of it, gangrene-gray and moribund, like a corpse summoned by my dance or some equally demonic force, was the gaunt, fetid figure of Koan.

Koan was smiling. "Hiroshi," he croaked, his head cocked to one side, love shining like beams from his eyes. "Hiroshi," he rasped again. "I forgive you."

Hiroshi, I observed, had, as if mirroring his lover, turned a similar porridge-gray color. "No," he said, shaking his head furiously. "No, Koan, you are dead."

"No, I'm not," Koan insisted. "Would I come here if I were dead? I don't care what they say. I'm alive. And I love you, Hiroshi. I have never loved anyone but you. I couldn't let myself be around you once I knew I was ill. I had to protect you. But you thought I had spurned you, and you refused all of my overtures. Now, that was so cruel. You hurt me more than anything I have ever known. I've been so unhappy, felt so wronged."

All the time Koan spoke he was inching toward Hiroshi, and Hiroshi was backing away.

"No. No." Hiroshi kept muttering, his fear of ghosts having gotten the better of him, the terror having tied up his tongue.

"Hiroshi," said the appalling Koan, stepping over me as if I didn't exist. "You love me, don't you, Hiroshi? I know you love beauty, but what does it matter that I look this way? Isn't there still a place for me in your life? Can't you forgive me? Accept me?"

There was one carpet in Hiroshi's apartment, a stupid thing to have in a place with such slippery floors. It was a red- and clay-colored kilim, no doubt from the same dealer as some of the horrible fetishes that the choreographer collected.

Hiroshi backed away far too quickly and his foot caught the edge of it. The carpet, which seemed at this point to have a life of its own, shifted magically, and I wondered, for one brief and terrible moment, if there weren't some dark force at work in the fetishes, in the rug, in the music, in my dance, and, most especially, in Koan.

Hiroshi staggered, tried to balance himself with his other foot, and only succeeded in losing his balance completely. Then he fell. He fell like a tree falls when it has been hewn down expertly—straight back and away from the woodcutter. That's how Hiroshi fell. Like a tree in the forest. But Hiroshi's head never hit the ground. It was stopped on its floorward trajectory by the gold-tipped spear of a particularly vicious little African fetish. He had the misfortune to catch it on the back of the neck in the area just between the atlas vertebra and the base of his skull. But he did not hit it straight on. The short spear pierced his neck, severed his carotid artery, and a pillar of blood sprang up and sprayed from the wound. There he lay, or more appropriately, sat, skewered by the fetish, his blood gushing from the spigot in his neck.

I watched it pump and pump, the red puddling on the smooth black floor. I crawled toward Hiroshi, put my hand in the blood. Yes, he was certainly dead.

"Now, look what you've gone and done," said Koan.

Only it was no longer Koan's voice. It was a voice that I recognized, one I'd heard too many times.

"Yes, it's me," said the ghoul. "Clément...oh, I mean karma... comes calling. You were expecting the dead man? Hiroshi certainly wasn't."

I felt my skin crawl at the sound of his voice. I should have known all along.

A Ghost Reflects on the Ninja

That night when the frogs were singing,
the nightingale floor went wild,
its creak-tweet warning us
of trouble in *tabi* afoot.

No one ignored it,
but we were too slow.
Assassins entered our bedrooms,
ushering in death.

It is true their swords, like water,
reflected the lanterns' false moonlight,
but we knew it was darkness that skewered us,
throats smiling in silence
as shadows leaked in
and the frogs continued to sing.

—Erin Orison

Note: The Nightingale Floor in Nijo Castle was laid to guard against intrusion by suspicious and dangerous ninja assassins. Suspended above the frame using special iron clamps, the floor moved up and down over the fixing nails when walked upon, creating a sound similar to the song of a nightingale.

Selections from Dead Love

A Kiss in the Dark

(excerpt)

My room was upstairs with a view of the courtyard, a quiet room with bright sunlight blaring in through the window. The walls were mint-green and calming, the sheets on the narrow bed crisp and pulled tight. The mean little nurse was gone but not without warning that I should stay put. Where would I go? Why would I leave? I was still dressed only in the hospital gown. I sat on the edge of the bed. Then, inexplicably, I started to cry—for the second time since I'd arrived in Kuala Lumpur. This time the tears were real. Earlier, laughter, now tears—all of this felt so strange to me. The teardrops—I have no idea what precipitated them—welled up in my eyes then spilled down my cheeks in a torrent. It felt like a tourniquet that was wrapped around my chest had been loosened. I was wracked with rib-jarring sobs. My lips shook, my nose, eyes, and sinuses swelled, and still the tears kept pouring from of me. I was drowning, caught in the pipeline of a huge wave of anguish. It carried me out to some tumultuous, wildly turbulent place then dashed me back again, emptied. Exhaustion and an enormous sense of relief overwhelmed me. I felt free. Was this happiness? I lay down on the bed and I slept.

When I awoke, it was to darkness. At first I didn't know where I was. Outside my doorway, the world was in motion, a train of wrinkly, cotton-haired residents on patrol in the softly lit halls. They drifted from door to door in aimless and perpetual motion. Now here was a line of true zombies. I moved into the corridor and joined the parade. One sad little woman clung like a newborn macaque to the waist-high railing that ran down the carpeted hall. Another blue-veined granny wagged a crooked index finger at anyone who dared pass her. There was an old man dressed in a sweatsuit who flapped his loose lips in imitation of a motor or engine, and there was a funny old gal who whooped like a crane if she managed to catch someone's eye. In a slow-moving conga line, they shuffled from bedroom to bedroom. The doors to the rooms were all open so that the ancient residents, with their terminally scrambled circadian rhythms, could walk. And they did—all night—under the watchful eye of a camera and the less watchful eyes of a night nurse whose attention wandered from the console to late-night British broadcast TV.

In a listless procession through the insomniac night, the aged and agitated population of Saint Ali traipsed through the halls until slumber caught them off guard.

In the darkened bedrooms, the small beds looked like coffins and their sleeping occupants looked like the dead. The ambulatory residents slipped in and out of the rooms. The sleeping ones shifted and snored. The hall was well lit, but the bedrooms were dark. Except for one. In that one a small cone of light illumined a corner where a silvery figure sat propped up in her pillows, the lamplight casting a pearly glow over her face. Shadows webbed the ceiling and walls all around her. She sat there, unmoving, an oasis of quiet and light in the midst of the shuffling darkness.

Mrs. Soren-Schmidt had been at Saint Ali for seven years. She had Alzheimer's but she was still able to call out to me and to speak. Her cry was feeble, but impossible to ignore. I leaned into the room toward her.

"Oh, you're here now," she said, and smiled. "Isn't it lovely? It's sunshine. You'll be safe here."

I sat down on the bed next to hers.

"You look so tired," said Mrs. Soren-Schmidt. "I recognize tired when I see it. I'm tired, my dear, so I know what I'm talking about. You, you look so young to be tired." She extended her hand, palm turned up. "Here, take my hand." It was cold.

"I'm an ice bucket," she laughed. "Where's the champagne?" Then she sank back into the pillows, her head resting lightly against the wall.

"I am the only Schmidt left here in the Highlands. Why do women seem to live so much longer than men? Do you know how old I am, dear? No? Me neither, but I'd guess a thousand years old. But it's nice here. I like it. The nurses and doctors are all troubled, poor souls, but for the most part, they leave us alone. Like roses," she said. "At Saint Ali we can rest." She closed her eyes as if trying to prove her point. I noticed how thin her eyelids were. Her eyelashes were wispy and white.

"We miss Ping," she moaned, eyelids lifting. "Do you know him? Who are you, dear? I don't believe we have met."

Mrs. Soren-Schmidt moved her hands through my hair, stroked my hand, her palsied fingers trembling like wind-shaken petals as they moved up my forearm toward my elbow. "We miss Ping, dear. But they leave us alone, don't they? And sometimes that's all that matters, especially when you're tired and all around you there are nothing but shadows.

"I used to dance out in the garden. It was quite a romance, I tell you. Then the next thing you know, all you want to do is to close your eyes. Look at those poor souls." She gestured out toward the corridor. "They can't rest. Those doctors and nurses, they are troubled. As for me, I just want to vanish. 'Don't hold onto me,' I say to them. I don't want to stay. We are almost there, though. Trust me, this is as close as it gets. Dandelion. Romance. A soft kiss in the dark. Then nothing. It's lovely, you know. You just close your eyes. A soft kiss in the dark, then you're sleeping."

Mrs. Soren-Schmidt's hands still fluttered over my arms, lighting here and there, never resting. And while she spoke, a dark, black-haired figure slipped in through the doorway and began to tiptoe toward me.

I stiffened.

"Oh, don't worry, dear, that is Khalid. Poor Khalid is terribly troubled. Khalid, tell us what you want. Why have you come here to visit?"

Khalid, with his smooth brown skin and curly black hair, was clearly not old like the others. His eyeballs were as white as cocktail onions, his irises like shiny black olives. His teeth flashed knife-bright in the half-light of the room, and he pulled a glass jar from his pajamas.

"I'm going to catch her, once and for all," he said.

"Who?" asked my frail hostess.

"Her," he said pointing the jar toward me. "That one, the angel. I'll put her in my jar."

"Oh, Khalid," the old woman said, "that's a brilliant idea, but what did you do with the last one?"

"She has made a cocoon in the courtyard," said Khalid. "That's all right. This one is better. She is bigger."

"Your jar is too small, then," said Mrs. Soren-Schmidt. "Khalid, you must go fetch another."

"But she'll get away..."

"No, she won't, Khalid, I'll watch her."

Khalid looked from me to Mrs. Soren-Schmidt, considering the puzzle and his options.

"I'll watch her. Run along," advised Mrs. Soren-Schmidt. "But hurry if you want to keep her."

"He'll forget," said Mrs. Soren-Schmidt when Khalid left the room. "Poor Muslim boy, he's so troubled. He sees angels everywhere, not the Christian kind. His are like *dakinis* or divas. Now where were we, dear? You're a doctor, aren't you? We were going to play the piano."

Once again the sheer eyelids barely curtained her eyes and the fingers kept moving, this time like a shaky pianist's, up and down my arm, up and down. Outside in the hall the slumberless cavalcade continued.

I must have fallen asleep in Mrs. Soren-Schmidt's room. It was late in the morning when I woke up. Mrs. Soren-Schmidt seemed to be sleeping soundly. She had loosened her hold on me and her forearm stuck out from the side of the bed, palm upward, the fingers still slightly curled. I got up from the floor where I'd apparently dozed off and stepped warily back into the hall. The sunlight from the windows of the wide-open rooms filled the corridor with buttery light.

No sign of Khalid. No sign of anyone at all. I was still dressed only in the hospital gown, which was loosely tied in the back, hardly covering me at all. I ran down the hallway in the creamy morning light, the hospital gown flaring out around me. The mean little head nurse apprehended me. She was terribly fast and vigorous and seemed to come out of nowhere.

"There you are," she scolded as she steered me back to my room. "I think you have enjoyed enough celebrity. It's one thing to act up outside of the hospital, but here we manage differently. Sit down," she commanded.

I sat.

"Do you want your clothes back?" she asked, regarding me with a look that I was certain was one of contempt.

I nodded.

"Then you have to behave," she said and seemed pleased when I did not budge.

"Sit still," she said. "Stay right there until I come back."

She left. I sat without moving, believing that she hid just on the other side of the door ready to pounce on me should I move into the hall.

When she returned, she did not have my dress over her arm. Instead she was carrying a simple blue chambray frock and white cotton underclothes, and she had the doctor with her.

"Have a seat on the bed, there," said Doctor Pilford Hodge. He wore a white coat over his tan shirt and slacks. His eyes were a placid blue-gray. "Your documents," he said, offering me the passport and photo.

I looked away. If I hadn't, perhaps I would have seen him raise his eyebrows, throw his head back ever so slightly, and exhale. I heard him exhale.

"As I thought," he said. "You have a problem. Maybe trauma, amnesia, shock, a reaction to drugs." He sighed. "Whatever the situation, we will endeavor to be of assistance. We are, frankly, confused about how you ended up on our doorstep, though it's clear that once more the ever-troublesome Ping has somehow gotten involved. No matter. I've phoned the authorities and the hospital's new owners, and I'm sure we'll have our answer before long. In the meantime, Ms. Orison—do you remember that name?—in the meantime, we will keep you safe and make attempts to diagnose your disorder. We cannot treat you without authority, but I suspect the police and our management will be able to locate your family."

Then he turned my head toward him—I didn't resist—and he used a little light to look into each of my eyes. Then he pushed the light thing up into each of my nostrils and peered into them. Then he looked into my ears.

As if he expected to find something there.

I could feel my lips curling back into something resembling a sneer.

"I do hope you'll cooperate and respect our rules," declared the doctor. "If you behave well, you may move about as the other residents do, without fear of restriction, until your family comes to your rescue. Otherwise, we will have to find ways to restrain you."

This speech of his was really more for the nurse than me, wasn't it? She seemed pleased by it, nodding her head, her squinty eyes like repeating horizontals.

I got up slowly, and turning my back to them, walked to the corner behind the bed. I felt the thin hospital gown billow out around me, chasing the hot, floozy breeze that came in through the open window. Who in the world invented this kind of clothing? I heard the nurse grumble something about my clothes. I turned to face them, narrowing my eyes, and smiled a thin, canine smile. I must have looked like a trapped dog, panting.

"I'm glad you've decided," the doctor said tiredly. He looked at me foolishly, than quickly away, his fingertips pressed on his temples.

"Nurse, perhaps you should give her the clothes."

And that should have been that, but before he could leave, a nurse's assistant rushed into the room in a panic.

"Nurse," she cried, "Doctor Hodge, I think we've lost one of the patients. It's Loretta," she gasped. "I do believe she is dead."

It seemed that one of the hospital patients had died. The staff and other residents were quite absorbed by this for the remainder of the day. One would think that the death of its clientele would be quite commonplace in a facility devoted mainly to the aged, but this particular death caused a veritable uproar. It seemed the dead woman, whoever she was, was a favorite within their community. I took advantage of the situation by wandering about with abandon and that is how I noticed Ping at one of the pools in the courtyard.

It was as bright and clear that day as it had been rainy and dour the day before. There were clouds overhead but they looked like white frigate ships sailing on a Wedgwood-blue sea. Under this gorgeous canopy, Ping knelt in the courtyard beside the smaller circular pool. I could see from the window that he had something in his arms. That something was small and pink and it looked like an infant. As Ping dipped it in the pool and lifted it out, the little thing seemed to put up a tremendous struggle.

Every Star Needs a Posse

Everywhere they looked there were pigs. The rainforest was full of them: fat pink porkers squealing around in the brush. This was, of course, very distracting to the dogs and an obstacle to the hunt. Between the canine trackers, the police, the remaining Consortium representative, recruits from the hospital staff, the angry villagers, and the pigs that Ping had released, the forest had morphed into a circus. At least, that is what Ryu thought as he fumbled along with the others, trying to pick up the fugitives' trail.

He hoped that this mob wouldn't find them. It wasn't so much that he wanted to protect Erin and Clément as that he had a sense of propriety, and a torch-bearing alliance of good citizens and bad seemed disorderly, undignified, and disgustingly unprofessional. He wanted to capture the quarry himself, to do it with grace and style and with intellectual relish. This was a free-for-all open to riffraff not much better, as he saw it, than the creatures they were after. And there was Erin. Clément had made it clear that she was the package in which the blackmailing microchip had been sequestered. Ryu had to make sure the *yakuza* got that back. And so he went along, more to ensure the safety of the pursued than the success of the pursuers.

He had watched them leave, had known they were hiding in Hodge's office. He could find Clément anywhere now. He had only to follow his nose. But he found it less than productive to discover them there at the hospital with a furious posse on hand to hijack the merchandise that it was his job to recover and trade. So he had sagely retreated, let them scamper away from the hospital, while he had gone upstairs to cut back on the competition.

In this he'd been rather successful. Hodge, he had dispatched in the hallway downstairs. The administrator was conducting his own furtive and timorous search for Erin and Clément after being advised by his new Consortium-employed superiors that he had better find them and fast. It had been a simple matter for Ryu to sneak up behind him, put one arm around his chest, and run his knife across the man's throat. He did this with the grace of a cellist. It was quick. It was clean. No longer would the good doctor worry about his failing prospects or lament his wasted promise. He was at rest, his head, nearly severed from his neck, propped up against the corridor wall, his body sprawled out as though at leisure, like a man enjoying his music.

There were two Consortium gunmen upstairs, and for them Ryu had to resort to a pistol. He used a Ruger S.A. with a silencer, waiting for one of the men in a resident's bedroom and plugging him right between his raised eyebrows. It was amusing to see the look of surprise, and Ryu couldn't help smiling as his finger pressed back on the trigger. Poof. Spliff.

The gunman's mouth fell open in a gaping "Oh," as the bullet hit his soft pillow of brain.

Ryu picked the other off near the stairwell, as the ruffian tried to interrogate one of the residents, a young Indian boy clutching a jar. Ryu shot this assassin first in the shoulder and then in the back of the knee. His first two targets had been too easily achieved. There was a lot to atone for. And Ryu wanted to play slightly rough for a while. The man responded with fury, rising up like a baited bear and turning on the much shorter Japanese man. But Ryu was unruffled, delivering the next three shots with deliberate satisfaction. He shot the weapon out of the big man's hand, he shot out the second kneecap, and when the man crashed to the floor in a paroxysm of pain, he blew off the top of his head. The *yakuza* still made it a point to finish both gunmen off with his trusty blade. That way he could be certain the deed was done right. He didn't want any comebacks. He stepped over the Indian boy who had curled up, uninjured, in a fetal position at the top of the stairwell, his body wrapped tightly around the jar.

Ryu had counted a third Consortium assassin, but he opted to save him for later. The police were on hand and with them an angry collection of plaintiff villagers, and his instincts told him to minimize damage, especially to anyone with no real idea of what was actually going on.

To the police, this was about an American girl accused of murder and smuggling. To the villagers, it was about their pigs. To the hospital staff, it was about a resident run wild. To the Consortium, it was about an obscene secret that needed to be kept. And to Ryu, it was about a mess, a courier out of control and a small spot of blood (he flashed back on the ladybug-sized stain on the Haitian desk clerk's white shirt) that was growing and growing and threatening to turn into an ocean.

Even before Ryu had dispatched some of the competition, the chase had moved to the rainforest. There the villagers fell upon the pigs as they found them, abandoning the search as soon as they'd secured an errant swine to call their own. The hospital workers, too, deserted early on, before the forest closed completely around them. The police, however, were determined and so were the dogs, but they couldn't pick up the scent. That's because they were trying to track Erin instead of the stinking ghoul. Ryu stayed just long enough to make sure that his quarry was not going to fall into the wrong hands. When he was certain of that, he made his exit. There was a big mess back at the hospital, and he didn't want to get mixed up in that. He would find them, but this wasn't the way.

The Time of Figs

I don't need to tell you that
we thought of you as we picked
figs, the smooth black bottoms
dimpled with dark pink
like a monkey's anus and
the way the fruit leaks milk,
there, where you break it off
the limb.

We must have eaten six or
seven in the garden, throwing
the dark tough skins into
the foliage.

By this time of year the apples, having
an early start, have turned
brassy. Even the leaves have yellowed,
scattered on patio stone or over
the rattan of lawn chairs.

Wasps comb the remains. Days are short,
stubby things now, barely utilitarian,
and the nights have stretched into
wide dark umbrellas folding us
into starry linings.

Enchanted Piazza

(travel essay)

It has been called Europe's grandest drawing room. Capacious and elegant, it is a great circle in which pigeons and people congregate. In winter, the waters rise and fill it. Gondolas slip through it.

It is the Piazza San Marco, center square of Venice, "La Serenissima," that most serene city that kisses the Adriatic Sea. Tonight the Piazza is awash in light. Over it, the full moon hangs like a Venetian glass globe. Ringing its vast perimeter, bandstands sparkle like bejeweled half shells, cupping dinner-jacketed orchestras and tuxedoed string quartets that fill the night with music. Mozart in one corner. Slow, syrupy jazz in another. Diners dawdle, pick at desserts, savor ports and cognacs, and sip at their last espressos.

We stroll through the moonlit piazza. Water colorists vending Venetian scenes sit, smiling tiredly, beside their portable stands. Other artists patiently complete the final portraits of the day. The campanile, the Piazza's famous bell tower, chimes the hour. A clock tower across the square responds—its medieval mechanical figures striking a tinny midnight. The smattering of ambient humanity stops, looks up, and smiles before moving on. Artists roll up their drawings and collect their pigments. Musicians put away their instruments. The restaurants grudgingly close.

It is at the Piazetta, vestibule to the Piazza San Marco, that our feet first touch Venetian soil. Disgorged by the fuming *vaporetti*, water buses that ply the Grand Canal, we have entered the city on a carpet of blue. Around us Venice gleams—bone white—a relic tottering upon its millions of wooden pilings.

Great façades, like old courtiers, crack-toothed and leering through years of paint, line the waterways. Venice is the merchant city, its heart perennially set upon the riches of the East. In the sixteenth century it was the largest empire in the West, controlling Crete, Corfu, and the Dalmatian Coast. Its arsenal could turn out a fighting galley in a single day. The breeze was one of piracy and larceny. Even the city's patron saint was shanghaied. In 829, Venetian buccaneers stole the bones of Saint Mark the Evangelist from his tomb in Alexandria, smuggling their booty back to Venice in a casket of pork. In 1204, Venice sacked the holy city of Constantinople, confounding its Christian partners on the Fourth Crusade. But Venice is also a place of dreams and mystery, home to adventurers and *bons vivants* like Casanova and Marco Polo, a giddy world of glass and masks.

We roam the Rialto in the early morning hours, linger on bridges, sip Chianti canal side, slip through the labyrinth of narrow streets to explore shops crammed with precious pieces of Murano glass, fine-blown from spidery filaments, or webs of Burano lace. But mainly we are drawn to shop after shop of *papier-mâché* masks. Maskers were the popular medieval and Renaissance celebrants and Carnevale was the Venetians' favorite masquerade. The faces of *commedia dell'arte* characters—Harlequins (colorful clowns), Punchinellos (quarrelsome hunchbacks), and Pierrots (sad-visaged mimes)—grimace on walls alongside Beasts and Sun Kings. The funereal guises of La Buatta, the Domino, with its black cape, white mask, and three-cornered hat, and the black mask and cape of Il Dottore suggest the sinister side of revelry.

Under evening's dusky cloak we glide through the canals in gondolas, the long, thin, black lacquer boats. Bats (the *pipistrelli*) crisscross the air space over the canals. Our gondolier, Paulo, is quiet and mysterious—pale hair, pale face, vermilion lips bright as the ribbon of his hat. The gondolas remind us of coffins, not surprisingly, for during the Black Plague of the Middle Ages, the Venetians painted their boats black, thinking the bright colors far too festive. As if in spite, the boats remain a mourning black—a dark joke in this city of dark humors.

It is this secret shadow side that contrasts so seductively with the carnival brilliance of Venice. During Carnevale, Venice becomes a madhouse, the Piazza flooded again, this time with revelry. In the weeks before Lent, winter's final grim gauntlet, costumed celebrants fill the Venetian streets. Maskers surge into the ice-bright squares. In recent years the count of party-goers has climbed to over a hundred thousand people. The cramped streets and bridges swell with them. They spill into the Piazza. In Venice all streets seem to flow into the Piazza San Marco, just as all roads once led to Rome. The parade is Felliniesque—sometimes a breathtaking vision, sometimes a hilarious nightmare—and the cast international. The exotic East sweeps onto the scene in a flurry of capes, turbans, scimitars, and curly-toed shoes. Party-crazed, profiling visitors mingle with the wise and wary Venetians. Plumes, hoods, and tricornered hats bob atop the seas of guests that crowd hotel lobbies. Greasepaint, crystal beads, and silk glint and flare in the candlelight of the city's restaurants. Phantoms veiled in tulle or wrapped in clouds of netting disappear around alleyway corners and reappear in neighboring squares.

But there is nothing more haunting than the sight of costumed celebrants ferried through the inky waters by a Charon-like boatman to the lip of another realm. During Carnevale to step into a costume, you remove the one you are wearing. The city is peopled with creatures of the interior landscape—the dreamy, the dangerous, and the archetypal.

This year Carnevale will be observed for nearly a month, but the celebration is such a part of the Venetian soul that in years past Carnevale lasted up to six months. Certainly, in those tiny shops selling masks, the carousel never stops. An atmosphere of transgression and excitement drapes Venice year round. It is present in strangers who share gondolas, and dinner, and then disappear; in restaurants like the Bai Barbacani—where the titillating conversations between guest and proprietor begin with a plate of plump gnocchi pillows, stained in cuttlefish ink, and an invitation to come into the kitchen, and end in breathless promises to "make marscapone together."

Our hidden and forbidden selves are reflected around us, as in the fractured glass of a funhouse mirror, on the walls covered with hundreds of carnival masks. We muse over those masks as we walk in silence along the Riva degli Schiavoni after midnight, just beyond the Piazza San Marco, where canal waters lap hypnotically like a subvocal command. We cannot leave Venice without one. Before we abandon the city, we must rush back to the shops to search for our favorites, seeking to take home with us a cherished touchstone to our secret selves, the lasting symbol of our enchantment.

This August

Now that we are descending down the stairwell
of the latter half of the year,
counting all of our aches and sorenesses,
collecting fruit like pomegranates, persimmons,
things with long names and histories to couple
with the widening mouth of nights,
I have so little to say to you,
considering how short the days have become.
The sunlight, growing watery,
is not shared easily.

You are opening up new spaces in the back of our bookshelves,
hoping the shadows filling them
will leave some kind of testament
to this other world of subterranean purpose.
The darkness is also full, albeit quieter,
of other things than us.

I believe there was a time when days were fat and round.
I'm not certain, having forgotten much
of what has passed us by.
Certainly, we have shared some secrets,
as if we knew what secrets really are.
Colors were rampant in that heyday, and fragrances
like new-mown grass and flesh.

I like, however, the way the thin skin of the sun
has stretched around us, tightening,
how things are not spent so readily or easily,

how we count among our treasures,
those organ vessels in this tomb containing heart,
or liver, or overburdened pancreas,
all that is lost.

If we could know that the days would, in fact,
again begin to lengthen,
after some corner critically turned,
finding our reassurance in a corbel, arch,
an architectural detail, some structure
that defies, through its own rules,
the larger set of laws like gravity and death,

if we could bring back tokens
from the journey down those steps,
say: newel posts, say: something tangible,
would we sink sensibly into that sunset,
would we believe in sleep,
trusting the eerie light of dreams?

I think decay becomes us.
Fading dresses us down,
and sunlight, never so savored,
becoming delicate in its dismissal,
yields another range of nuance in this gloaming.

Perhaps we will become resilient,
snake our way toward eclipse,
or maybe we will whisper toward
the very back of the house where promises
and priesthoods balance on phenomena,
the room of pulleys and infernal machines.

I follow you, the trail of hieroglyphs, of gloves,
hands pressed against walls,
the confidence that these recede, opening into
a larger and more uncontroverted space.

Part 4: The Edge and Beyond

The Dragon

I am
the dragon,
the serpent coiled,
torpid,
at the base of your spine.
I twine,
slither upward,
lengthening,
long,
stretched like a chord
from coccyx to cranium
my head
the medulla oblongata.

I will speak for you
from now on.

You are a cavity,
hollow,
swallowing shoals of gold coins,
bright fish,
smelt for this gullet.
You are gelatinous
under me,
each nerve a string.

I play you well,
cast up knights
and virgins,
whatever I find
in my black box.
My smile
draws the chimera,
my breath
the quivering mirage.
I animate the flame.

Mostly I sleep,
easily bored.
I yawn.
My jaw unhinges
like a python's
and the squealing piglets,
saints,
the vast array of shadows that I paint
slide
in.

Lost in the Okefenokee

(travel essay)

When I was a blithely disobedient little girl, my father would always threaten, with a malignant air, to throw me into the Okefenokee Swamp. He could not know then, and doesn't know to this day, I'll bet, how thrilling a prospect that seemed. O-k-e-f-e-n-o-k-e-e. The very name was magical, and I rolled it around in my mouth with other delicious words like "Ubangi" and "Kilimanjaro." It is, in fact, possible that my unspoken desire for that forbidden place was the secret font of all my future misbehaviors.

Years passed, and I almost forgot about the Okefenokee and about swamps in general. That is, until I arrived one midnight at the Valdosta Airport on a then all-important corporate job. Dead beat and cranky, I sarcastically asked my cab driver (that's how I channeled my hostilities in those days) what sights there were to see in Valdosta, Georgia.

"Well," he drawled, "not far from here, there's the Okefenokee Swamp." He said this, I think, with the same tone that my father had used on his ill-behaved daughter, but the subtlety was lost on me at the time.

I had enough sense not to insist that the cab driver, to whom I'd just been so rude, drive the 120 miles west so that I could try to wander into a swamp at midnight. But a flame had been fanned on a very old fire. A new Okefenokee fever consumed me.

The Okefenokee Swamp is one of America's largest wetlands. Covering 438,000 south Georgia acres, an area roughly a third the size of the Everglades, it is really not a swamp at all, since it fills, flows, and drains, but an enormous watershed around twelve feet above sea level, and the source of two large rivers: St. Marys and the famous Suwannee River. The name Okefenokee is of Native American origin. It means "land of trembling earth." As the Native Americans discovered, "land" in the Okefenokee is not land as we know it. The swamp is comprised of over sixty spongy, peat moss–formed islands, bearing colorful names like Blackjack, Roasting Ear, Broomstraw, and Bugaboo; a similar number of lakes, innumerable watery glades called "homes" or "hammocks," and around sixty thousand acres of grass-covered marshland.

You will know when you're nearing the Okefenokee Swamp. If you are driving up from Orlando, through well-manicured north Florida, for example, the scenery will go through a dramatic transformation. On either side of the road, you will notice narrow channels that widen into still ponds of mahogany-colored water. You might see the snakelike silhouette of an otter clinging to the trunk of one of the skimpy cypresses that rise from the ash-colored muck, or an egret, neck curled into a perfect question mark, poised on the grassy marshland. Towns will become tiny and haphazard, the landscape increasingly savage.

The Okefenokee Swamp can be accessed through any of three entrances—the western entrance, at Stephen Foster State Park, is just off Highway 29, on Jones Island, near Fargo, Georgia. It is wilder than the parks situated to the north of Cowehouse Island, fifteen miles from the town of Waycross. This was the stomping grounds of cartoonist Walt Kelly, creator of Pogo, the savvy comic strip possum, and ancestor of Opus, whose arcane speech and strange wisdoms, along with those of his swamp critter cohorts, edified a generation. The eastern entrance is at the Suwannee Canal Recreation Area, headquarters of the Okefenokee National Wildlife Refuge. All three entrances are wild and beautiful points of ingress, which include picnic areas, nature trails, guided boat tours, canoe rentals, and interpretive centers where you can gather an assortment of free and purchased literature about the Okefenokee. You will need this information to penetrate the swamp's mysteries—chances are much of what you see will be new to you. Or you can opt for one of the guided boat tours, and a well-informed ranger like Pete Griffin will introduce you to this watery world.

Beyond that, you will need all of your senses, for the swamp of flora and fauna is as rich as a great bouillabaisse, and as profoundly satisfying. It is a strange mixture of the dreadful and the sublime—a place where three-hundred-pound black bears tread the same cypress and mulberry glades through which black-tailed deer delicately spring; where seven-hundred-pound alligators cruise canals in which egrets, ibis, herons (yellow-crested and great blue), and sandhill cranes gingerly wade. Regal flags of purple iris spring from the same mud that nourishes the hair-covered, liquor-filled basins of carnivorous pitcher plants; and lilies open like celestial white crowns next to the sticky tongues and yellow flower-lipped chambers of sundews and bladderworts, floral prisons baited for insect prey.

A fly fisherman's heaven (the season is year round) the waters teem with catfish, bluegill, bass, walleye, trout, and pickerel. A clever fisherman will study the webs of orb weaver spiders and see what's caught in them to know just what lures to tie.

If you are wise, you will gather the literature, study it, walk the trails, bring in a picnic, and take one of the guided boat tours. If you are of a more adventuresome spirit, you will rent a two-person canoe and paddle in on one of the several trails. Some of these run the breadth of the swamp and take one to five days to traverse. Platforms along the way at five- to ten-mile intervals have been set up for camping. The longer trails are regulated and limited to one canoe a day. This is really the best way to see the swamp, but not something to embark upon lightly.

When I finally made my journey into the swamps, our canoe barely squeaked past a fourteen-foot alligator, hogging a narrow channel. Less than a paddle length away, it watched us suspiciously as we tried to maneuver past, snorting water from its nose flaps and submerging like an enemy submarine until only its eyes were above the water. It was as long as our canoe. I imagined I would have fit comfortably into its gullet, more so after a couple of snaps. We capsized in a bog. The water was warm and brown and I couldn't get out of it fast enough, finally finding a foothold on spongy earth. It was an experience that lends new meaning to the expression "up to your armpits in alligators," one that I do not regret, but don't care to repeat. In a way, it fulfilled an old prophecy. I lost a roll of film on the muddy bottom and had to right the canoe and paddle on, in an attempt to recapture some of the shots. Paddling on was no problem. The swamp draws you into it. It's easy to become disoriented, absorbed in the hypnotic twist of its labyrinthine waterways, in the molasses-dark mirror of its waters, in the operatic grandeur of its tattered curtains of Spanish moss, its golden carpet of grasses, its wildlife cast of thousands.

In your small boat, you are pulled toward the center. Its silence surrounds you, a silence broken only by the screak of insects, the muffled splash of an alligator moving into the water. The swamp has a delectable languor that is soporific. You lose track of time. And you can lose yourself there. In fact, it's easy to get lost in the Okefenokee, and once you do, it's easy to stay lost, even though you think you have left it behind, and you are thousands of miles away.

Selection from Namako: Sea Cucumber

akishima/autumn island

The florist's wagon bounced along in silence on the rough, gravel lane that approached Akishima. On either side of the roadway early plantings of cabbage, radish, turnips, and rice stretched across valley and hillside, in earthy brown squares neatly banded by watery ditches and dotted with green.

The byway became rocky, still more uneven. To the left, twenty feet from the road, an eight-foot stone wall rose and followed a course roughly parallel to the car path, dipping and climbing with the contours of the land. Above it, apple boughs poked out from the interior side. The dark branches were pricked with shiny green buds. A tangle of tall blackberry bramble, in some places as high as six feet, barbed the exterior surface. To the right, a knoll crowned with a big tree stump, backed by orchards and, past these, a thick forest of pine, dominated the landscape. Regarding it, Sara remarked wistfully that they had hacked down the three-hundred-year-old persimmon tree that she had fretted under as a small child. "There was a *kami* in the tree," she said. "Who would do such a thing?"

"A *kami*?" I asked, hoping to elicit a response, to lead her into a conversation. Sara's silence and distance disturbed me.

"Yes," she said. "You know, a *kami*. A spirit. When I was a little girl I used to wait under that tree for the ripe persimmons to fall. I was alone so much. The *kami* of that tree was my first *amma*, my nanny."

"Where was Grandmother?" I asked.

"Oh," Sara said with a pensive smile. "She was away. She was always away. She was with my father in Shanghai. But look at that, they have cut the tree down and the *kami* will be so unhappy."

"Maybe the tree was already dead," I offered, trying to console her. "Maybe the *kami* had already left it."

Something about what I said got through to Sara. She looked at me sharply. Then her face became distant. I felt her drifting away again.

"Maybe," she answered laconically.

By this time, we had skirted the entire eastern wall and the road took a sharp turn, driving into the enclave that the wall surrounded. Once inside, the route became straight and unbending, leading inward past lines of budding apple and plum trees. Gravel gave way to loose dirt on a narrowing causeway that gave the impression of not being much used. At the end of this track, which was really more like a drive, was a meadow-like expanse of low grass, and in the center of that—boarded by outbuildings, forest, and garden—stood the house.

The house itself was an old-style dwelling, not the lordly fortress of a *daimyō*, but a rustic samurai homestead, made of wood and roofed in thatch. Still, it was grand. The large exterior doors were of dark red mahogany and the enormous *genkan* was made entirely of stone. Sliding interior doors led up to the central hall, a large room carpeted in creamy *tatami*, in the center of which sat a huge table surrounded by *zabuton* cushions of pewter-colored silk. The table was situated over a pit. Over one-foot deep, the stony floor of this pit was covered with ash, as coals were placed there in the winter to provide warmth for the house. The columns that supported the house, great soot-covered beams in the central hall, had been polished to a mirrorlike blackness by centuries of women. Those columns disappeared somewhere into the darkness above us.

"Your samurai ancestor had a fight with a demon," Sara explained. "He vanquished the demon, but the demon swore he'd take vengeance. 'You can't keep me out,' he had howled at his samurai conqueror. 'If you close all the windows, I will come in through the chimney.' So the samurai ancestor had built his home without a chimney, and the smoke collected for centuries up in the rafters. In this century, tired of choking on smoke for some silly old story, they finally opened a chimney. And the war came, and Akishima was lost in the war. But Mother bought it back for the family. Who knows? Maybe they lost it because the demon had finally found his way in, because they had opened a chimney."

I looked up into the rafters to where the chimney had been cut and tried to imagine a demon hurling himself down through the narrow opening. I tried to imagine the demon's appearance. He would be red and blue and golden, the color of flames, and he would leap and cavort the same way flames do. A chimney demon would certainly breathe fire.

But even with the chimney, the house was very dark, brightened only by the small windows and by the dingy pink and vermilions of the camellias and peonies that faded on the black lacquer screens in the corners. This house, like my grandmother's house in Tokyo, was muffled in silence. My great-uncle, Shiro, the oldest of Grandmother's brothers and the only one who still lived on the land, was the man who had greeted us when we arrived. Grandmother had died unexpectedly. There hadn't been time yet for the family to gather. This man looked like Grandmother, tall and quite thin, but there was a depth and gentleness in his eyes that seemed to soften the severity of his manner. He was very formal with Sara—the two bowed when they met and exchanged no more than names. Every syllable of the names seemed to carry some meaning.

"Furigawa, Sakura," my great-uncle said, using Sara's full name with a slow and precise articulation that gave it great significance.

"Honorable Uncle," Sara responded, bowing in the way a flower bends when touched by a strong, late summer breeze.

Then, looking down at Sara, my great-uncle had inexplicably smiled, and the smile seemed weighted with a profound sorrow and a profound understanding. I suddenly felt quite unlike myself. I felt as Gray might, like rushing up to this man to collapse against him in search of some solace—abject, overwhelmed, and unable to cope. But I am not Gray, so naturally I did not express myself in that manner. Instead, I bowed, and my uncle reached out and took my hands in his and held them, regarding them closely as if he were studying them. His hands were strong and warm.

"Kaze ga fuku," my great uncle said. Then he let go of my hands, told his servants to escort me into the house, and turned, with Sara, to the florist's wagon.

"What does '*kaze ga fuku*' mean?" I asked Sara later in the garden on the left-hand side of the house where we stood, mesmerized by the fish that swam around and around in one of the fish ponds.

"Well, it means 'the wind blows,' in its simplest form," Sara answered. "But your uncle meant it a different way. He also meant we are carried away by the wind, that it is stronger than we are and that it presages change. In that way, he acknowledged a force that is greater than we are. That statement is the last line of an old expression. It is a form of resignation to the natural movement of all things."

"Oh," I said, pondering Sara's explanation. It seemed like a lot of meaning for three little words. I turned my attention back to the fish. There were three ponds in the garden in which large koi circled gracefully, silver and gold torpedoes moving under the green, algae-furred surface.

"They look like giant goldfish," I observed, still deliberating over all those multiple meanings.

"They are something like goldfish," Sara affirmed. "They are beautiful scavengers. They live for a very long time."

"How old are these?" I asked, trying to imagine what a long time was for a fish.

"Well, the large white one is probably twenty years old."

"Twenty years old," I repeated. I was only thirteen. That fish was older than me. "Has it been in the pond all its life?" I asked.

"Yes, I imagine so," Sara said thoughtfully. "Just swimming around and around." Sara's eyes were far away, dreamy.

"How old was Grandmother?" I asked. "Wasn't she sixty-three?"

Suddenly it seemed very important. If a fish could be twenty, it didn't seem fair that Grandmother should live only until sixty-three.

"Yes, your grandmother lived to be sixty-three." Sara said this with finality. It sounded like a book being closed or a drawer being pushed shut. But I didn't want to shut the drawer yet.

"That seems young," I said irritably. "It doesn't seem fair." I paused as another question formed in my mind.

"Sara," I asked. "What do you think happens when a person dies?"

"I really don't know," Sara said honestly.

She was never one to feign knowledge.

"It's best to keep an open mind. Your grandmother, for example, hedged her bets. She practiced Buddhist, Christian, and Shinto rituals from time to time. I think if she'd known more about Hinduism or Judaism, she'd have practiced those too. I went to Catholic schools when I was a little girl, just like you. I suppose that makes me a Catholic." She didn't sound very convincing.

"I don't know what to believe," I confessed. Sara laughed. It was good to hear her laugh.

"Well, Ellen," she said, "you are only thirteen. There is still plenty of time for your belief to find you."

Sara was holding something back, some deep truth. I could feel it. She wasn't really a Catholic. She believed in something else. I looked back into the pond and watched the big white fish swimming around in the shadows. I didn't know what I believed, but I knew it had something to do with that fish.

"You are a *kami*, aren't you?" I said to the fish. Then I cast a sneaky look over at Sara. Her faced was filled with a mysterious pleasure.

"Oh, I see," she said sagely. "Maybe you believe in the *kami* way. Maybe I am American, Ellen, and you are the one who is Japanese. How strange that would be. How thoroughly unexpected."

Grandmother's funeral was simple. She was cremated. Death is no good thing in the Shinto religion. That religion celebrates life. Death is a state that requires purification, so the ceremonies were Buddhist instead. Sacrifices were made to the spirits of the ancestors in the Shinto way. Family members arrived for the funeral. My uncles divided and redivided the land. Sara gave a big bronze bell in Grandmother's name to the village. She decided to stay at Akishima in respect and mourning until Grandmother's soul joined that of her ancestors. I tried to walk through it all untouched. The household seemed to be caught up in a quiet river of sorrow. When the somber undercurrents became too much, I escaped outdoors.

To the right, on the kitchen and bathroom side of the house, was a small well that the household used for its water. Beyond that a dirt path led back past the barn and stable, past chickens and ducks, to a small murky pond choked with blue stones, catkins, and tall purple iris. Skirting this, the path led directly into a large stand of bamboo, a fourteen-foot-high wall of green that had been cut back to allow for ingress and exit on the opposite side. Upon leaving this bamboo forest, one arrived at the stone wall that surrounded the house, except that at this point, hidden by the rangy curtain of green, stones had been removed from the wall to create a gap that opened onto an almond orchard, two small stands of cherry trees, and field after carefully cultivated field. The path skirted through the trees and continued weaving along on the margins of the fields.

The earth directly on the opposite side of the wall was wet, black, and pungent. It smelled of mushrooms and moss. A large number of the fields, dedicated to rice, had already been flooded to encourage the rice seedlings, and the shining surfaces of those paddies gave the landscape the appearance of an uneven green surface upon which a huge mirror had fallen and shattered. It was toward these fields that I headed, surveying the property and patrolling the boundaries as my Japanese forebears must have done for as long as the lands had been theirs. From a certain point on the far side of the paddies, I could see the village where the field workers lived and the backside of the wall that surrounded the dwelling as it rose and fell with the face of the land, for a mile or so, on its serpentine crawl back to the village.

It was still too early for fruits and berries, and the rice was still young because, unlike the farms in the southern part of the country, Akishima would only have one rice crop each year. It was quiet out in the fields, so I roamed, unhindered, around the whole territory, exploring it bit by bit, charting its contours until I felt that, uncles or not, Akishima was mine. It was mine, not in the way that those yellowing old documents said, but in a deeper, more significant way. It was mine in the way the morning air rushed, sweet and apple-crisp, into my lungs; in the way new hay and manure filled my head with their sharp-scented aromas; in the way hyacinths opened like small stars in my heart and peeping quail filled me with curiosity and delight.

But there was one part of Akishima that I didn't explore, and that was the wooded shrine just inside the wall on the left-hand side of the property. From the garden and the fish ponds it was easy enough to follow the flagstone walk that meandered the quarter-mile toward it, but this was a sanctuary to which my uncle would often retire, and I didn't want to disturb him. I wanted very much for him to like me. It was my guess that the best way to do this was to stay out of his way. However, snooping has always been one of my weaknesses. In the end, I simply could not overcome my old inclination to spy.

"Why does Uncle Shiro go to that shrine every day?" I asked Sara one evening. We'd been at Akishima for nearly two weeks. The place had cast some kind of spell over us. Sara still showed no signs of rousing herself from the trance-like world of her sorrow. She didn't even seem really to miss Gene, Samuel, Mimi, and Gray. I didn't either, but I knew they missed Sara, and I was beginning to believe that we would never go back.

"He goes there to pray, Ellen. You are very nosy," she added, regarding me with a stony glare.

It was true. I was very nosy, and that is why I followed my uncle and, crouching in a thicket of pines, watched him bow twice, very deeply, and raise his hands, palms level to his face, clap four times, and bow again after lowering his hands. That's also why, when he left, I entered the grove and did the same thing that he had in front of the shrine in which a *kami* surely resided. I waited, breath held. Nothing happened. I waited, hoping for contact with a *kami*, but the only feeling I experienced was a wave of certainty that I had actually done something terribly wrong. It grew—a tiny panic, ripening and swelling in my stomach.

It was a sour and sickening feeling. It bubbled into my throat and filled my mouth with a nauseating cottony taste. I felt like I was being watched by hundreds of eyes, hidden up in the pines, like the big eyes on the tail of a peacock. I closed my eyes and tried to inhale. The wind around me seemed to get stronger, seemed to move through the trees with a sound like a rattle, like a waterfall, like the dissonant clang of small bells.

Then I heard a soft drumbeat, a gentle thumping that threaded its way through the sounds of the wind. I stood very still, listening intently. The noises wound around one another in a hypnotic way. They created a mystical music. I listened harder, bewitched by the sounds. It felt like the music was blowing right through me, as though I were riddled with holes. I realized then that the wind and my breath were one and the same and the timpani was my heartbeat.

I opened my eyes and looked up at the pines that towered above me. They seemed to look down on me in sadness. I felt like a prawn at the bottom of a very big bowl. The bowl opened up into the sky. The pine trees were nothing more than hand-painted images, climbing the gentle slope of its sides. Outside me, outside my body, the grove was so quiet I could feel the silence in a rhythm like the ripples that form when you drop a rock into the water. Silence has its movement. I lifted one of my hands and watched it float like a white cloud, past my face and out, settling downward at my side. My other hand repeated the pattern, reaching out to the opposite side. Then I stepped and stopped with a little bend of my knee—in one direction first, then the other. The movement wormed into me, pulling like a string. I swayed this way and that, let my head go limp, a big flower lolling on its too-thin stem. It felt good to let myself drift back and forth like a petal tossed on a wind.

I had closed my eyes, and behind my lids a dazzling white light was dancing like a silver koi. It twirled and swayed in the darkness. *The sun. The sun. It must be the sun*, I thought, opening my eyes.

Poised on the stone walkway that led into the copse, my great-uncle stood, astonished, an expression of consternation occupying his narrow face. My eyes met his, and I felt my mouth open, but no sound came out of me. I looked at the great circle of sky above me, at the pines that surrounded the shrine. I looked at my uncle, at the thick carpet of grass under my feet. There were very few options for action. In fact, in my heart, I could see only one. My eyes found my uncle's and locking upon them held there, fiercely focused, like someone navigating by compass and star. Wary at first, then encouraged by the strong sense of clarity that seemed to be widening inside me, I continued my very strange dance. My uncle watched me in silence, then he, too, closed his eyes and turned, walking slowly back up the path toward the house.

A few days later Sara woke up from the lethargy that had possessed her. When Gene called and she heard the voices of Samuel, Mimi, and Gray, a look of alarm spread over her face.

"I miss my babies," she confessed, aghast, like a sleeper who has been roused from a coma and discovered that months have gone by.

In no time at all our bags were all packed. Sara communicated to my uncle her desire to go home.

"Stay, Sara," he implored. "You have not been here long enough."

"Uncle, I cannot, I miss my children," Sara said.

"Then I shall miss you," my uncle replied, acquiescing with a slight nod of his head. A sad smile tugged at the corners of his mouth, then resumed its position of waiting. "Please, then will you leave Ellen?" my uncle requested politely.

"Oh, Uncle, I can't," Sara apologized. "Ellen has already missed far too much school. I'm afraid she has to go back with me."

"A pity," he replied, "but I think," he added, "she has also learned something here. So, Ellen?" he asked, addressing me directly.

"Yes, Uncle," I responded, my eyes meeting his.

Sara stepped closer to me. I felt her hand on my elbow. "Ellen has school," she repeated, this time a little more firmly.

"Yes," my uncle said, closing his eyes and slightly inclining his head.

"Ellen, you will come back?" he asked kindly, moving closer to me, his melancholy smile forming for my ambush.

"Yes, Uncle," I promised. "I will come back."

"We will be here," he said, and I knew he would, knew that Akishima would always be there, waiting for me to return. Sara finished her packing. My uncle showered us with gifts. I prepared for my final farewells.

I did not want to leave Akishima. Spring was stirring in the forests and fields teasing the land into bloom. Dazzling sunlight seemed to halo the farmlands, its brilliance mirrored on the shimmering surfaces of the flooded rice paddies. Following my favorite path, I crossed behind the well and cut past barnyards and stables, whispering good-byes to the chickens and ducks, to the black-maned horse, to the dragonflies and the water spiders squatting, pontoons afloat on the pond's brackish surface. Climbing out through the broken part of the wall, I threaded my way through the almond and cherry orchards, heading out toward the water-soaked paddies. It was quiet, the farm nearly unpeopled except for a handful of workers who waded through water-filled rice fields bending and standing, replanting the young rice shoots that were already thrusting their way up through the mud.

A woman with a child on her back and another at her side walked along the margin of the fields, headed home, probably to make lunch for her family. It was very warm out, and it felt more like summer than spring. "Time passes so swiftly," I thought.

I was picking my way along on the network of muddy paths that girded the fields, watching the sunlight ricochet off the water when I saw her. At first I thought she was just a mirage, a figure clad in diaphanous white flickering on the horizon. No one else seemed to see her. The workers continued their stoop-and-bend over the flooded earth, unaware of her presence. From where I stood, she seemed thin, but also quite tall even from that distance, and she appeared to watch me as thoughtfully as I was watched her. It was all very odd. I couldn't imagine why this woman in a flowing formal kimono would be standing in the middle of a rice paddy, but something about her struck me as very appropriate, the way a lotus looks floating on the face of a lake. She turned away from me as I watched her, and I noticed that her long black hair had been gathered, midback, in a ribbon. The ribbon seemed to be white as well, and her dark hair fanned down from the point at which it was gathered, falling far below her waist in a shining ebony column. She was actually moving away from me, seeming to glide over the watery surfaces of the paddies. She progressed for some yards, then paused for a while, stopping to turn and look back at me.

She was very beautiful, shimmering there in the distance, like a lily rising from a swamp. I wanted to catch up with her and find out who she was. I started out after her, picking my way along the fields' muddy margins. The mud splashed up, covering my shoes in sediment, oozing into them and staining my socks.

Meanwhile, the woman seemed to hang there on the water's surface, like a thing rooted, waiting for me. As I got closer, I could see framed in the jet-black wings of her long bangs a Kabuki-white visage. Her face was expressionless. Something about her reminded me of my grandmother, though she didn't look like her at all. Grandmother was sixty-three. This woman was young, twenty perhaps, the same age as the koi in the fish pond. She observed my awkward progress with the greatest of patience, as if she were used to counting time in centuries. Her lips were a very bright red. Pursed, they looked like a Chinese seal. Her eyes were like bits of dark glass. The sunlight poured over her in a halo of brilliance, but she seemed much brighter than the sun. She waited until I was only a few yards away, then turned, and moved on, as if expecting me to follow. I did.

We were far from the house. I wasn't sure where. The rice paddies seemed to stretch out in their endless watery jigsaw. The sun was directly above us. It was probably noon. There were no longer any workers about. The woman moved very quickly. I was getting tired of trying to keep up with her. And although she would wait, and although she was very compelling, I was ready to give up and stop following her. As if reading my mind, she stopped. She did not move until I was almost upon her. I got very excited as I drew nearer, stumbled on the muddy bank at the paddy's edge, slipped in the silt, and fell into the water, which came up past my knees.

Now that I was close, I saw that her feet did not seem to break the water's surface at all. Her kimono appeared to float over it. It was clear that she had no feet. I was shocked. I nearly fell one more time, my feet sliding again on the mud of the bank.

She was moving away from me again.

"Wait, Lady. Wait," I called out to her. "Are you a *kami*?" She spun around quickly and faced me.

Her face was stern. Her hair glinted blue-black as a myna bird's wing in the sunlight. Again I was reminded strongly of my grandmother, although this young woman, with her starkly classical features, didn't really look anything like her. She held up a hand as if warning me not to come closer. "Look," she said. "Namako. Look at you." She was speaking in Japanese, but I seemed to understand every word she said. In fact, it really wasn't like speaking at all. She didn't have to say anything. I seemed to read her mind.

I rushed forward, stumbling toward her, slipping again in the clay-colored mud. The woman moved back as if afraid to get near me. "Do not defile me," she warned.

"Wait, Lady," I pleaded. "Why are you here? Who are you?"

Shaking her head, she reached into the bodice of her kimono and pulled something out. It was a sea cucumber, and it was alive. She held it aloft like a talisman. It was wet. The wetness trickled down her arm and disappeared into the wing-like sleeve of her kimono. Then she spoke again. I was shocked by the intensity of her speech.

"Do you know what this is?" she asked, holding the sea cucumber high over her head.

I nodded my head yes.

"Yes," she said tersely, without waiting for my verbal reply. "This is a sea cucumber. Namako. Na-ma-ko. Raw child," she added. Her thin eyebrows, joined like caterpillars making an inverted V in the center of her forehead. "Namako, the world will devour you. Yes, the world will devour you, so you'd better be tasty."

The words burst from her with great passion. "You'd better be tasty. That way the gods will be pleased."

She closed her eyes and bowed her head slowly, as if waiting for some mysterious ax to fall. The sea cucumber wriggled about in her hand. Then she held it out to me, and I grabbed it. I could feel it struggling. It was slippery and powerful. It had a very strong smell. I gripped it tightly, amazed that it should feel so incredibly real when the lady herself was clearly a ghost.

"Lady," I asked breathlessly, "are you a *kami*?"

The lady regarded me narrowly. "Perhaps I am a *kami*," she offered reluctantly.

"Which *kami* are you?" I asked.

"Why?" she asked. "Why do you wish to know?"

"Because I want to ask you a favor."

"What might that be?"

"Have you seen my grandmother? She is new to the *kami* world. I'm wondering if she is there?"

"Your grandmother," the lady said, "is newly dead. She has not yet purified her soul in a way to join her ancestors."

"Can I speak to her?" I pleaded. "I have things that I want to ask her."

"Of course you cannot speak to her," the lady responded,

apparently appalled by my audacity. "You are human, so dirty. Clearly, she cannot come near you. You hang on to that cucumber," she warned. "It's a gift, do not lose it."

I didn't really think it was such a great gift. It was one thing to study a sea cucumber, dead, in a jar, and quite another to hold one in my hand.

"It looks like it wants to bite me," I muttered.

"Don't be ridiculous," the woman said. "You are far more likely to bite it than it is to bite you.

"Listen," she said, "when the soul is pure, the water will always turn clear."

She said this quickly and with a great deal of feeling. Then she turned her back to me again and set forth once more over the paddies. Her retreating form quivered in the sunlight like a desert mirage. I didn't follow this time. I watched her disappear into the haze of the horizon.

When the soul is pure, the water will always turn clear, I repeated to myself, looking down at my mud-soaked shoes and socks, at the dirty wet hem of my skirt.

I was a mess, and Sara would not believe that I'd gotten this way in pursuit of a *kami*.

A *kami*. I had seen a *kami*, a beautiful *kami*, and she had spoken to me. Soon my grandmother would be with her, too, with the great rock-earth prince *kami* and the princess swift autumn *kami*. I would have to tell Sara that. Grandmother would be with the *kami* of the winds, the *kami* of the mountains, the *kami* of the rivers and ponds.

When the soul is pure, the water will always turn clear.

I chanted this to myself as I slogged back to the edge of the mire-filled paddy and clambered up onto the bank. Standing, rooted again on the slippery ribbon of land that bordered the fields, I suddenly felt as though I were racing along on my bicycle—going fast, very fast. I threw my head back to look up into the sky and then twirled around in a slow full circle, scanning the landscape in every direction.

All about me spring was forcing its way into the world. Everywhere I looked, nature was exploding—robust and unforgiving. The tender grasses were already pushing their way up through the clay. Soon the fields would be green, and rice would cover the land. I could feel my own body stirring and changing. The pinch of the air, the stabs of bright green all around me were intoxicating. I drew several sharp breaths and realized, with a start, that the sea cucumber had, at some point, ceased struggling. I looked down at my hand in alarm, expecting to find a dead creature hanging there, throttled in my grasp. There was no sea cucumber in my hand at all. In its place I clutched a fistful of rice and mud. Rice and mud, what was that? It was Akishima. It was me. It was my grandmother's world.

I squinted back into the distance at the path that the *kami* had traveled. The shining jigsaw of water-soaked paddies swam together into a single bright lake that mirrored the sky. It was as if the pieces of a puzzle had finally fallen together. At that moment I wanted to laugh. I wanted to laugh and shout and run. I wanted to sing, and I wanted to dance. I wanted to celebrate wildly because out there in the fields, in the violence of spring, I had left the sadness and the severity of that ancient house and my mother's mourning far behind me. I had found a *kami*, a *kami* who filled me with hope for my grandmother, for myself, for every part of the world, one who promised that the water would always turn clear. It seemed I had finally found a trail through the lies and the secrets. I had found a place to come back to, and I knew, at last, the way that I must go to get there.

The House

Do not own the house;
you may become it.
You may become dark
as the stairwell
or cramped
as the basement garage.
You may love the sunroom
too dearly.

A hole in the roof
could cause
overwhelming despair,
the faint odor of mold
disturbing your dreams.
You might collect mice,
voracious squirrels,
relatives.

If your family had homes,
being sufficiently
created by them,
live in rented rooms.
Look for high ceilings,
avoid carpeting.
Allow no window coverings.

If you must own a house,
do not live in it.
If all else fails,
travel often.

The Lure of Hoodoos

(travel essay; excerpts)

Sedona is due north of Scottsdale, a straight shot up Highway 179, but this little town is easy to miss. At night its sprinkling of lights is no match for a big desert sky studded with stars. By day, the soft hues and lines of its predominantly Southwestern-style architecture are lost in the shadow of a landscape where three-hundred-million-year-old cliffs of limestone, shale, basalt, and sandstone climb to form sheer walls, towers, and elegant minarets.

We arrived at the Scottsdale Airport in the late afternoon, rented a car, and set out at once on our drive through the twilit desert. Not even our California backgrounds in wide, wild expanses could prepare us for the magic of that scrub-strewn terrain. We saw ten- and twelve-foot saguaro cactus that looked like lonesome cowboys heading on home to the ranch. Twilight played coyote trickster with shadow and light. In the gathering gloom, squat scrub chaparral—manzanita, mesquite, and shrub live oak—began to take on the forms of various animals: jackrabbits, prairie dogs, and ring-tailed cats. The rocks themselves seemed to come alive, twisting and snaking upward. Then darkness fell like a tomahawk, stars opened up like tiny eyes in the sky, and a full moon rose over the desert. It started to rain—a fast, snappy splattering. We found out later that this was the monsoon season, and these feverish bursts of precipitation would prove to be one of the kernels of our private set of myths. But back to the trip.

We were hurtling down that rattlesnake of a road. We screeched to a halt on a crescent of gravel and dust at the roadside and got out of the car to stretch our legs. It was humid and cool. The moon was a smudge behind a halo of moisture. On either side of us, the desert rose in fabulous hoodoos, in snaggle-toothed spires. We thought we heard a wolf howl, an owl hoot. We found ourselves speaking in whispers, like kids at a campfire. A spooky feeling came over us. We got back into the car. It wouldn't start. Not even the comforting cough of the ignition greeted our efforts. Only silence. Two ordinary women on a desert road—was this the Twilight Zone? Since Samantha could not start the car, I tried. It started right up. We turned nervously to one another, eyes as big as saucers, eyebrows jumping to the top of our foreheads.

"We're almost there," I said.

Samantha nodded.

We thought we missed Sedona completely. In the inky darkness, the eerily lit entrance of Los Abrigados, a luxury resort that we'd investigate later, seemed to mark the town, and we were quickly past it. But the road went on to a form a T. At the top of that T was Highway 89A, main street, Sedona. Our hotel, rather inappropriately named L'Auberge de Sedona, was tucked off this main thoroughfare. A labyrinth of rustic cabins and oaks obscured our approach to the lodge. Great for families, I noted, thoughtfully regarding Samantha's soon-to-be-showing stomach. Our room for the night was an aerie of an apartment perched on the hillside overlooking a canyon. It was ten o'clock by the time we sat down to eat and midnight by the time we got back to our room. We went out like a couple of well-used candles.

By six the next morning, the sun had already muscled its way into our room. Along with the heat, we were showered in an incredible wraparound sound. I couldn't place it. It sounded like cards being shuffled over a P.A. system. It sounded like a million maracas being shaken at once. The sound seemed to swell from the forest below, a beckoning mystery. Within minutes the more proximate hiss and splash of my shower joined it.

In our room, a plethora of newsletters and brochures promised Disney-like adventures, replete with Native American rituals, wildlife encounters, spiritual awakenings, and pink Jeeps. Sideshows and extravaganzas. We were ready to meet Sedona head-on, but like any good scouts, we first opted to explore our more immediate surroundings. We had to walk down the hillside into Oak Creek Canyon and discover the source of that sound.

The rattling rose and fell around us on our short descent into the canyon. The fat faces of daisies gazed up at us. June bugs as big as hummingbirds buzzed us. It grew cooler as we closed in on the creek. Irises grew in the small patches of shadow. Oak Creek was so clear that we could see the flat gray-green rocks resting like turtles beneath the water on the opposite side. Ducks cut slow ciphers into the water's glassy surface. I began to feel drowsy. That's when I met it—my first denizen of the desert. I came face to face with a fat grasshopper with leopard markings and pearl-gray eyes at the top of its head. It was clinging to one of the green rushes at the side of the creek that cut through the canyon, and it was staring at me, its thorax heaving. I bent closer, until it was inches away from my cheek. Clearly, this was one of those monumental meetings in which creatures from disparate worlds connect spiritually and exchange greetings. It didn't seem frightened. Why had it singled me out? What did it have to say? Suddenly, I was aware of hundreds of similarly bead-like eyes. I had not even seen them—thousands of grasshoppers. They perched on all of the rushes around the creek. They peered from the short grass at my feet. They were the source of the ocean of sound that rolled in great waves through the canyon. It seemed as if some great truth had just been revealed, but I wasn't sure what. I was overwhelmed with the sense of missing some significant point. I looked around for Samantha. She was sitting on a red rock some distance away, looking over the creek, still as a sandstone statue, already one with the landscape.

My second encounter with a denizen of the desert occurred after breakfast, when our guide arrived. Samantha and I had selected what we thought was the most interesting tour. Affiliated with the local bookstore, it promised smudge sticks, cornmeal offerings, and prayer-feather rituals. For a guide, we did not get a sun-burned mercenary or a native mystic; we got Jill, a tiny transplant from Tennessee by way of New York, street-smart, trouble-scarred, and tough as a prairie chicken.

"Look," Sam said, trying to explain our slightly cynical point of view, "we're not Woo woos."

"Woo woo?" Jill asked, raising her eyebrow.

"You know, New Agers," Samantha explained.

Actually, I was beginning to have my doubts, after my brief communion with the grasshopper.

"Yeah," I seconded heartily.

"Well, good," said Jill. "Neither am I. Now that we've got that out of the way, let's get going."

We set out in our minivan through a landscape that, because of its beauty, has been a pilgrimage point for generations. Jill explained that the Native Americans measure time in worlds. The rock face that towered around us accurately recorded these incarnations—ocean five times, freshwater lake two times, swamp twice, desert twice—and each incarnation had sculpted another layer of personality.

"So why did you guys choose a Vortex Tour?" Jill asked with studied carelessness, squinting into the sunlight.

Samantha piped up, "We want to know more about the vortexes."

"Vortices," Jill corrected with a snakelike hiss of the sibilants. I pictured the warning flick of a rattler's tail. "I prefer 'vortices.'

"Well, you picked the right spot. The vortices are power spots, places where energy collects and swirls. The Bermuda Triangle is a vortex. There are vortices all over the world. You know about them. They're where mysterious events occur. People are naturally attracted to them. We have seen vortices in Sedona. Some are negative, some are positive. Let's start right here. See that rock over there."

Our eyes followed the apocalyptic point of Jill's finger to an enormous bluff that rose like a callused red giant from the low plane of the desert.

"That's Apache Leap. It's a powerful negative vortex. I tried to climb it once." Jill frowned. "I couldn't. Fear gripped me. Do you know what happened there? The story goes that when General Crook was rounding up Native Americans to put them on reservations, the few free remaining Apache got wind of it. The braves, all the men, got on their horses and rode. They rode right up to the top of that cliff where it looked as if they had nowhere to go, and then...they leapt over. All the braves in the party plunged to their deaths rather than face white man's captivity. Maybe they stayed free.

"And see that beautiful swathe of green stretching beneath the leap. You'd like to say it's a well-tended Native American burial ground, a kind of memorial, right? Wrong. It's a golf course. Yep, a golf course. I guess some people are immune to bad vibes."

Our guide was silent for a while. She seemed deep in rumination. Suddenly she stuck a thin arm out the window again, gesturing toward an immense dome-shaped rock formation up ahead, to the left of us.

"That over there's Bell Rock," she said. "Remember 1989, the Harmonic Convergence, when all of the planets supposedly lined up and big things were supposed to happen? Well, some of the people let on that Bell Rock was a spaceship that was meant to take people away from this planet, which was slated to be destroyed. They even sold tickets. And people bought 'em! But, as you can see, old Bell Rock never took off, and I don't think those ticket holders ever got their money back.

"Yeah," she laughed, "it can get pretty weird here, and if you ever want that kind of action, you just go to the Coffee Pot Restaurant in West Sedona. You'll find them there any day of the week, those Woo woos you're talking about, playing flutes and dangling crystals. Heck, these people have to consult a pendulum before they go to the bathroom."

...The desert was silent and still. We looked back at Jill, who was leaning against the minivan taking long slow pulls on the rest of her cigarette. The midday sun washed over us, warm and soporific. Lizards blinked up at us. Time seemed to stop. Jill had told us that Cathedral Rock was a feminine vortex. A holy place for the Native Americans, the women had come here for centuries to bear children. Shaped like a coronet, it's several turrets encircled a lower, rocky center. I watched Samantha, my dear friend, framed in the months before motherhood, as she moved ahead, picking her way past walls of rust-colored stone, a solitary figure climbing up into the high lap of that natural sanctuary. I could feel it—a kind of gentle tug. Sedona was pulling me into another dimension. It was a wordless dimension of feelings and a heightened sensitivity, a sense of interconnectedness with everything around me. It scared me a little. Perhaps this is what Jill felt on the trail to the summit of Apache Leap. The terrain I hike through is generally one of physical landmarks, of objective reality. Here, in Sedona, things shifted into a kind of double exposure, the external and internal landscapes seemed to have superimposed...

Let's Phosphoresce by Intellection

(after a painting by Roberto Matta)

Matrix or matrices

revision

etching or mezzotint
soft sound
intaglio

revision

paper color, surface texture, relative absorbency

revision

composition
age

manipulation of the plate and ink

revision

red hair and inky skin

revision

soft yellow sky

revision

more age, more age

revision

dry point

Snake Karma

(travel essay)

The fer-de-lance is an extremely venomous snake. More deadly than a rattlesnake, this pit viper is also missing its genetic cousin's one redeeming virtue—a warning rattle. It strikes suddenly, and when the *terciopelo* bites, it injects into your system, with the deadly syringes of its fangs, a substance that is part neural toxin, part anticoagulant and part digestive enzyme, so that the process of digestion can begin at once. You don't have long once it bites: a minute, maybe two.

We were not looking for snakes. My friend Dixie and I were looking for quetzals, for scarlet macaws, for beautiful birds. We were just north of Panama, on the Osa Peninsula, often called the armpit of Costa Rica, known for gigantic Corcovado, one of Costa Rica's most imposing national parks. Comprised of acres of virgin rainforest, it's the slithering grounds of some of the world's most dangerous *serpientes.* Our eyes were fixed on the thick, epiphyte-laden jungle canopy overhead, but in the back of our minds lurked serpents. Was that an eyelash viper that we saw snaking its way up the side of a tree? A *terciopelo* waiting patiently for us in the tall dry savannah grasses?

I'd just finished reading a cautionary tale by biologist Donald Perry. In his book, *Life Above the Jungle Floor,* Perry relives his encounter with a local who was bitten by a fer-de-lance. The last time he saw this man, the fellow was in a rowboat being taken back to the mainland, bleeding from his mouth and all of his pores. This is a gruesome image. I shared it with Dixie. Dixie and I were staying at Lapa Rios, a resort built in the middle of snake territory. We'd been told the snakes were in abeyance, that they used to turn up in the rooms.

Before I left home, Lawrence, my husband, who is entertained by these things, shared all of his snake stories. He told tales about rattlesnakes and boa constrictors. He recalled a National Geographic special that he'd seen about the Amazon. In one exciting sequence, he recounted, one Native American guide went upriver to fish, leaving the main party. The Native American didn't return. The party began to worry. Later, a twenty-foot Anaconda came floating down the river with a big bulge in its center. Unable to move, it was easily caught and killed. The party, suspecting the worst, cut open the snake, and there, of course, was their Native American guide—all in one piece, but no longer alive.

"I'm not going to the Amazon," I said dryly.

"There'll be plenty of snakes in Costa Rica," Lawrence assured me.

I was outfitted, I thought, against snakes. Dixie, in spite of my warnings, wore high-top tennis shoes which she replaced with rubber boots for wet, jungle trekking. But I was prepared. I am the happy owner of the world's most perfect and attractive pair of waterproof Timberland hiking boots. These boots have hiked through the Death Valley Badlands. They have been immersed in the muddy bottom of the Okefenokee Swamp.

"I'm safe from snakes," I announced to Augusto, our guide, proudly tapping my boot. He smiled and shook his head slowly.

"They bite through animal skins," he laughed. "Your boots cannot stop them."

I must have deflated like a week-old balloon.

Then, suspecting the impact his comment had made, and in an effort to hearten us, he whipped out a snakebite kit to give us a demonstration of his medical prowess. This kit consisted of a small plastic glass, a match, and a piece of cotton. According to Augusto, all jungle guides must carry them. To demonstrate, Augusto doused the cotton in alcohol, threw it into the bottom of the glass, lit the match, threw it in too, and applied this to the selected body part—in this case, his side. Instantly, all of his flesh was sucked up into the glass.

The whole operation took only a few (maybe thirty) seconds—fast enough, he assured us, to prevent the poison's spread.

Later that day, on our hike through the rainforest, Augusto grew suddenly very serious. We had reached the edge of the forest. Strangler figs retreated from land that had been planted and cleared. Banana palms formed long, leafy corridors edged in high, sun-bleached savannah grass. Augusto walked ahead of us, arms stretched out dramatically. He was muttering something in Spanish. I asked him what he was doing. "I am clearing the path," he said, his eyes sparkling like obsidian beads.

"Tell me what you are saying," I pleaded. He tried to teach me his chant. It was a strange poem in which Jesus figured. I repeated it in Spanish and promptly forgot it, trusting his odd mix of Native American and Christian lore to see us through. It worked like a charm.

That night Dixie and I prepared for bed in the usual way. We washed and hung out the clothes that would never dry because of the damp. Every day they made great progress toward further fermentation. Every night we rinsed them out to reduce the thick, yeasty smell that swelled through our bungalow and threatened to throttle us. Then we filled the room with the muffled tattoo of our palms slapping against the sheets, condemning to perdition the insects that had managed to permeate our protective membrane of mosquito netting. We sat up in our beds with our maps, our reference materials, and our Deet, an insecticide strong enough to remove lacquer and melt plastic. The rainforest night and breeze blew in through the rattan walls. It was quiet. Suddenly, high and tremulous, a scream broke the silence. It was right outside our door.

"Of course, a woman's scream breaks the silence," I snapped. "How predictable. How stereotypically lame."

"Maybe she saw a cockroach," Dixie offered, bringing to mind a particularly large specimen that we had encountered on one of our late-night rambles.

"Well," I observed snottily, "if she's afraid of bugs, she shouldn't have come to a rainforest."

Dixie and I decided to ignore the scream and the commotion right outside our door—footsteps, yelling, muffled noises. Sensationalism. We didn't want to be bothered. Besides we had, by now, managed to kill every bug that crawled, wriggled, or flew within our protective netting. Our seals were complete. We didn't want to invite further intrusion by breaking the mosquito net barrier. At breakfast the next morning we heard the whole creepy honeymoon story. Two newlyweds had taken a moonlit walk down the winding resort steps, so reminiscent of *l'escalera de mono*, a vine called "monkey ladder." The new bride told us that she turned her flashlight on right outside our door. I had to wonder what life-saving instinct had prompted this action. There, inches from her sandaled foot, was a six-foot fer-de-lance. She backed up slowly. Then she let out her scream. Hotel staff arrived and dispatched the snake. They were sorry they'd done this. Toxic snakes are a fundamental part of rainforest ecologies. It's best to adopt a laissez-faire attitude. I told the new bride that we'd pegged her for some sissy girl, squealing because she'd seen a bug. She told us about the time a poisonous green snake slid across her belly at a beach in Indonesia.

"Everyone says I have Snake Karma," she added with pride.

That same morning a group of surfers reported killing a fifteen-foot boa constrictor at a spot a few miles up the coast. It had a cotamundi still in its stomach. The cotamundi is a pleasant animal that looks like a cross between an anteater and a raccoon. It's bite-sized for a fifteen-foot boa. This cotamundi's eyes were still open. The surfers said they'd cut up the snake and eaten some of it. It tasted, they said, like very tough chicken.

Snake stories intrigue me. My favorites are those that others have shared. Swapping tales one night with Kevin, a friend of mine, I was told what must be a classic. Kevin was on a hike somewhere in the northeast portion of the U.S. He had fallen behind his group. He was shocked to find a rattlesnake on the trail in front of him. He saw it in time to leap for the bushes. Shaken, he gave the snake and the trail a wide berth.

He quickly caught up with the group. That evening, at home, when he took off his clothes, he noticed two fang marks right over his boot. The rattlesnake had bitten him (fortunately, it was a dry bite; snakes only inject venom some of the time). It had bitten him, and he hadn't even know it. The snake was that fast! I flashed back on my own snake encounters: the cobra I'd seen trailside on a run through a Malaysian cemetery; the highly poisonous European adder I'd encountered one morning when I was running alone on a mountain called Ramundberget, in Sweden; the green mamba that liked to camp out on the top of my tent in Kenya; the rattlesnake I met one fine Easter morning right here, in my Bay Area home. I'd narrowly missed them. Or they had missed me. I shuddered.

Give me the prayers and charms and chants. Snake karma—who needs it?

Running the Lion City Hash

(travel essay)

"Want to run the hash with me tonight?" Doug asked on my second morning in Singapore. We were driving back from the wet market near Bukit Timah, having breakfasted among hawkers' stalls, bean curd, spices, and produce. It seemed an odd question. We'd only just met.

"All right," I heard myself answer. Doug was a pleasant, easygoing guy. I was up for a little excitement. Besides, my husband, Lawrence, had vouched for him. Lawrence and Doug were colleagues. I'd be in good hands.

By the time Doug came around to my hotel to fetch me at six that evening, I'd worked myself into a state of mild agitation.

"We're meeting the others just outside the city in the outback, the wilds," Doug announced as I slid gingerly into his car. We were going to run the Lion City Hash—five miles through thicket and jungle. I burrowed into the seat next to him, very nervous. It was my first time running the hash.

A drinking club with a running problem

It all began in 1938, north of Singapore, in Kuala Lumpur in what is today Malaysia. Several residents of the Royal Selangor Club, a watering hole affectionately known as the Spotted Dog, decided, in the spirit of mockery and mismanagement, to start a runners' club. It's believed that the group of colonials from Britain and Australia—Albert Stephen Ignatius Gispert, Cecil H. Lee, Frederick "Horse" Thompson, and "Torch" Bennett among them—launched the enterprise as a way of prolonging their drinking and fornicating capabilities. They patterned their runs after the eighteenth-century English children's game of Hare and Hounds (ahead of the others, the "hare" sets a trail using bits of paper, then the "hounds" give chase, following the paper), and christened their club the Hash House Harriers—Hash House in honor of the lackluster food at the Selangor Club chambers, Harriers for the hounds.

An international running club—part secret society, part frat party—the concept caught on among expats assigned to out-of-the-way parts of the Far East like Malaysia and Brunei. WWII induced a hiatus; the flame flickered until it was rekindled in 1962 when the Singapore Hash House Harriers formed. Today, the popularity of the enterprise has spread well beyond Asia. An alphabetical list of the community worldwide will take you from Aalborg, Denmark, to Zagreb, Croatia with around two thousand hashes in between. There are around a hundred thousand participants, or hashers, involved. But the Singapore hash is the second longest consecutively running hash on the planet; the first being the Mother Hash that began in Kuala Lumpur.

If you have half a mind to join a hash that's all you need

I had no idea where we were. Clearly well beyond Singapore's carefully groomed dominion—a weedy bushland of woodlet and scrub stretched before us. The hare had chosen this spot. Somewhere through the tangle of frond and vine lay the one true trail and several false ones designed to confound us. It is the hare's job to set a spectacular and surprising trail. Preceding the pack, sometimes by minutes (Live Hare), sometimes by days (Dead Hare), the hare scatters four by four inch pieces of paper—these days hares also use lumps of flour—over the designated miles. Hares have been known to go overboard. Hashers have fallen into manure pits. Once, in Kuala Lumpur, hares got an entire pack of forty runners lost. The runners had to spend the night in the jungle.

Doug and I rolled in at the start site much later than planned. Most of the runners had gathered, and the hash was just about to begin. I noticed that the air was fraught with a strange tension that seemed to spark into short bursts of hilarity. Furtively, because I only knew Doug and we'd arrived late, I checked out my running companions. They were a motley collection of women and men—tall and short, heavy and thin. No one looked particularly gazelle-like, although there were several obvious athletes in the crowd. We milled about for a bit in vaguely social disorganization, then before I knew it, we were off.

The pack thinned almost immediately, the front running bastards, as they are referred to in hash parlance, darting forward to lead the chase. If there is a false trail, they are the first to encounter it. If there's a dead end, they are the first to be fooled. Doug followed paper. I followed Doug. Up ahead I could see runners sprinting off into the bushes, turning maddening circles at checkpoints, yelling "checking, checking" to let the pack know that they'd lost the trail, then "on on" to let us know that they'd found it. Doug and I were somewhere in the middle of the runners, dodging the rocks, mud, and trees that sprouted up from the path. We broke through forest and into a clearing. The hare's trail took us around an old cemetery, seemingly abandoned, all overgrown. Then we were back in the woods again, climbing hills, jumping streams, huffing and puffing our way to the finish. The heat was oppressive. Mosquitoes, attracted to our perspiring persons, swarmed us. *Malaria*, I thought briefly. *Dengue fever*. Then I brushed those thoughts from my mind. It was loads of fun, the scenery superb, I was having a wonderful time.

Doug was behind me; I had decided to pass him on the previous slope. My eye caught a movement at the side of the trail. A large snake quivered to life and rose to watch me run by.

"Did you see that snake?," I yelled to Doug as he panted up the rise behind me.

"Yeah," he wheezed. "Cobra."

No one on a run, I was subsequently informed, has ever been killed by a viper. An Okinawan hasher was bitten by a poisonous snake once, but he received antivenin and lived. I tried to pay closer attention to the immediate landscape, but it was useless. It was starting to get dark and everything—twig, boulder, curling liana—was beginning to look like a threat.

Beer is the punishment for a shortcutting bastard

Dusk was falling by the time we arrived at the final checkpoint, also known as the "on in." Cars had been moved, and the sweaty band was clustered about them in a roughly circular configuration. There was a bonfire burning. It looked as if some mysterious ritual was about to commence. In the back of the circle was a hatchback car. In front of the car were a couple of coolers. The coolers were filled with beer. Next to the coolers stood the Religious Advisor, or RA, a kind of master of ceremonies who was about to administer "down-downs." Down-downs are punishments for various infractions. Misdemeanors can include anything from wearing new shoes to saying something stupid like, "Don't you find the outdoors refreshing?" Designer running clothes are an infraction, for example, as is having a serious discussion. The hash is supposed to offer release from day-to-day pressures. Bringing these into the hash is a major offense. The most popular down-down is chug-a-lugging a twelve-ounce beer, but down-downs can also include belting out a bawdy tune for the congregation or sitting bare-bottom on a block of ice.

Of course, I knew none of this at the time. It was my first hash, and Doug had been very stingy with details. All I saw was a guy in the middle of a beer-thirsty group singling people out to come up and do ridiculous things. Doug had a big grin on his face.

"This is weird," I said.

He laughed. "This is my favorite part."

I remember once, when I was in high school, going to a religious rally with a girlfriend. It was held in a football stadium. At one point everyone in the stands went down to the center of the field to be saved. The cute guy sitting next to me and I were the only ones left in the stands. "Don't you want to be saved?" I asked archly, thinking I'd found a friend. He smiled broadly.

"Don't need to," he beamed. "I already have been." Uhhh... that was the same feeling I had just experienced with Doug.

The whim of the pack is the only rule

By this time we were surrounded by darkness. People were seriously loaded, and the RA's accounts of embarrassment and misadventure sounded like one long slur to me. In these far more judicious times, the imbibing of copious amounts of liquor during hashes is no longer strictly required. Water and soda down-downs are allowed, but some teetotalers prefer to simply pour their beer on themselves and on others. Songs were sung. Everyone started chanting "down, down, down" as more of the reticent stepped into the raucous circle. Then the RA began baptizing people. He started handing out nicknames. Hash names are generally earned. They are bestowed upon new runners as the pack becomes familiar with them, usually because they've acquired notoriety through some foolish act or characteristic trait. These monikers are a form of honor and recognition by the collective. Fortunately, I hadn't distinguished myself in any way, and I relished my anonymity. I hadn't turned heads either by my performance or my lack thereof. I was safe. But now something else was happening. As the activity began to reach a crescendo, the group started calling out for a virgin. I had a very sick feeling in the pit of my stomach. I felt like the happy little pig at a luau when she suddenly realizes that she's the star of the show.

"What's a virgin?" I asked Doug warily.

He took a long, slow swallow of beer and leered down at me. "You are," he smiled.

"I don't think so," I argued, shaking my head.

"Yes, you are," said Doug. "You've never run a hash before. You're a newboot, a newbie."

I looked up at Doug, distrusting him mightily. Suddenly everything came clear. I'd been invited to the run as a sacrifice.

"What if I don't want to be," I pleaded.

Doug took another long swallow of beer, as if weighing the situation, my fate at that moment engaged in a precarious dance with his conscience, then he winked. Doug did not turn me over to the hounds that night.

Meanwhile, two more members of the pack had taken center stage. They were merrily dousing one another with beer.

Doug turned his attention back to the frenzy.

I took a deep breath and stepped deeper into the shadows.

Bali Belly on The Bukit and the Zombie Apocalypse

(travel essay)

I blame myself for introducing the zombie into the circle of elegant guests gathered at Villa Cahaya. The whole undead concept had no place in the paradise that our generous hosts had prepared for us, and yet the lonely Bukit Peninsula, or The Bukit, as it is often called—that desolate and surprisingly flinty clubfoot of land at the southernmost tip of Bali—did seem a likely setting for just such an appearance. There, at the end of a maze of unmarked roads with ultra-tight turns, the villa sprawled on a small cliff above the Indian Ocean. Remote—its access confounded even our host, who is one of the planet's most famous and experienced travelers—it sported a decidedly post-apocalyptic air.

I was in Indonesia because of a novel I'd written about zombies (*Dead Love*), which was a finalist for a Bram Stoker Award, and because of a workshop, a festival, and a wedding. The wedding was the reason we were all on The Bukit; it's a popular place for the type of fête that is by special invitation only, the kind so off the beaten path that only the invited guests—and perhaps the occasional walking corpse—will jet, motor, or stumble toward it. I was the only working stiff in our party, with almost daily commitments hours to the north at the Ubud Writers & Readers Festival. I was exhausted, having just finished co-directing a group of astoundingly energetic writers; I was consumed by the lurid characters in my book; and I was sick.

> We found the Zombie in the hospital yard. They had just set her dinner before her, but she was not eating. The moment she sensed our approach, she broke off a limb of a shrub and began to use it to dust and clean the ground and the table, which bore her food. The two doctors made kindly noises and tried to reassure her. She seemed to hear nothing. The doctor uncovered her head for a moment (she had covered it with a cloth) but she promptly clapped her arms and hands over it to shut out the things she dreaded. Finally the doctor forcibly uncovered her and held her...and the sight was dreadful. The blank face with the dead eyes.
>
> —Zora Neale Hurston, *Tell My Horse*

Can you call contagion to you? I read somewhere that you call your fears. If this is the case, I was guilty, and I was certainly suffering for it. I believe my malaise began in Jakarta, where I had been careless. I should explain that I have an almost unbelievably finicky system. I am highly allergic to numerous substances, and they are the kind of allergies that require epinephrine and, sometimes, hospitalization. Infectious agents and bacterial enteropathogens find hospitable terrain in my gut. In high-risk destinations like Latin America, Africa, the Middle East, and Asia—heck, even at home in the U.S.—I have to mind what I put into my mouth. So, whether it was contaminated water or food, nonpasteurized dairy products, a toothbrush improperly cleansed, or something I handled during my visit to the largest dumpsite in the world (my must-see on Java), my system had been breached. I was a walking Petri dish.

I was armed, of course, with an arsenal of prophylactics: loperamide, ciprofloxacin, chloroquine, and more—the kind of things designed to fill you up with antiviral, antibacterial, and antiparasitic protection. To no avail, by the time I arrived on The Bukit, my belly was the size of a beach ball, and while that thing that would turn me into one of the living dead had not yet overwhelmed me, I could feel it crawling around inside me like a centipede soaked in hot sauce, making my stomach cramp, my head hurt, my vision narrow.

This affliction had no place here, amid villas so exquisite that they are like gemstones cut out of the heart of the rugged peninsula, in a company so illustrious. As the glamorous women and dashing men sipped cocktails and chatted, strolled the estate's massive grounds, and stroked their way slowly through the glassy waters of an infinity pool that seemed to be waterfalling into an ocean at the end of the world, I sat nauseated, my innards roiling, like an aging and unraveling Gustav von Aschenbach, the unfortunate protagonist of Thomas Mann's *Death in Venice* or—like a zombie.

The cocktails, the meticulously served banquets set up under the stars on terraces and wide lawns, came and went. The talk swirled around me like a mad carousel, the food—what little I'd swallowed earlier—was dancing a tarantella in my belly.

"Linda, a cocktail?"

"No, thank you."

"Try the prawns."

"No thanks."

"Champagne?"

"I don't think so."

"This grilled fish is delicious. Some *nasi goreng*?"

The smile on my face had turned into a corncob grin, my teeth clenched tight as prison bars. I ate and drank nothing, hurried back to my sumptuous quarters to lie on the bed in a state of alarm, breathing hard, waiting for the next god-awful spasm.

How long could it go on? In the evenings while the others feasted and drank, I tried to converse amicably, manage what little was left of the "me" that once was, and stave off the indignity of the ultimate "transformation." Let's face it, ill health may be unpalatable, but a lack of control over basic bodily functions is a serious social disadvantage.

By day, while the others visited temples and beach towns and ran about and shopped, I sat, like one drugged, in the backseat of the rented vehicle on my daily trip north, watching the landscape race by and listening to my stomach burble. It was the only noise in the car. Outside, the pocked and scaly landscape of Uluwatu and Ungasan, where skeletal livestock picked at the meager furze that stippled the barren fields, gave way to a fecund paradise. Inside the car, I did not move. I munched on pills and wrestled with intestinal demons. I was in hell in Paradise. I admit, there was definitely something vaguely poetic about being miserable in the midst of all that beauty, so I may have wallowed in it—in the same way, I think, that a zombie wallows in brains.

Meanwhile, well-meaning locals recommended natural cures for what they called Bali belly: tamarind juice, simple white rice, and so on. None of them worked.

> A mirror hung on one wall. I approached it as one might approach a window, trying to look out onto a landscape, objective reality: physical, solid. The mirror was darkness framed in gloom, and the door to the room did not admit enough light to brighten it. I crossed to the window. I pushed back the drapes. I turned back to the mirror. A weak wash of moonlight invaded the chamber, animating the face there. I looked at a stranger, myself, for a brand-new first time.
>
> My eyes were dark, but they had a surreal brilliance, like a couple of coals suddenly ignited. Under each eye floated a blue thumbprint of shadow. These two bruise-like marks never vanished. They were the result of my near extermination.
>
> They are also the mark of a zombie.
>
> —Linda Watanabe McFerrin, *Dead Love*

I suppose that it comes as no surprise that, feeling "crappy" in the true sense of the word, and absorbed in what felt like complete disintegration, I found some solace and comfort in the miseries of the undead. Call it schadenfreude; it was no accident that I turned the conversation to zombies and, incidentally, my novel. In fact, we had joked about it earlier—about the living dead, about our desolate setting, still a backwater but for the sprinkling of villas, being ripe for a zombie apocalypse, the perfect place for the undead to stagger toward their inevitable end... Paradise lost before it is really found. Our host, who is also a writer and terribly imaginative, introduced the concept of were-cats and were-dogs. And as the others, more newly arrived than I, began to take ill, a kind of zombie fever soon had us all in its grip. We exchanged medicines, worried about electrolytes, dispensed advice, and exhibited copious communal concern.

There is something romantic about dying. And coming back from the dead is the ultimate romance. So, I suppose even my story ends romantically. I did not die on The Bukit. I returned—feeling horribly rotten—to the U.S., to doctors who saw me and saved me and billed me for the resurrection. As for the others in that Balinese party, of course no one died, but they were in some way affected. The zombie had walked among them, and they all—every last one of them—bought the book.

Hunger

I want to eat trees.
I reach out, grabbing.
They are crunchy,
and the trunks have a nutty taste.

I want to taste bridges.
I drag my tongue along the surfaces—
rough,
cold, something like ice.

I want to drink the Mississippi,
the Nile, the Amazon at once—
a mixture thick as a milkshake
with a slightly exotic flavor.

I want to try those people
and those.
They slide down my throat—
26, 100, 3698,
4,285,192—
slippery as sashimi,
each one more subtle than the first.

I want, in fact,
to devour the universe.
I pluck out each planet
like a small Swedish meatball,
swallowing whole,
every swallow punctuated
by a tiny burp.

I am a bag without a bottom.
Nevertheless, I am optimistic.
I want to go on eating.

Selections from Dead Love

Grave Matters

(excerpt)

He was dressed like a ninja, wrapped in darkness. And his friends, silent as shadows, were clothed as ninjas as well. No one would have seen them in the garden, crouching and creeping among the pots. They cat-footed their way up the paths on *tabi* feet in the rubber-soled, two-toed, black cotton socks that ninjas wear. They knew exactly where we were. It was as if they had GPS, their on-board computers preprogrammed, the address fixed in their minds. Not so much as a board creaked when they set foot up on the *genkan*. They were as invisible as bunraku puppet masters, as the dressers in a Kabuki play.

He picked the locks—all of them—quickly, moving around the cottage until every door and window could be opened soundlessly, easily. Then they invaded, the way smoke permeates a room, through cracks and crevices—a door barely opened, a window only slightly raised. Dropping to the *tatami* floor, one through six, they stole toward the bedroom where Lou Lou and I were dreaming. Cat burglars? Thieves? Assassins? Terrible as assassins, better as cats—they dawdled on their prowl to run gloved hands over objects, to examine photos, look into lacquer bowls. Shipu was awake and uttered a welcoming meow, rushing up to greet them, purring and pushing against one of them, drawn no doubt by the faint aroma of decomposition that floated about them like a cloak. Carefully, inch by inch, the gang members made their way toward our beds. Shipu was ahead of them, pleased to be in the vanguard, his tail rising up over his back in punctuation. Exclamation point. Question mark. Slash. Slash. Slash. Shipu hopped up onto the futon first, purring loudly, so loudly that I opened my eyes.

I found myself staring straight into his eyes. Not the cat's, but the burglar's. His face was over mine, his legs straddling me, knees on either side of my hips, his pupils thin slits ringed in amber in lidless eyes that bored into mine. He pulled down the mask that covered the lower half of his face to reveal a wide nose and cruel mouth.

"We meet again," he said huskily. "Not really the outfit I'd planned."

I knew that voice.

The scab upon his left temple was gone. His face had been altered entirely, but I recognized him at once. Clément. I opened my mouth.

"No noise, zombie-girl," he said quickly, covering my mouth with black duct tape. There was a struggle going on next to me. I looked over to my left. Lou Lou was awake, sitting up, a ninja sitting behind her, his legs wrapped like arms around her naked hips, one arm vise-like around her chest, one gloved hand over her mouth. The futon and sheets were pooled about her knees in confusion. Above the black glove, her blue eyes danced, wide, frantic and signaling, desperately darting right, to the area just over my shoulder.

The ninja ringleader got the message when I did, but I was fast and the brass lamp came crashing down on the side of his head. In the split second after the impact, I wriggled out from under him, trying to get up and head for the front door. He was up and in motion before I could jump to my feet, somersaulting over my head, like a funereal saltimbanque, landing impossibly on the wall next to the window with his feet planted squarely upon it, his body perpendicular to the floor. I froze and gaped at him jutting straight out from the wall, fiendishly defying gravity like a gargoyle on the spire of a church.

That's when the third ninja pounced. He'd been up on the ceiling, crouched on all fours, watching me like a black spider in the corner of its web. He landed on my back and shoulders, bringing me back down to the bedding with a soft thud. Then he and a fourth went to work on me, wrapping my ankles in more duct tape, binding my wrists with tape behind my back.

For the second time in twenty-four hours I was trapped. It was maddening, much worse than the handcuffs, and I thrashed about helplessly on the ground, nearly dislocating my arms and neck while three ninjas stood above me laughing. The leader, who had by this time descended from the wall, kicked the bedclothes in my direction. "Wrap her up," he commanded, "before she does physical damage."

They moved very quickly, these ninjas, and my struggles ended in almost instant mummification. Next to me, Lou Lou, naked and duct-taped, looked on in terror until one of the ninjas kneeled down beside her and, making an elaborate ritual of it, decorously folding and refolding the blindfold, covered her eyes with a kerchief. Then they made tea.

Two of them sat in the kitchen sipping the steaming green liquid while the other four played their gravity-defying games. They climbed up the wall like flies. On all fours, they walked upside down on the ceiling, sprang back down to the floor, tumbled across the *tatami*, then somersaulted back up to the ceiling again. Shipu jumped from chair to chair, delighted, neck craning, crooning in pussycat pleasure at their splendid antics. In the process, one of them lost a foot, and this seemed to fill them all with glee, especially when Shipu ran and tried to take a few bites out of it, turning it over and pushing his nose into the foot's *tabi* sock.

"For God's sake, get your foot," the lead ninja said tiredly, sipping the last of his tea. "And get them. We wouldn't want them to keep this appointment." He walked over to me where I lay on the futon, wrapped tight as a chrysalis in the bed sheet. My face was the only thing not totally covered.

"Your 'friends' will be here any minute," he sang merrily and he winked. Then he pulled the mask back up over his face. His henchmen hoisted Lou Lou and me and, as soundlessly as they had entered, they soft-footed it back through the garden.

They carried us easily, like very light bags, hopping the five-foot-high fence when we got to it, one of them preceding the others and catching us when they tossed us over the top. I was not blindfolded, so I saw the black sedan waiting out on the narrow street, watched the fat driver open the trunk so the ninja could throw us inside. I recoiled when the lead ninja ran a naked finger down the side of my cheek and purred, "Let's see you get out of this one." Then he closed the trunk. I felt as if I were suffocating. Low and constant, I could feel the growl of the engine, feel its vibration against my chest. Then there was a knocking sound; I thought I heard doors opening and someone yanked Lou Lou out of the trunk...

It was not a traditional graveyard, though there were a number of them nearby. It was, instead, one of the tiny Buddhist cemeteries that line some of the narrow streets of Shitamachi, a kind of historical district in Tokyo. The small yard was chockablock with graves and *toba*, the tall wooden funerary slats with sacred texts trickling downward in black ink. But we were inside and, I might add, underground, in what could once have been a bomb shelter. It was dank and mildewed and cluttered with paraphernalia: blank markers, small wooden chairs, grass sandals, bits of ceramic, pots of ash, wooden buckets, and dippers for cleaning the graves.

The ninjas, whom you may have guessed were actually ghouls, had deposited us in this basement room, which I suppose I should call their "dorm," although I've since learned that they never sleep. Lou Lou, duct-taped, still nude, but no longer blindfolded, was writhing about. Cocooned in the bed sheet, I couldn't budge and I lay there on the concrete floor, looking like a large white grub or a mummy.

"Booty," sang out the head ninja, who also happened to be Clément. He threw his arms upward and all the ghoul-ninjas, even the one with one foot, began prancing around him in a dance. One moment they'd be balancing on the rim of a bucket, the next stumbling and clumsily tumbling to the ground. They seemed to ignore Lou Lou's pointless thrashing about, though I suspected it was the cause of their very obvious excitement.

"Welcome to our humble home," said Clément. He had plucked a few flowers—carnations—from one of the newer graves and tossed them our way. "You are safe here.

"Boys," he commanded, addressing his slovenly ninja cohorts, who seemed held together by the black rags wrapped around their bodies, "dress them in finery. Show them every comfort."

In response to this order, his fellows dragged forth a bag from one corner of the cellar and began to pull out old clothes. Men's shoes. Suit jackets. Ladies' blouses. A coat. A pink skirt. An aqua-colored, beaded cardigan sweater. A short, salmon-colored shift. They tossed the pink skirt and aqua sweater at Lou Lou. The garments landed on top of her wriggling form. The colors, so different from her ever-black, must have shocked her. She froze, and her blue eyes widened. The ghouls, meanwhile, had started a tug-of-war with the salmon-colored dress. The victor in the tug-of-war held the garment over his head like a flag, then lowered it, and marched solemnly toward me at a ceremonial pace, the other ghouls falling in step behind him. The ghoul with the dress knelt by my side and carefully placed the garment on top of my sheet-bound body as if dressing a paper doll, smoothing out any wrinkles. His eyes, above the mask that covered the lower half of his face, looked momentarily sad: melancholy and rot—not exactly a winning combination. Then he quickly tore the tape from my mouth. I immediately let out a wail that could wake the dead. It rang through the cellar and up into the temple above us, no doubt confirming any lingering graveside superstitions once and for all.

"Enough," yelled Clément. He was beside the kneeling ninja in an instant, cuffing him on the side of the head. The poor creature's temple caved in like the shell of a very old pumpkin. "Just what do you think you are doing? Damn you," he growled, slapping the tape back over my mouth.

The other three ghouls started to giggle. Clément towered over the ghoul at my side, his gloved hands in fists and let out a world-weary sigh. "Well," he said, "I suppose you're already damned...as are we all." He touched the head of the kneeling ghoul somewhat tenderly. "Sorry," he mumbled. "We'll get you something..." His apology was interrupted by a rustle on the stair and the appearance of a rather old monk.

The ghouls were not the least bit surprised by the monk's appearance and he, in turn, seemed not at all surprised by theirs. He glanced over at us—the ghouls, the bound women—and shook his head. Then, shuffling over to a corner of the room, he retrieved a pot of black paint and took down a box from a shelf on the wall and extracted a brush. The ghouls watched him. One even waved. The old monk ignored them and carried his supplies back upstairs.

"He thinks we are figments of his imagination," said Clément. "We can do whatever we like. He pretends we do not exist, though he does seem to chant his prayers with increasing vehemence."

Something to Rave About

(excerpts)

The old houses of Amsterdam were built with economics in mind. That is why they are tall and thin. Taxes were charged for the street space, so homes were built narrow and deep. The restaurant we'd entered was situated in a nest of five of these buildings and the staircase allowed access to a warren of gloomy wood-paneled, low-beamed rooms. In the first of these rooms a host of exotically attired men and women milled about amid antique chairs and white-clothed tables set with elaborate towers of food. Music rained down on them from speakers sequestered in the beams, and this, together with their chatter, created a deep, panting din. There were makeshift altars everywhere, jostled up against northern European finery, upon which little statues of various gods—Shivas and Kalis and Buddhas and Ganeshas and Kuan Nins and Christs—frolicked, prayed, and writhed in perpetual pleasure and pain. The altars were decorated with candles and flowers and fruit and mirrors and jewelry and bits of colored silk. Albert was in this room...

In the kitchen, two tall women with red hair stood at an enormous industrial stove, stirring soup. They looked like twins. Both wore short black cocktail dresses, chef's toques and threateningly pointed, six-inch stiletto heels that made them appear taller still. The chef's toques were stiffly starched columns topped with a poof that made them look like they had their red heads up in their respective clouds.

The cook sat at the table, pale as a ghost, his arm out in front of him as if he were giving blood.

"He's tired," said one of the twins as she stirred her soup.

"Yes, yes," laughed the other.

Suddenly it was clear to me: the wine casks, the pale cook, the twins.

"You are all vampires," I said.

"Really, no, I am not a vampire. I am Trekka," said one of the women.

"Yes, ha, ha, ha," laughed the other. "Have a drink. Have some borscht." She pulled a large spoon, full, from the pot. The spoon dripped a hairy mixture of beets and red cabbage.

"Oh, Greta, you have ruined it. You know now I will have to pull the cabbage out of my teeth."

"Critic, then you get no soup, you will have to subsist on wine." Greta winked at me and went back to stirring the soup.

The cook at the table groaned and shook his head.

"Oh, darling, you are exhausted," said one of the twins. "Here, have some of this soup that you helped us to make. It's delicious." She walked over to him and spooned the red mixture into his mouth.

To say that he found it energizing would be a gross understatement. The man's eyes opened wide as if he'd been shocked. His hair stood on end and he hopped up and began waving his arms and yelling in high-pitched and unintelligible Dutch.

"Shhh, shhh, quiet, darling," said Greta, wrestling him into a headlock. "You'll be fine in a minute. Calm down." She kissed him on the top of his head. Then she looked up at me and smiled. She did indeed have red cabbage stuck between her sharp little teeth. "They always react this way at first. Then they like it. Such an energy burst."

The man continued to struggle, but Greta, the muscles on her wiry arms bulging, had him completely under control. She dragged him over to the stove and shoveled another ladleful of the soup into his mouth. The man spasmed again, but Greta held him tight.

"This will go on for some time," explained Trekka while Greta continued to force the borscht into the man. "Then he will rest. Are you hungry? Do you want some of our soup? Or are you just a voyeur?"

I was hungry, but I didn't want any of their bloody borscht. I backed my way from the threshold.

"Leave the girls alone."

It was Gilbert. He'd found me, and his tone was thick with malice. Then he smiled, his elastic mouth stretching into another ominous bow-like grin.

"They are just playing."

Once again he wound his hand in my hair and he pulled me to him, very close, his wide lips spreading before my eyes, his teeth glistening like a row of tiny white lights. He had removed his suit jacket, loosened his red tie. I could hear the music pounding a few rooms away. I could feel the tempestuous whoosh-whoosh of his heart.

"Ah, Erin, you know about something I want. But you won't talk, will you? I can see that. You listen. How unusual to find a woman who actually listens. It makes me wonder what kind of woman you are. Not a real woman surely. Something else?"

The hand not in my hair moved to my throat, lingered there tapping lightly as his other hand pulled back my head. The wild tattoo of his heartbeat quickened. "I can have anything that I want," he gloated.

Of course he could. He was a vampire, too.

"A vampire, perhaps," he said reading my mind, "but that title is purely metaphorical. I am a banker, a venture capitalist, and a commercial success. I create nothing. I live off the productivity of others. I accept their money, their hopes, and their dreams. I invest. I suppose in that way I'm a vampire. We are all vampires at root, aren't we? Isn't that why the concept is so enticing? Show me someone who doesn't eat, who doesn't feast, on the living? My crime, if there is one, is in owning it.

"Are you listening, Erin? Good. Listen well. I have received a phone call and that is why you and your partner are here. It seems something that I deeply desire is very close at hand, some information, something well worth the investment. Do you know what it is? Of course you don't. I was told you know nothing about it. You thought you were simply carrying drugs. But your partner Alain, he knows, doesn't he?"

Now my heart was racing. I could feel it rising in tempo, matching his, beat for beat. This was sounding complicated, arcane. There was a hellish signature in it.

"What if I told you that a nest of hypocrites was about to be unmasked, or could be, if certain facts were revealed—facts that implicate them in a greedy plan more destructive and diabolical than any invented devil could devise? What do you suppose such creatures would pay to have that information suppressed? We are in the midst of an interesting moment in history, a moment not unlike the old eras of terror. All rules are about to be broken and new ones made. Walls will come down. The vast plain of possibility will unfurl before us. It is mind- and soul-boggling," he said, "and we are in the vanguard of that change." His voice had softened, become something akin to a purr. He drew a finger the length of my windpipe; then he tightened his grip on my hair. "You have a powerful patron and he insists that I leave you unbroken," he mused and cocked his ear to the music. "Ah, an evening raga, I think, an exquisite evocation of night." The music, which had softened, laced its way through the restaurant's rooms with soporific results. Gilbert's heart rate had slowed, was quiet and deep and powerful.

"In the end," he continued, "It all comes down to the truth. Such a nebulous thing, the truth, easy to twist; some will do anything to suppress it. And that is where I come in. You see, there is a record that implicates certain men who seem above reproach. A record stored in a microchip. You did not know it was quite so important, did you?

"It has been sold and is out for delivery. That is where I come in. I'm here to intercept it. The forwarding agent, your patron, is double-crossing his blackmailing employers. He doesn't want much in return: a paltry sum and...you. But now he says he's lost track of the chip. But he's given us someone who knows: the photographer fellow, Alain. He says we just need to get him to talk."

Forwarding agent, blackmail, patron, Alain—it was all horribly clear. If this was about the microchip, it was certainly nothing Alain could know anything about. This was just another play in Clément's stupid game, but to what end? What was really at stake?

"What's at stake?" asked Gilbert, surprised, as he meddled around in my thoughts. "For us, the very nature of reality is at stake, the safety of the world, the illusion around which everything else revolves. The truth will blow the lid off the concept of good men and bad. And if we get beyond that, there is no fact, no fiction. No truth or lies. Then every creature consigned to the world of imagination can truly exist—in this one. We will step from the pages of books, from the recesses of the mind, and onto the stage of life. It is revolutionary. And we, my dear friends and I, are the first creatures of the new revolution."

Gilbert's dark eyes turned nocturnal, his black pupils slitting like a cat's. Still holding my hair fast in one fist, he pulled at my arm. Very quickly, expertly, he stabbed a needle into a vein. Then that stretchy mouth of his opened onto my neck, formed a rubber-tight seal, and he bit me...

Limbo

All of that is another lifetime ago, she thinks. Then she wakes up.

Who is the man sleeping beside her? A banker, he'd said, a Belgian banker—just a man who had taken her in.

Who is the woman in bed with him? It might be her.

When she gets out of bed, the other woman stays there. Is she a ghost, then? Or is the woman in bed, who looks so much like her, only a body? The two of them, man and woman, are curled toward one another like the petals of a tulip. They appear to be dead. They are sleeping. Tulips are beautiful flowers.

The house is cold. She moves her hand to her cheek. This is accomplished without hands really, only the feeling of moving one's hand. There is no cheek to meet the hand. There is only the cold. The cheek is cold.

She performs the usual movements gratuitously since they have no physical counterparts. Just as she dresses, eats, out of habit. None of it has any basis in physical reality. She has begun to think of herself as a ghost. The body that follows her around, vaguely attached, annoys her. She makes an attempt to ignore it, to pretend it doesn't exist.

Perhaps it is the overwhelming sense that a certain thing is spoiled or tainted and should be thrown out. She meets herself occasionally, a shudder down the other woman's spine. How long can she go on in this way, in a kind of limbo?

The early morning hours are quietest. Quiet before the household gets up. She roams the yard then, and climbs down to the creek to sit under the huge bole of a tree. The mosquitoes move away.

Her most vigorous action is, once, to collect an armful of irises from the soft bank, but, as with all things, she grows listless, leaves them strewn all over the yard. No, she does not feel pointless; that would assume a point.

Sometimes she wanders out from the gates. She is looking for graveyards. It is pleasant to sit on the grass and survey the headstones. Sometimes she loiters among them, reading the names as though from some checklist. She is looking for one name really. One name. She forgets what it is. The only thing she recollects is a number. "I am number 421," she says sadly. There was a time when the dam broke in Amsterdam. The houseboat exploded, too. It rained money. They were all so surprised by that.

Sometimes she finds a nice headstone and stops, as though reflecting upon something. This is silly, because she is reflecting on nothing. Not even searching her mind. There's nothing there. Oh, yes, a number.

"I am number 421," she says and she sighs. There was a time when the dam broke in Amsterdam. The houseboat rained money. Everyone was surprised about that.

The housekeeper, assigned to watch her, finds her disturbing, very strange.

"What is she doing out there in her nightdress?"

In this, as in other things, there is no connection between the outward appearance and what is actually going on.

That is when *he* appears in her garden. Or maybe it is in the graveyard. One way or another, he is digging. She knows him—a trickle like ice water down her spine.

"I am your savior," he says. He is the gardener maybe. Perhaps he is the undertaker. He smells bad. She looks into his wheelbarrow. It's full of worms. Worms.

Someone is calling. She shivers. She goes back to the house.

Worms.

When she returns to the garden, he is back. This time he is wearing a shin length tweed coat and a cap. He looks as if he has grown a beard. The beard keeps growing after you die. The lower half of his face is in shadow.

"Nice dress," he says when she approaches. She sees she is wearing a white satin nightgown. The hem is covered with creek mud.

"Why are you here?" he asks. She does not know how to answer that.

"Run away," he says.

"Go away," she slurs back.

The defiance exhausts her. She is in bed for a long time after that. When she rises, she goes to the window. He is still there, in the garden.

Worms.

She realizes that she hates him.

The man in the bed has become the man at the breakfast table. He ignores her mostly. He calls this tenderness.

Everyone in the house ignores her. That is what she sees. But there is the man in the garden. He watches her. Always.

Worms.

"It's time for you to leave. Run away," he says. "You like to run. Run away."

Every day now, he is in the garden. The garden used to be so peaceful.

Now she is wearing a light blue dress. The gardener is back, digging another grave. She thinks she must hate him.

"You are fucking a Belgian banker," he says with contempt. "You can't hide anymore. Vacation is over. Run away."

She thinks she will run away from him, from the gardener, from the gh... she can't seem to finish her thought. Instead another thought fills her mind, then another time, another place.

There is a girl in a schoolyard. The school is in Ireland, set on the coast upon acres and acres of loneliness. And there is a gardener there as well...

"I'm not sorry I did it," he says. "You only knew him for one day."

"I'm number 421."

"Come off it. You only knew him for one day."

She is sure now that she hates him, the gardener, the ghoul. It's November. The weather has turned cold.

The gardener is dirty. He's dirty and he smells bad.

"You stink," she says.

There's a film of white frost on the lawn.

"You're shivering," he says. "Take my coat."

The house and the garden have turned into a prison. She finds four dead ducks by the creek bed—a new dead duck every day.

"Death is all around you," he says.

Why won't he leave her alone?

Worms.

She wants him to go away, but he won't. He comes every day for the garden.

The man says, "I like the job that gardener is doing."

What job? She wonders and pushes her hair back from her forehead.

"What have you written there?" asks the banker.

It's a number: 421.

They won't let her go outside anymore. The gate that opens out onto the street is locked. She has become a prisoner.

She is wearing the blue dress and it's cold outside. In the autumn garden, *he* is pruning the trees. Bare branches drop one by one.

She decides she will run away. She has the blue dress, his tweed coat. It smells bad.

There is no such thing as time in her world, but it's late, very late. There was a time when the dam broke in Amsterdam and the houseboat rained money and everyone was surprised about that.

The sun is like a persimmon. It's a fat, orange globe. It's setting behind the bare branches.

"Could you give me some water?" he asks. He stands at the blue kitchen door.

"Wait outside," the housekeeper grumbles. "Gypsy," she mutters in Flemish.

I am wearing the blue dress and I smooth down the skirt. I have found my hands in the pockets of the coat and I use them. In the pocket of the tweed coat, I've also found a plane ticket. It is a ticket to Malaysia. I stand inside the blue door to the kitchen. Better. Myself again. At least more than I was months ago. There he is. There he is. I have my eye on him. He's not going to trick me again.

"I will leave the gate open," he whispers.

The housekeeper returns with the water. "Here's your water," she snaps at the gypsy gardener. "Back to bed with you, ma'am," she says.

I have my hand on the ticket. I remember how the dam burst in Amsterdam. It is all so terribly sad. Everyone said that it rained money.

Worms.

The Tunnel of Light

The manicured front lawn of Saint Ali was crawling with big black vehicles. Daimlers, BMW and Mercedes sedans, and SUVs—there must have been eight or nine of them parked like gargantuan beetles hunkering amid the rose bushes. I tiptoed around them and crept to the back of the building. Alas, the gate was locked, so I circled back to the front and found the main entrance wide open, the atrium space deserted except for a lone fellow with a camera and recorder, his nose pressed against one of the glass cases as if the better to ponder its contents.

The long corridors, too, were quiet, oddly so, but I heard noise at one end of the building where the passageway ran into the lecture hall that formed one of the arms of the U. A crowd of cotton-headed residents was assembled at the door of the auditorium, and no one shooed them away, so I joined them, peering out over the sea of their hoary-haired craniums at a collection of men, women, microphones, and camera equipment engaged in what appeared to be a press conference.

On the stage in the front of the auditorium, a table had been set up. Behind the table, decked out in a powder-blue cardigan sweater and shell set, her face dusted a disturbingly bright magenta shade, was a frail and much-changed Mrs. Soren-Schmidt. Where once she was delicate, she now was brittle. Where once she'd been gentle, she seemed harsh. The silvery aura that had distinguished her seemed to have been transformed by some crude alchemy into lead. Understandable for a woman who had, as I was about to discover, recently come back from the dead.

To her right sat an ebullient Dr. Pilford Hodge, to her left the mean little nurse. Staring up at the table, trailing wires and assistants, cameras, microphones, and tape recorders extended, were the journalists.

"Dr. Hodge. Dr. Hodge. Are you certain that she was dead?"

"Of course we are certain."

"What was the time of death?"

"She died between three and four a.m. on the night of November seventh."

"Dr. Hodge, how long did you say she was dead?"

"Mrs. Soren-Schmidt was dead for thirty-four hours."

A hush filled the room, but only for an instant, and it exploded again into questions.

"Was she ill, Dr. Hodge? Who found her? Has her family been notified?"

"Mrs. Soren-Schmidt was the last of the Schmidts here in the Cameron Highlands. Distant relatives in Europe have been notified. Our head nurse found her in the morning," he lied. The head nurse sat up very straight and smiled. She beamed at the doctor.

"Of course, this is astounding," Pilford Hodge continued. "It is a medical and metaphysical miracle, if I may be so dramatic," here he crossed some imaginary line. "Never before," he said gravely, "never before have scientific and spiritual data been so perfectly co-joined as to give us absolute proof of an afterlife."

At this lofty proclamation, Mrs. Soren-Schmidt stirred. She threw back her head and stuck her arms up into the air like a puppet on the end of taut strings. "I was dead for thirty-four hours," she gasped in a wheezy and breathless falsetto. "It was marvelous, I tell you. Do not be afraid of your death."

"Mrs. Soren-Schmidt. Mrs. Soren-Schmidt..." The journalists turned their attention to her. "Were you conscious? Could you feel anything? What happened? What did you see?"

In tune with the drama of the moment, Mrs. Soren-Schmidt rose from her chair. She gazed out over the upturned and expectant faces with a look of superiority and relish. My elderly neighbors held their breaths, waiting for her pronouncements. She paused for a long time for effect, and an eerie silence drifted in over the room.

"It was dark at first," the old lady began, standing ramrod straight, her arms extended before her now like a woman walking in her sleep. "And I did not know I was dead."

She stopped her narrative and engaged the reporters and onlookers again, this time with a look of mystery.

"I was cold, very cold, but that feeling passed, and I felt as though I were floating, floating up in one corner of my room. Do you know what it feels like to be lifted ever so gently, like a feather on a breeze, up, up, and away? It was like it was when I was a child and my father took me up in his arms and carried me away to my bedroom and my slumbers. That is how it felt. Lovely. Safe.

"I could see myself on the bed below me." Mrs. Soren-Schmidt stared down at the table before her, as if she could see herself lying there. "I looked so tiny, so frail, and I felt an overwhelming compassion for the woman on the bed. 'Poor woman,' I thought, 'poor, poor woman, she has tried so hard and she's tired. She is so very tired.' I wanted to reach down and comfort the woman on the bed, but I couldn't. I didn't seem to have a body at all, but I felt complete, fully sentient.

"Hospital staff came and went. I could see them all, running here and there, calling out to one another, so concerned. Doctor Hodge was so solicitous. I could feel his care. You were heroic, Dr. Hodge."

She turned to the doctor, who beamed at the compliment, saying humbly, but loud enough for the recorders to catch, "I am a doctor. It is my calling to care."

"And the staff," Mrs. Soren-Schmidt added, "they were all so efficient."

The head nurse straightened and smiled.

"But they couldn't see me. All they saw was a dead woman there on the bed. I wanted to call out to them, tell them I was all right, but I couldn't. And that is what I want you to know," said Mrs. Soren-Schmidt, gazing out over the crowd. "I want you to know that the body dies, but you, the parts that make you who you are, live on."

She took a deep breath and beamed her message out to every being in the room, her eyes moving soulfully from one person to the next—the journalists, my elderly neighbors—searching each face until her gaze met mine and she stopped.

My throat constricted. My stomach turned.

"Yes, now, where was I?" asked the much-pleased old woman.

"Oh, yes, I was floating above the dead woman and the staff, but I couldn't tell anyone I was there. Then I wondered, 'Am I a ghost? Is this what a ghost feels like? Am I doomed to float forever, alone and unnoticed in a disembodied limbo?' I'm sure you've all wondered about this. Wondered and worried. I was filled with a great melancholia."

Again, Mrs. Soren-Schmidt paused for effect, her cupped hand placed over her heart. She had arranged her visage into a look of profound sorrow, so profound as to be nearly comic.

"And then, as they wheeled my body away..."

"Mrs. Schmidt, you were ill, weren't you? Alzheimer's, wasn't it? Isn't that what Dr. Hodge said? Late-stage Alzheimer's?"

"Mrs. *Soren*-Schmidt," the old lady corrected. "You are far too impatient, young man, and rude to interrupt in that way. What are you trying to say, anyway? I am in the middle of telling my story."

Her mood changed dramatically. She became suddenly irritable, testy, but she calmed down a bit, put a hand to a brow, and continued. "I wondered, 'What will happen to me? Is this what death means? Is it an eternity of loneliness?' And that, my dears, is when I saw it. 'What?' you might ask. Why, a tunnel of light.

"They wheeled the body away and I felt abandoned, but

just at that moment I saw, felt, came to know, what I can only describe as a tractor beam of warmth, light, and bliss. It opened above me. It was pulsating, too, as if it were alive, made of sentience, filled with love and compassion and every good thing I have ever imagined. And it was calling to me. Not in a voice, you understand, but in a language so pure and clear that it defied misapprehension. It was beauty and truth, and I knew that it was the center of my—of everyone's—highest good. 'Come, come,' the voices seemed to say, and I longed with all of my being to join them."

Mrs. Soren-Schmidt had us; we were all in her hands and she knew this as well, as surely as she knew what the voices desired. She closed her eyes, those thin-lidded eyes, her face suffused with satisfaction as she continued.

"Of course, this is the point we have all heard about. The point at which one must decide whether we want to live or move on. Many have come to this gateway, returned, and told others about the experience. But you see, I didn't want to return. There was nothing left to bind me to this world: the worn-out husk of a body, an enfeebled mind. All my loved ones were dead. I was ready.

"So I did it. I let go, and when I did, I could feel myself being pulled—slowly, tenderly—right into the source of the light. What was it like? It was like the embrace of millions of arms, the touch of countless hands. I felt welcomed and loved and whole. I felt like I'd just been born. Soft centers of energy pressed up around me and I recognized them. One by one the entities made themselves known. Subtle greetings. There was a sound like a murmur, like a heart shushing blood, or the roar in the inside of a shell. I felt myself spreading, thin and wide and forever, like a blanket stretched out over the universe, and then I was the one embracing the others with compassion; they were all part of me."

Mrs. Soren-Schmidt opened her eyes. Hodge proffered a handkerchief and she brought it to her eyes. When she removed it, her eyes glistened with tears. They rolled down her rouged cheeks.

"There was warmth; there was light; there was movement. There were constant comings and goings and the excitement of souls embarking on new journeys and others coming back—such a sweet, single-celled celebration. Who knew?" she sniffled, dabbing her eyes again with the handkerchief. "And I'm back now, you see, to tell you about this. To tell you that there *is* a heaven."

Mrs. Soren-Schmidt seemed to cave in at that point. She collapsed into the chair like a marionette, a creaky shell of a woman. Through much of her speech she'd been staring at me and the sour feeling in my gut had been growing. One moment she'd been animated, full of fire and intent, and the next she was broken and doll-like, like a battery-driven plaything run down. The end of her talk was greeted with a thunderous new round of questions.

"Mrs. Soren-Schmidt, what religion are you?"

"Is the Alzheimer's gone?"

"Did you want to come back?"

"How do you feel now?"

"Do you think there's a god?"

"Will you stay at Saint Ali?"

"Is there some way we can get an exclusive?"

"The patient is tired," said Dr. Pilford Hodge. "She has had a very big day...days, in fact," he corrected. "We must get her to bed, but of course, I will stay. I'll be happy to answer your questions."

"I am just thankful," said Mrs. Soren-Schmidt, raising herself from her stupor, "to be able to bring back this news to you all, to allay your fears, calm your spirits."

The muscles in her face worked powerfully, as if holding back a huge wave of emotion. The ancient crowd at the door began moving forward, pushing their way into the room. The journalists yelled out more questions. Two certified medical technicians mounted the stage with a collapsible wheelchair, which they opened behind the old woman. The nurse seated at the table stood up to assist. Mrs. Soren-Schmidt threw one last glance over the room with its hopeful and attentive masses. She dismissed them all with a look of contempt, then her eyes caught mine and I knew that every word in the story she'd told was a lie, that this was not Mrs. Soren-Schmidt at all, but Clément, and that the emotion that he was holding back was not gratitude or reverence. It was laughter.

Serendipity

> And hand in hand on the edge of the sand
> They danced by the light of the moon, the moon, the moon...
>
> —Edward Lear, "The Owl and the Pussy-Cat"

The beach, with its crescent of crystal sand and its fringe of palms, was a South Sea cliché except for the sand flies that patrolled it. These flies swarmed Clément even before he had disembarked, though he paid them no heed.

"What land is this?" he muttered rhetorically, losing his too-big shoes to the sand, the dead skin shredding on his feet amid the pumicing dunes. He drove on toward a point in the distance, a place where a break in the line of palms created a natural gate into the surrounding jungle. Even here, in a place that he hadn't planned on, he seemed to know where he was going. I followed at a reluctant distance. I was very tired. I wanted nothing more than to sleep.

Clément paused at the frondy forest portal and waited for me to catch up with him.

"After you, my sweet," he murmured with a gentlemanly bow, "I wouldn't want to lose you."

The landscape was lush. The walls of trees with their thick liana- and orchid-fretted canopy made one feel as though this were a leafy house full of elaborately flowered rooms.

"Bower-like, isn't it?" smirked a much-subdued Clément, taking my hand. "The perfect place for a honeymoon." He was joking of course, but when I gazed at him, he looked away quickly, almost shyly, muttering, "Onward" and pulling me along.

We plunged deeper into the forest and the rain began to fall again, lightly at first, then in the drenching sheets that characterize monsoons. The ground beneath us became slick, then viscous, and Clément began to lose the fleshier parts of his feet to the sucking mud. A few of the flies still buzzed around him, although most of them had been driven off by the downpour. It was amazingly quiet, the usual jungle cacophony silenced by the insistent splatter of rain. Water dominated the rainforest. Mist rose up all around us even as the torrent slapped through the treetops, sluiced down skinny trunks, and waterfalled from the fat, waxy platforms of leaves. Monkeys, insects, birds—all took shelter, hunkering down for the moment under leafy umbrellas. Clément forged on in spite of his rapidly deteriorating feet. A monsoon is not hard to outlast. Almost as quickly as the tap is turned on to full blast, it is shut. The rain stops; hoots and screeches once again fill the canopy; the creatures of the forest re-emerge.

I was drowsy, drugged by the low drone of the flies, which had returned with the end of the shower. I don't remember sitting down to rest, but we must have done so because the next thing I knew I was nodding awake, head bouncing on my chest, a thin line of drool casting a spidery line from the slack side of my mouth. Clément was seated beside me, his butt in the mud, picking at what was left of his feet.

"You are beautiful when you are sleeping," he said, looking at me sideways, smiling at the long thread of spit.

I blinked at him, closed my mouth and swallowed, exhausted all over again by his company. I opened my mouth as though ready to speak and nearly surprised myself with a verbal response, but Clément quickly shushed me.

"Shshshsh," he commanded, stifling my attempt at speech. "You can hear that, can't you?"

I could indeed. I heard voices and the rhythmic crash of gongs and cymbals coming from somewhere further along in the forest.

Clément was already standing. "Come on," he whispered, pulling me to my feet. "This is good, very good. Let's see where this leads."

THEY WERE A MOTLEY PROCESSION. They marched along in single file: a man, a woman, a child, and an elephant. We were spying on them from behind a small tree. The first man in the procession was dressed like a clown—the world's largest clown. He was enormous, around six foot eight, and he wore bright yellow bloomers that failed to blouse out around his hammy thighs, curly-toed shoes, and a sleeveless tank top that showcased biceps that bulged under the weight of a very large suitcase. The clown with the suitcase was followed by a veiled woman with something tied around her neck. She was carrying a boom box that was playing gamelan music. Behind her waddled a fat, somewhat large-headed child leading an elephant pulling a colorful litter upon which was mounted a coffin.

"Jimor, are we nearly there? It's muddy and wet," groused the woman in veils in a voice that carried over the orchestra.

"Yes, very nearly," said the oversized clown. "The gravesite is just around the bend."

Clément leaned forward in his hiding place next to mine. "Delightful. A corpse," he whispered. He had not taken his eyes off the casket on the bier, which was rapidly disappearing into the distance. "Come on, then. Let's follow," he directed. "My feet are a mess. This is just what the doctor ordered."

We tiptoed through the forest behind them, Clément totally noiseless in spite of the wet mud and his crumbling feet. He was the perfect stalker.

The large-headed child who, we discovered, was really a dwarf, kept looking back at the elephant and the coffin as if something were terribly wrong.

"Something smells bad," said the dwarf.

"Maybe it's Brent," the big clown replied. "Or Bila. I told you not to feed her any more bananas. You may have given her gas."

"Gas? I don't think so," the dwarf argued back. "I give her bananas all the time and she loves them. If you fed her once in a while you'd now that. Bananas don't give her gas."

I knew of course that it wasn't the elephant's fault. It was Clément who was stinking up the rear. I was used to the smell that surrounded him most of the time, but that didn't mean others were immune.

"Gas," muttered Clément, "I'll show them gas."

By this time the funeral procession was starting to unravel at the ends. The big clown was way up ahead and the dwarf and the elephant, only a few yards beyond us, though the dwarf couldn't actually see us. The elephant was in the way. If I'd been alone, I would have run into them when they halted.

"Okay, we're here," the clown announced, seemingly to his suitcase, as he set it down next to a hole in the ground. One by one the other members of the funeral procession arrived at the gravesite. Clément and I scuttled into the nearby bushes.

The suitcase fell over, opened itself, and a tiny Chinese girl unfolded herself from within it.

"Thanks for the ride," she said to the clown as she bent forward at the waist, hooked her elbows around her ankles, and stretched. Then she stood up, threw her thin arms to the heavens and, bending backward, placed her palms on the still-steaming ground. She wore a sparkly blue swimsuit and was only around four feet tall, though she looked even shorter next to the huge man who'd been carrying her around in the suitcase.

The clown nodded and stepped to the elephant's rear. He untied the litter, lifted the casket, and let it drop with a thud to the earth.

"This coffin business, what a chore," he complained.

"Yeah," said the dwarf. "I still say we should have cremated him."

"He was a Christian," said the little Chinese girl, putting one foot behind her head. "This is the way they like to be buried."

"And Muslims, minus the coffin," said the veiled woman, setting the music down and unwinding the thing around her neck. It repositioned itself, coiled its way up her arm. It was a very large snake.

"Whatever," said the dwarf. "Let's just put him in the ground. We don't need to bury him deep."

"We won't," said the clown, as he dragged the coffin toward a shallow pit apparently prepared for the purpose. "Bila," he called, "Bila, down." And the elephant pushed the box into the hole.

The clown, the dwarf, and the two women fell into silence. The woman with the veils kneeled, scooped up a handful of mud, and tossed it into the hollow.

"Brent was a wonderful leader," she said.

"What will we do without him?" sighed the miniscule contortionist.

"A friend, a mentor, a talent," said the clown.

"The best trapeze artist in the Pacific," added the dwarf.

Then the veiled woman turned up the music and they all began dancing while the big clown spackled the hole in the ground with more mud.

"Very touching, but I wish they would leave," said Clément. The flies that buzzed around him seemed to have multiplied. He swatted at them with impatience.

By this time the woman had shed her veils and was dancing quite provocatively with the snake.

"I wish Brent were here to see that new dance," said the Chinese girl.

"He'd want Nidi to throw in a cobra," said the clown.

"And a poisonous adder," added the dwarf.

"Yes, I guess so," sighed the tiny contortionist.

Nidi said nothing. She was in her own world. She kept dancing until the clown finished covering the coffin. Then she rearranged the snake and her many veils and turned off the music.

"All right, that's enough," she said gruffly. "Let's go."

And with that, the troupe headed back through the forest.

Clément didn't wait long to come out of hiding. "About time," he grumbled, approaching the grave. "Here's where I take over."

Then he threw himself upon the freshly mounded earth, digging in frenzy, with claw-like hands. "Don't watch me," he hissed, bent over the gravesite and digging down, like a dog, throwing the wet dirt back over his shoulders. A finger or two flew back with it. When he got to the casket, he used what was left of his hands to pry open the lid, huffing and puffing and cursing. He wrenched the top off at last and stepped back, clapping his palms together in glee.

"Ooooh," moaned Clément. "Oh, look. This is nice, so nice." He beckoned to me. "Erin, look. So fresh, nearly perfect, and, oh, what an outfit."

I inched toward him, and when I was within reach, he pulled me to his side and pointed with his remaining middle finger. "Do you like him, Erin?" he asked breathlessly. "Oh, he is lovely, isn't he?"

The man in the hole did not look dead. He appeared to be merely sleeping. His sun-streaked hair had a sleep-tousled quality, his handsome face flushed beneath a warm tan. He was not especially tall, but he did look very fit, and his body, even lying cushioned in the casket, still exuded a powerful vigor. "A king of a corpse," as Clément might say, but I knew that the thing that most enamored my constant companion was not the man's physical composition, but his clothing.

Brent, the trapeze artist and ringleader to his recently departed cohorts, wore a turquoise jumpsuit with an Elvis-slick sparkle. It had trumpet sleeves, a deep V-neck, and was made of a very sheer spandex. His broad shoulders were spangled in turquoise sequins. Gold threads traced the deep cleft of the neckline, arrowing down toward his waist. This accentuated a veritable codpiece of an erection, which further contributed to his lively presentation. He was dressed to perform, and as we stared down into his last resting place, we could almost see him up on his trapeze, knees hooked over the bar, arms stretched gracefully up over his head, ready to make a catch.

"Now that is a costume," Clément whistled admiringly, and he fell upon the body like a lover.

The body of the Chinese man sagged and seemed almost

to pour off the corpse. The dead trapeze artist spasmed as though an electric current had hit him, then his mouth and eyes opened, he bolted upright, and he let out a low-pitched roar.

"Oh, god," gasped Clément, "that is so much better." He stood up, turned, and then stooped back over the grave. Once again I was treated to the oily suck, slurp, lip-smacking sound. He rose with a mouth full of offal. "Uuuh," he breathed, "that is so good. Sometimes I forget that I'm hungry."

I had not yet seen a ghoul feed on a corpse. It is a disgusting and mannerless thing. Like a ravenous turkey vulture, Clément had fallen upon the Chinese man's remains, gorging as though time were short. It didn't take long for him to consume a good piece of what was left in the casket. "Just like a stew," he said. "This stuff really sticks to the ribs. But check this out," he added, admiring his new physique. "I've definitely traded up." He gazed down at the penis that was still standing erect. "I have a hard-on, too."

I was squatting at the edge of the grave, my hands over my mouth.

"Help me out," he ordered and stretched out a hand.

I wished the grave had been deeper. If the grave had been deeper, perhaps I could have left him there. Maybe I could have run off, tried to escape. But the grave was not much deeper than the casket was tall. Clément's demand for assistance was a mere formality, a way to exert his authority. If I didn't assist, he'd have easily climbed out. There was really no way to break free. So, I lent him a hand, and he pulled himself up. It was better to have no illusions.

On the San Joaquin

(travel essay)

"You look lonely."

The waiter stops at my table, leans across it.

I am sipping a Bloody Mary in the dining car of the San Joaquin, a train that runs daily from San Francisco to Bakersfield and back. I am on my way home to Oakland.

He puts his hand on my arm.

I realize at that point, sunlight insinuating through the scratched window of the train, that loneliness is a feeling I'm comfortable with. Like an old bathrobe—one that's not particularly attractive—it's a feeling I've worn so long that I don it with the greatest of comfort, sometimes unaware of the fact that it's not the correct dress for dinner and social interaction, that it's not really appropriate for any company or any place outside the home.

Yes, I think, *at this moment, I am lonely—but only for this moment, and certainly not as lonely as Iggy.*

Iggy is the iguana that bit me earlier in the day. Iggy has become so lonely that he cannot be handled. He is seven years old and has spent all seven of those years in a thirty-six-by-twelve-inch glass case. Iggy is angry and he'll bite any hand that comes near him. I imagine myself biting the waiter who has just put his hand on my arm.

Outside the train window the sun is setting like an egg yolk on the edge of a bowl. The windows look like they have glue smeared on them. Twilight filters through the panes in an irregular fashion.

Iggy belongs to my niece and nephew. He sleeps in his glass case at the foot of Eileen's bed. She can watch him as she lies there with her head on the pillow. Iggy is a fabulous green color. He has beautiful, long, curved claws, and although my niece and nephew claim he has none, he has a set of cartilaginous teeth that make an imprint like a small choker upon contact with skin—a one-inch circle of flesh wounds beaded with blood. Iggy has no mate. He has soft little spines all along his back, a beautiful neck that puffs out and puffs in, and a habit of poking his head directly under the sunlamp to soak up the heat.

I have a mate, and I love him dearly. I have long, dark hair and skin that's beginning to age. Like Iggy, I'm exceedingly fond of sunshine, although I'm aware that it greatly accelerates the aging process.

Darkness is falling, and the chatter in the dinner car gets louder. I love the dusky mood of the place—white tablecloths, lamplight. There are a lot of foreign travelers on the train. Europeans, people from other countries, enjoy train travel. You always find them in the dining cars. They know that's the best place to be.

According to my nephew Peter, I am supposed to turn into an iguana. I have only a few days left. Then, my face will begin to point; a tough, scaly skin will start to form over my body; and I will turn green. As a matter of fact, my finger is throbbing. It is swollen. The veins on the back of my hand stand out as if overtaxed, straining to convey the iguana enzymes to other parts of my body. Maybe it's my imagination or just a coincidental discomfort. I cough and a sticky, tobacco-like substance comes out of my mouth. A syrup-like trickle escapes from my nose. I am freezing. I put on my jacket. I am still cold.

When I become an iguana, I will be a giant iguana. I will not be able to take the train anymore. I will need to get away. There is really nowhere for a five-foot-two iguana to go. I don't think there's a glass case big enough.

Iguanas live for a very long time. I don't know how long Iggy will live. I think he will just get crazier and crazier. One day, maybe, he'll try to run off. Where can an iguana run? I will book a ticket to Mexico or rent a car while I still can, and hide out in the Sonoran Desert. I'll become a legend—the Giant Iguana of the Sonoran Desert—like Nessie, the Loch Ness monster.

I am feeling green—very green—and very alien in spite of the Bloody Mary, in spite of the salmon dinner and the incessant questions of the woman sitting at the table across the aisle from me.

"Do you know when we'll be in Modesto?" she asks.

Unlike the European travelers, she seems ill at ease on the train.

"At seven thirty, I think." I try to sound charitable. "Here, have a look at the timetable," I add, handing it over to her. I notice that my fingernails look like claws. The skin on my hands looks scaly. In the lamplight they appear to be almost chartreuse. All of the Europeans are smiling. I believe they're aware of my dilemma. I miss my mate.

The waiter is bustling about my table. He is very solicitous. He brings me dessert. He brings me coffee. He finally brings me the bill.

"Phew," he says, "it usually doesn't get this busy until summer. I hope I haven't neglected you." He brings back my credit card, asks for my signature. Once again he puts his hand on my arm. Things get hazy then. I am no longer responsible.

"Iggy," he says with an understanding smile, looking at my receipt, at the place where I've signed for the meal. I am gazing out into the darkness, feeling terribly lonely, not minding at all.

"Iggy McFerrin, you've been very patient. Thank you."

Inside the White Gorilla

(travel essay)

We are sitting inside the White Gorilla, the conversations around us rising and falling like the chatter of birds in an aviary, and I am mesmerized by the writer who sometimes wears dark glasses, sometimes a pirate patch over his left eye, his mood mercurial, while outside the rain plashes down.

> *...Il pleure dans mon cœur*
> *Comme il pleut sur la ville...*
>
> —Paul Verlaine, "*Romances sans paroles*"

> *...It cries in my core*
> *Like it pours on the town...*

The White Gorilla is Le Gorille Blanc, a bistro in Paris's fourth *arrondissement* on the right bank—the Marais—once home of the French royals and the *grand hôtels particuliers*, its fashionable comeback from a postwar decline evident everywhere in the clatter of commerce, the digestibility of its arts.

The restaurant is named after Snowflake, Copito de Nieve, the albino gorilla who, for decades, tantalized children and adults in a Barcelona zoo, or so the handsome son of the restaurant's Spanish proprietor tells me. Snowflake was captured in Equatorial Guinea in 1966 at the age of two by a Fang farmer who shot Snowflake's mother and massacred the rest of his charcoal-black band. Snowflake had eyes of the palest blue, so light they seemed nearly transparent, like ice. He is gone now, after forty years of captivity—the only albino gorilla known to man. From the chalk-white stone walls of the bistro, his ghostly image in deft outline presides over the restaurant, at once at home and tragically out of place in this European enclave so far from the land of his birth.

I could be Snowflake. I feel lost, untethered, as I always do when I am in Paris. The wine, the platters of *foie gras*, of *confit de canard*, of *fricassée de lapin* come and go. The conversation continues. The rain is counting the afternoon down. I feel like a Dali watch melting over the edge of the table. I feel like a white gorilla in a Barcelona zoo. I realize that Paris is playing that old trick on me again: Reality is shifting in the strangest way...minutes bumping into centuries, people, places, and philosophies sprouting poems.

> *...Que lentement passent les heures*
> *Comme passe un enterrement*
> *Tu pleureras l'heure où tu pleures*
> *Qui passera trop vitement*
> *Comme passent toutes les heures...*
>
> —Guillaume Apollinaire, *"À la Santé"*

> *...How slowly the hours pass*
> *crawling like an eternity*
> *You will decry the hour when*
> *You mourn what passes so quickly*
> *As every hour must pass...*

I first came to Paris by way of the surreal. It was a Cocteau moment in my life. I was a shipwreck washed up on the shore. I stayed at the Crystal, 24 Rue Saint-Benoît, with my husband, Lawrence. We had come from Hydra, from Greece, where we'd run to escape our loss—the death of our infant daughter. There, at the Crystal, the wallpaper in our room was speaking to me, "*Courez! Courez!* Flee! Flee!" the curlicue shapes of its brown and mustard fronds insinuating madness, insisting upon release.

...Dans une fosse comme un ours
Chaque matin je me promène
Tournons tournons tournons toujours
Le ciel est bleu comme une chaîne
Dans une fosse comme un ours
Chaque matin je me promène...

—Guillaume Apollinaire, *"À la Santé"*

...In a pit like a bear
Every morning I pace
Around and around and around here
The blue sky, a chain
In a pit like a bear
Every morning I pace...

La boule Miche, le Quartier Latin, les Tuileries, les Jardins du Luxembourg, Saint Séverin, le Trocadero, Montmartre, Versailles—where didn't we wander and weep? The soles of our shoes wore thin.

The next time we visited Paris we came to see the Greek Surrealists exhibition at the Centre Georges Pompidou. This time we were coming from Sweden, where the ever-simmering caldron of the midsummer sun denied us repose, and the thirty-four-hour train ride cramped in close quarters with a quartet of libidinous Finns left us exhausted. We stumbled from the train station and onto the Paris streets nearly comatose and holed up in the Hotel Lutetia. Matisse, André Gide, Antoine de Saint-Exupéry, and Picasso have all either stayed or made their home at the Lutetia, as have Josephine Baker and Alexandra David-Neel. It was exquisite. I fell in love with our bed.

At some point we did catch up with our mutual friend and mentor, Greek surrealist poet and essayist, Nanos Valaoritis. Nanos, who writes in English, in French, and in Greek, had introduced me to the Surrealist Movement and the work of André Breton and his antecedents: Rimbaud, Apollinaire, Lautréamont, and Jarry. This exposition featured the surrealist contributions of Greek artists, Odysseus Elytis, Andréas Embiricos, Nikos Engonopoulos, Mayo, Gisèle Prassinos, and Nanos himself, among others.

> *...Under the restful rule of electricity*
> *Surrealism raises its transparent head*
> *From now on we shall all see through*
> *The bodies of people hanging in mid-air...*
>
> —*Nanos Valaoritis, "Ermenonville"*

Every subsequent visit to the French capital city seemed to be similarly colored by the surreal: chance meetings with missing and much-missed friends, sudden descents into the underworld, sudden ascents to join the Aesir—the catacombs, Le Jules Verne in la Tour Eiffel.

This trip is no different. I am again at a crossroads. Friends from afar have congregated, their proximity fleeting, dreamlike. At the Musée national du Moyen Âge, the old Musée de Cluny, I descend into third-century Roman Paris, or Lutetia, to the frigidarium, part of the Gallo-Roman thermal baths over which the museum is built. I climb the stairs to confront a unicorn and a maiden in a room full of exquisite tapestries. I have lost my analytical compass. I can no longer distinguish between what I have forgotten and what I falsely remember: this street, that museum, these gardens—have I walked here, lingered here, laughed here before? At one point I stop, arrested by the façade of a handsome edifice. French flags, the *tricolore*, flap in the breeze before it. I snap a photo.

"Such a beautiful building," I observe.

"Yes," says Joanna, who is witnessing my confusion. "The Lutetia. Didn't you stay there?"

And now here I am inside the White Gorilla. The Marais comes rushing back at me: an inquisitive amble arm in arm with friends down the rue de Rosiers; French onion soup on a chilly day a few steps from the Musée Picasso; shopping at a boutique in the Place des Vosges where I bought an enormous hand-woven black hat.

Our umbrellas leak puddles. It's still raining when we step outside. The leaves run off the trees in colors. Russets and ochers are pouring onto the ground. History sluices down the walls of the buildings. The writer speaks into the weakening light. His words fly off and are lost. I fill the pages of my mind with new symbols. Everyone's wings are drying. The long-limbed horses in the caravan awaken and blink. The white gorilla closes its ice-blue eyes.

Navigating the Divide: Selected Poetry and Prose by Linda Watanabe McFerrin is the third volume in ASP's Legacy Series, following *Other Voices, Other Lives: A Grace Cavalieri Collection* (2017) and *The Richard Peabody Reader* (2015). This series is devoted to career-spanning collections from writers who meet the following three criteria: the majority of their books have been published by independent presses; they are active in more than one literary genre; and they are consistent and influential champions of the work of other writers, whether through publishing, reviewing, teaching, mentoring, or some combination of these. Modeled after the "readers" popular in academia in the mid-twentieth century, our Legacy Series allows readers to trace the arc of a significant writer's literary development in a single, representative volume.